Investing in China

Investing in China
New Opportunities in a Transforming Stock Market

By Winston Ma

Risk books

Published by Risk Books, a Division of Incisive Financial Publishing Ltd

Haymarket House
28–29 Haymarket
London SW1Y 4RX
Tel: +44 (0)20 7484 9700
Fax: +44 (0)20 7484 9800
E-mail: books@incisivemedia.com
Sites: www.riskbooks.com
www.incisivemedia.com

ISBN 1 904339 84 0

British Library Cataloguing in Publication Data
A catalogue record for this book is available from the British Library

Publisher: Laurie Donaldson
Assistant Editor: Hannah Berry
Designer: Rebecca Bramwell

Typeset by Mizpah Publishing Services Private Limited, Chennai, India

Printed and bound in Spain by Espacegrafic, Pamplona, Navarra

Contents

To Angela, who gave me love and support

Acknowledgements

I have been blessed to work with and learn from a uniquely, high-quality group of mentors in business and law. The Chinese capital markets are such a complex and fast-moving topic that this book would not have been possible if it were not for the dozens of friends, mentors, and colleagues who provided expert opinions, feedbacks, insights and suggestions for improvement.

My deepest thanks go to Dr Rita Hauser and the New York University School of Law. My investment banking and practicing attorney experiences in New York, the global centre for capital markets and corporate law practices, all started with your generous Hauser scholarship in 1997. My time at the NYU School of Law has reshaped my way of thinking as well as myself as a person. I see a universe of opportunities as a result of my Hauser experience, including an ambitious project like this book.

Special thanks to Professor John Pagan who, as the then Director of the Hauser Global Law School program at NYU, encouraged me to apply for the Hauser Scholarship when I was a graduating law school student in China 10 years ago. You transformed my international professional dream into a reality. Thank you also for inviting me to your University of Richmond Law School in 2000 as an international visiting professor on China law: many ideas in this book date back to those quiet weeks at Virginia.

Many thanks to David Hsu, Chief Executive of JF Asset Management Ltd. The earlier insightful conversations with you regarding my "China and US, law and business" background helped me develop the fundamental approach of this book. As a result, I endeavoured to capture the fast transforming Chinese markets by synthesising my Chinese background and US experiences as well as integrating discussions on financial innovations and regulatory reforms.

My sincere appreciation to Linda Simpson, senior partner and my former boss at the New York office of Davis Polk & Wardwell. Thank you for encouraging me to pursue MBA studies and a more business-oriented career when you really needed me for your booming structured equity practice group. You have been a tremendous mentor and I thank you for continuously being a great cheerleader.

My gratitude to many outstanding practitioners and academics, whose insights give *Investing in China* its distinctive character. Among others, I would particularly thank Professor Bill Allen at NYU Center of Law and Business, Professor Zhiwu Chen at Yale University School of Management, Yuanfang Du and Jun Huang at Haitong Securities Co., Dingyuan Gu at China Securities Regulatory Commission, Youqiang Li at Te Bon Securities Co., Xiongying Lu at Shanghai Stock Exchange, Joe O'Mara at KPMG, Owen Nee at Orrick, Herrington & Sutcliffe, Lester Ross at Wilmer Hale (Beijing), Pengfei Su at Paul Hasting (Shanghai), and Dr Peter Zhang at China Bank Regulatory Commission.

I thank everyone at *Risk Books*, who has made publishing this book a joyous experience. Special thanks to Laurie Donaldson, editor extraordinaire, who truly "got it" the first time we spoke when China had just launched the first pilot program of the full-flotation reform in May 2005. You immediately recognised the historical transition that China's capital markets are experiencing and directed the book through initial ideas to final pages. Thanks also to the whole *Risk Books* team including book editor Hannah Berry and head of marketing Rainy Dhillon.

Many chapters of the book began, in some sense, with the "Learning Curve" column I wrote for *Derivatives Week* magazine. Many thanks to Jeremy Carter and Matt Tremblay, who invited me to regularly contribute to the Column and also challenged me to follow the burgeoning financial innovations in China's capital markets in real time.

And last in the lineup but first in my heart, I thank my wife, Angela Ju-hsin Pan, who gave me love and support, thank you for the patience you had while I wrecked our weekends and evenings working on this book.

About the Author

Winston Wenyan Ma, CFA and Esq., is one of a small number of native Chinese that have worked as an investment banker and practicing capital markets attorney in both the United States and China. He is currently a Vice President at a major multinational investment bank based in New York, where he is a member of an investment banking structuring and solution team across equity, fixed income, M&A and rating advisories.

With Bar admissions in both China and New York, he worked as a corporate lawyer at Freshfields' Shanghai Office and Davis Polk & Wardwell's New York office until 2001. In the spring semester of 2000, Winston was an international visiting professor at the University of Richmond Law School, teaching a course on China's Corporations and Securities Laws.

As a capital markets attorney at Davis Polk, he excelled in structured equity transactions with his strong quantitative background. To pursue a more business-oriented role, he studied at the University of Michigan Business School for an MBA and joined the major investment bank thereafter. The *New York Times* detailed his career story in a Sunday Business issue.

He frequently publishes articles on financial innovation in industry magazines, and he has spoken at a number of global conferences on structured products, convertible bonds, and emerging markets securitisation.

Winston has an MBA degree from the University of Michigan Ross Business School and a Master of Comparative Jurisprudence (MCJ) from the New York University School of Law, where he was a Hauser Global Scholar. Before that, he graduated with a Bachelor of Science and a Bachelor of Law degree from Fudan University Materials Science Department and School of Law respectively in Shanghai, China.

Winston can be reached at WinstonWMa@gmail.com for comments and feedback on *Investing in China*.

Foreword

When I arrived in Shanghai in 2004 to lecture Chinese MBA students on the development of financial institutions and markets, I was struck by two things. First, the Chinese economy was booming, and everyone knew it. Second, Chinese stocks were mired in a bear market that began at the turn of the millennium, and everyone knew that, too. It was puzzling. Financial history, my speciality, finds that financial development usually precedes and then promotes economic growth. As an economy grows, for example, its companies tend to earn more, and rising earnings ought to show up on higher stock prices. China appeared to be a counter-example to such forecasts.

To explain the Chinese conundrum, various analysts pointed to a number of shortcomings of the Chinese stock markets. There were deficiencies in self-regulation and formal regulation. The markets themselves and the products they offered were limited. Compared to other countries, there were not a lot of institutional investors. Market behaviour was speculation-driven, and possibly manipulated. And since the government and its representatives retained majority ownership of many Chinese companies in the form of shares that did not trade, investors had to worry about control and other corporate governance issues, as well as the possibility that the large overhang of government shares might one day be dumped into the market.

Winston Ma's remarkably informed study of China's recent stock market developments and the emerging opportunities they are providing to investors is a most welcome contribution to modern financial literature. He demonstrates that not only did the Chinese realise the deficiencies of their markets fairly recently, but that they also decided to do something about them. Regulation has improved. There are more investment products. Institutional investors are a growing presence, and foreign institutions are finding that Chinese markets are increasingly accessible. The government is addressing the problems of segregated equity ownership – the buckets of A, B, H, and N shares – and thinking about a gradual privatisation of government-owned shares.

As I read this book, I quickly understood two things, namely, how rapidly things are changing in China, and how on top of these changes Winston Ma is. Although I was in China again in late 2005, I learned from Ma that important changes have occurred during the several intervening months to make participation in the Chinese markets more attractive to foreign investors. No doubt the changes will continue, and probably rapidly. To understand them as they unfold, one needs to have a base, a set of coordinates from which to start. Winston Ma's book provides just such a base.

Of course, given the conundrum of the Chinese markets not reflecting China's growth as well as the rapidity of the changes now taking place in them, one might well be tempted to stand aside and let things shake out before taking an interest or investment position in China. That would be understandable for investors with high-risk aversion. Others, however, will be searching for opportunities to get in on the ground floor of developments that will most likely align Chinese stock market performance with China's remarkable economic expansion. Investing in China is the place to begin that search.

Richard Sylla
Stern School of Business
New York University

Introduction

More than ever before, "investing in China" is a dominating theme in the international investment community. China has enjoyed near double-digit economic growth for more than a decade, and investors in every corner of the globe are seeking opportunities to participate in China's economic miracles by investing in its stock market.

The year 2005–2006 has been a major milestone in the history of China's stock market. Three interactive driving forces – namely, the state share reform (also known as "full-flotation" reform), continued legal and regulatory liberalisation, and ever-active financial innovations have opened up interesting opportunities for foreign investors. While foreign investments were basically limited to straight equity investments (or ADRs) in Chinese companies listed in overseas exchanges, investors today have access to many new investment vehicles with a wide spectrum of risk and reward profiles.

Firstly, the state share reform launched in mid 2005 has been indisputably the biggest ever reform for China's stock market. It aims to solve the so-called "segregated equity ownership" in listed companies, a deep-rooted issue that has been plaguing the stock market for years. Together with the newly revised corporate and securities laws, the reform is a major step to structurally transforming the once state-dominated market to a true investor-oriented stock market. It will have profound implications on valuation and the trading behaviour of existing financial instruments going forward, and it is leading to fast-paced financial innovations in the "post-reform" era.

Secondly, China has also liberalised its regulatory framework recently to increase foreign participation in its stock market. The

QFII system opens up the domestic public stock market to foreign institutional investors. This system's I trading mechanism further creates an access product market for broad off-shore investors. At the same time, China's multiple regulatory bodies have issued a flurry of important new regulations to reopen foreign investor access to the non-tradable shares of the listed companies, providing foreign investors greater market entry options.

Finally, the stock market has seen active financial innovations as a result of market reform and regulatory liberalisation. Over recent years, China's stock market has embraced a variety of new financial products and transaction structures. The former consist of warrants/options, exchanged-traded funds (ETF), listed open-funds (LOF), principal-protected investments, convertible bonds, and treasury-bond repurchase agreement (buy-out repo). The latter includes foreign private funds acquiring controlling interests in state-owned companies and different structures in management buy-outs.

This book will provide a practical roadmap for this important, fast transforming, yet somewhat mysterious market. With the stock market at this critical point in its history, the three powerful driving forces are creating new opportunities as well as complexities. As is often the case, financial products in China are not always exactly what their names would suggest to a westerner.

As such, a thorough understanding of the "Chinese characteristics" of those investment vehicles is extremely important for foreign investors. With investment banking and practicing legal experience in both China and the US, I am uniquely equipped to present the cutting-edge opportunities and distinctive risks in China stock market today. Using a "China *versus* developed markets" approach, this book aims to bridge the gap between foreign market experience and Chinese local knowledge for foreign investors.

The book is both accessible to the lay reader and challenging to the experienced market professional, as it delves into the unique characteristics of this market. Instead of models and pricing theory, the book focuses on the framework – the fundamental issues investors must appreciate before investing in this uniquely complex market – by integrating financial and legal analysis throughout the book.

Divided into three major parts, Part I summarises new trends in China's stock market post re-entry into the WTO and discusses the new QFII system, which provides the platform for foreign investors to gain direct access to China's domestic market (also known as A share market) and subsequently the off-shore access products market.

Part II will cover the latest financial innovations in China's A share market. These investment products are similar to their foreign counterparts, but they exhibit certain "Chinese characteristics" because of the existing economic and regulatory infrastructure, and in particular, the unique "segregated equity ownership" structure in Chinese listed companies. Those features will be analysed from both financial and legal perspectives.

Part III reviews two investment alternatives in the non-tradable share market, management buy-out (MBO) and mergers & acquisitions (M&A), which exhibit enormous potential but still involve substantial uncertainties. These two areas have seen successful precedents, but more fundamental reforms are needed to make them effective investment tools for foreign investors. The chapters will examine the current practices, analyse the existing issues, and discuss the prospects in light of on-going reforms.

Because the book is intended for interested foreign investors, it is organised by the different investment vehicles, and I have tried to make each chapter stand. On the other hand, all chapters are connected by the same three major driving forces in China's stock market today: state share reform, regulatory liberalisation, and financial innovation. The on-going full-flotation reform will eventually bridge the gap between the tradable share market (Part II) and non-tradable share market (Part III).

2006 is poised to be a critical and dynamic year for China's stock market. The state share reform program has entered a significant phase; aiming to reach the key state-owned enterprises that have yet to launch the programme. The drastically amended securities and corporations law became effective at the beginning of the New Year. The newly introduced warrant/option market has led to a new wave of financial innovations among exchanges and securities firms. As a sign of optimism, both the domestic currency A share market and the foreign currency B share market closed sharply higher since the first trading day of the New Year.

It will be exciting to watch a completely new stock market in China unfold.

Part I

Market Trends and New Foreign Access

One distinctive feature of China's listed companies is their complex equity ownership structure. The different types of shares creates an alphabet soup mix that may be sub-categorised in multiple ways by currency denomination, listing place, access restrictions, and most importantly, transfer restrictions. Above all, the dichotomy of public-owned tradable and state-owned nontradable shares is the single most important characteristic of China's stock market. It is frequently referred to as "segregated equity ownership", and it has led to the unique trading behaviour of many financial instruments, complex structures in equity transfer transactions, as well as serious corporate governance issues.

To improve the ownership structure in listed companies, China's government has initiated two powerful reforms in recent years. On one hand, it promotes a stronger institutional investor base in the public A share market, which could potentially become a counterweight to the dominating shareholders of the nontradable shares. On the other hand, it also takes steps to reduce state-ownership through privatisation, which culminated at the 2005 full-flotation reform that aims to ultimately make all nontradable shares of listed companies tradable.

Both approaches have opened up foreign participation in China's domestic stock market. In institutionalising the stock market, China introduced the QFII system, which permits large foreign institutional investors to participate directly in China's domestic RMB-denominated capital markets. Together with active financial innovations in China, the QFII system provides foreign investors with a number of new financial products that represent a broad spectrum of investment styles and risk reward profiles.

On the privatisation front, China's multiple regulatory bodies have issued a flurry of important new regulations to bring the framework closer to international norms. Those regulatory developments reopened foreign investor access to the nontradable shares of the listed companies. Following the state share reform, the new "full-floating" equity ownership structure of listed companies will offer foreign capital more opportunities to acquire controlling interests through capital markets transactions.

1

Overview and New Trends

2005 marked the fifth straight year of slump for China's stock market. The Shanghai Composite Index reached an eight-year low of 998.23 points in mid 2005; falling through the 1,000-point mark has long been regarded as a vital psychological level for investors. The market rebounded afterwards, but nevertheless posted an above 8% loss by the end of the year. Since hitting historic highs in 2001, China's stock market has diminished by approximately half its value.

This dismal bear market is in sharp contrast to China's booming economy, whose GDP growth has surged forward in the high single digits for the past two decades. From its modest inception merely 15 years ago, China's stock market has made tremendous progress, but a complex array of issues has impeded its next-stage developments. These issues range from poor disclosure and financial reporting, excessive speculation, and above all, the convoluted shareholding structure that involves the state owning two-thirds of the equity of the listed companies that create an overhang on the market.

On the other hand, 2005 was a critical transition year for China's struggling stock market. Despite great disputes, the regulators launched, in mid 2005, indisputably the biggest-ever reforms in China's stock market history, the reform on the "segregated equity ownership structure" issue of all the listed companies. The reform has been executed at an astounding pace: over 300 holdings had already completed the divestment reform by the year-end and another 400–500 are expected to complete the programme by mid 2006.

Manifesting the fundamental transformation of the stock market, China's Securities Law – by no means coincidently – made sweeping changes via a long-awaited amendment in late 2005. Few Chinese laws as recent as the Securities Law have experienced such an extensive revision, nor have they attracted the same wide public attention domestically and internationally. The gradual liberalisation of the stock market, post China's WTO accession, has finally culminated in the 2005 equity ownership structure reform: China's stock market is in a new era.

CRITICAL POINT

China's stock market accounts for less than 1% of the world's total, yet "invest in China" has dominated the international investment community in recent years. China's exceptional economic growth definitely justifies the enthusiasm: at roughly 10% a year, it doubles or trebles the rates currently achieved by most western economies. While it has already earned its reputation as the supplier of the world with its low costs and vast labour force, China is also poised to create unparalleled demand with more than 1 billion domestic customers.

For many investors, however, whether domestic or international, China's economic growth has failed to convert into investment returns for them. The Shanghai Composite Index, the most widely used benchmark, has fallen 50% since it peaked in 2001. In an economy enjoying high growth rates, such a poor performance in the stock market can only reflect deeply rooted structural problems.

Remarkable growth

The Shanghai and Shenzhen stock markets were established in China in 1990 and 1991, respectively, and they jointly created an integrated national equity market. With a mere 15 years' history, China's stock market has enjoyed remarkable growth. From a modest 14 listed companies in its inception year, there are approximately 1,400 listed companies from various sectors (see Table 1). The total market capitalisation as a percentage of the national GDP has constantly risen (with corrections in recent years as a result of the multi-year bear market) as shown in Table 2.

With its current US$350 billion or so market capitalisation, the total capitalisation of China's domestic stock market is equivalent to just 30% of China's current GDP. Compare that with the US ratio of

Table 1 Sector distribution of listed companies (as at the end of December 2003)

Agriculture/forestry/breeding/fisheries	30
Mining	20
Food/beverages	60
Textiles/garments/fur	63
Wood/furniture	2
Paper-making/printing	25
Petroleum/chemicals/rubber/plastic	139
Electronics	67
Metal and non-metals	121
Mechanical equipment/instruments	178
Medicine and biology	72
Other manufacturing	18
Power/steam/water production and supply	51
Construction	26
Traffic/transportation/warehousing	56
IT	76
Wholesale/retail	99
Finance/insurance	10
Real estate	41
Social services	42
Broadcasting and culture	11
Miscellaneous	80
Total	1,287

Source: China Securities Regulatory Commission

Table 2 Ratio of market capitalisation to GDP (1992–2003) (100 million yuan)

	GDP	Market capitalisation (A and B shares)	Market capitalisation/ GDP (%)
1992	26,638	1,048	3.93
1993	34,634	3,531	10.20
1994	46,759	3,691	7.89
1995	58,478	3,474	5.94
1996	67,885	9,842	14.50
1997	74,772	17,529	23.44
1998	79,553	19,506	24.52
1999	82,054	26,471	31.82
2000	89,404	48,091	53.79
2001	95,933	43,522	45.37
2002	102,398	38,329	37.43
2003	116,694	42,458	36.38

Source: China Securities Regulatory Commission
1US$ = 8.1 yuan

110% of GDP or Japan's 70% of GDP; there is clearly room for further growth. To bring the market's general efficiency and liquidity to a higher level, however, requires innovation in the stock market's fundamental infrastructures. A sweeping reform of its fundamental structure is a critical prerequisite for its next-stage leap.

Profound issues

The development of China's stock market vividly reflected the "trial and error" approach widely seen in its two-decade market economy reform. When China experimented with reform measures in earlier days, many regulations and mechanisms were temporary designs intended to operate for a stage or step in developments, instead of making it a long-lasting regulatory guideline. Chinese leaders described this process figuratively as "crossing a river by feeling the stones underneath."

Trial and error theory – the highest level
China's late leader, Deng Xiaoping, provided macro-guidance on China's Stock Market in his famous "Southern China Tour" in the early spring of 1992:

Are securities and the stock market good or bad? Do they entail any dangers? Are they peculiar to capitalism? Can socialism make use of them? We allow people to reserve their judgment, but we must try these things out. If, … they prove sensible, we can expand them. Otherwise, we can put a stop to them.

Unofficial translation of excerpts from Talks Given in Wuchang, Shenzhen, Zhuhai and Shanghai (18 January–21 February, 1992), in *Selected Works of Deng Xiaoping, Volume 3.*

For the stock market in particular, the "trial and error" approach has left many fundamental issues unresolved as the stock market continued its remarkable growth for years. For example, although stocks listing and trading started in 1990, the market operated without a securities law until seven years later. Furthermore, the Securities Law, initially enacted in 1998 (and numerous securities regulations following it), was curiously silent on what constitutes a "securities instrument" until its recent amendments in 2005.

Among others, the single most important overhang on the China stock market is the so-called "separation of equity ownership" feature. When China's traditional state-owned enterprises (SOEs) were restructured to become listed companies on the stock exchanges, their share structure was segregated into ownership by the state, the state-owned controlling entities and public individuals. This peculiar phenomenon is also known as the separation of equity ownership and will be discussed in detail later in this chapter.

The segmented share ownership structure and the ongoing reform effort on it will have a profound impact on China's stock market in the new century. It is the ultimate driving force for the liquidity, valuation and trading mechanisms with respect to the innovative financial products to be in discussed in Part II of this book, and importantly, leads to complex issues with respect to transferring the controlling share ownership such as mergers and acquisitions (M&As) and management buy-out (MBO) transactions in Part III.

In recent months, the regulators' commitment to fundamental market reform has given investors grounds for optimism. Extensive reform measures are being carried out, as the persistent bear market in recent years has convinced the regulators and market players that quick fixes are no longer possible. The share ownership structure, not surprisingly, is at the core of this fundamental reform.

ALL SHARES ARE NOT CREATED EQUAL

The segregated share ownerships, together with currency inconvertibility and domestic/overseas listings, have created a variety of share categories for China's listed companies. Foreign investors, however, should note that these share categories are different from the share class concept that they are familiar with. In developed markets, respective investors for different share classes have different dividend expectations, voting rights and priority in liquidations, but within each class, shareholders are entitled to equal rights and equal benefits, irrespective of the investors' legal format or citizenship.

In China, the issue is that there are different rights for the "same" class of shares, even though China's Company Law explicitly provides that "shares of the same class should have equal rights and equal benefits." Below is a chart illustrating the typical shareholding structure for China's listed companies, the various share categories will be explained in detail below.

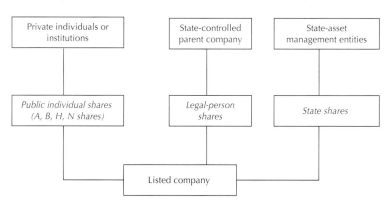

Typical share ownership structure of China's listed companies

Individual, legal person and state shares

To fully understand the segregated share ownership in China's listed companies, a brief history lesson may be helpful. At the inception of the stock market, most of the listed companies in China were previously large SOEs, which were viewed as the basis and symbol of a socialist economy. When they were restructured into shareholding companies to be traded publicly, continued controlling ownership by the state seemed to be politically essential.

Upon listing, an SOE is typically restructured to have three macro-categories of share ownership. Firstly, approximately one-third of the equity ownership is allocated to "state shares" (*guojia gu*), which are held by state-asset management entities or other authorised institutions on behalf of the state, which are mandated to protect state assets from depreciation and misappropriation. Secondly, another third or more equity ownership is held by a parent company with a "legal-person" status in the form of "legal-person" shares (*faren gu*). The parent contributes productive assets to the listed firm in exchange for the legal-person shares. The local government is typically the ultimate holder of the state share and legal-person share interests.

Finally, the remaining one-third or less equity ownership is placed with the public in the form of "public individual shares" (*shehui geren gu*), which could then be held by individuals and institutions. Only the public individual shares (also known as tradable shares) are freely tradable on the stock market whereas the state shares and legal-person shares are not (for this reason, they are generally referred to as nontradable shares in aggregate). The nontradable shares, however, may be transferred upon regulatory approval, including the transfer to foreign investors that has been made possible by recent legal developments since China's accession to the WTO.

Nontradable shares (China) *versus* restricted stocks (US)

In the US stock market, a few types of shares are known as "restricted stocks", which cannot be traded freely. The nontradable shares in China, however, are quite a different concept.

The restricted stocks in the US, for example the restricted stocks received from a private security offering, typically could be traded freely after being held for a sufficiently long holding period. In a case where the restriction could not be completely removed by a holding period, for example the shares held by the corporate insiders such as the board of directors, those restricted shares could still be sold with specific volume and manner limitations.

By contrast, China's nontradable shares are subject to a much stronger restriction. In fact, the nontradable shares could not be traded publicly "at all" before China, in 2005, reinitiated the reform on the separation of equity ownership issue. Even for those companies that participated in the full-flotation pilot programme, their nontradable shares could not be traded until the public shareholder meeting and regulatory bodies approved their shareholding reform plan.

On average, about one-third (33%) of the shares of listed companies are traded publicly. In other words, about twice as many, ie, two-thirds of the shares, are held in the form of nontradable shares. Table 3 shows the amount of tradable shares as a percentage of the total shares of the listed companies (the so-called "float ratio") for the 12-year period covering 1992 to 2003.

Table 3 Tradable share ratios of the Chinese market (%)

	Tradable shares (100 million shares)	Nontradable shares (100 million shares)	Ratio of tradable to total shares (%)
1992	21	69	31
1993	108	388	28
1994	226	685	33
1995	301	848	36
1996	430	1,220	35
1997	671	1,943	35
1998	862	2,527	34
1999	1,080	3,089	35
2000	1,354	3,792	36
2001	1,813	5,218	35
2002	2,037	5,875	35
2003	2,268	6,428	35

Source: China Securities Regulatory Commission

Subclassification among individual shares

The public individual shares are further divided into more subcategories.

Currency inconvertibility: A and B shares

Depending on the eligible buyers and the reference, the listed shares on the two stock exchanges in China are traditionally divided into A shares and B shares. A shares are basically limited to domestic investors, with both the principal and dividends denominated into the local Chinese currency yuan, also known as Ren Min Bi (RMB). Since China implemented the Qualified Foreign Institutional Investors (QFII) system a few years ago, a small number of qualified foreign investors have also gained direct access to the A share market, which will be discussed in detail in Chapter 2.

Like the A shares, B shares are listed on exchanges in China and are also denominated in yuan. However, they are bought and sold in foreign currencies, and foreigners are allowed to invest in them directly. Dividends and other distributions on the B shares are also paid in foreign currencies, though calculated and declared in yuan.

Historically, the separation of A and B shares is largely due to the lack of free convertibility of yuan and the so-called "restricted foreign currency" policy. The B share market was specifically created for foreign investors at its inception in 1991, but Chinese individuals

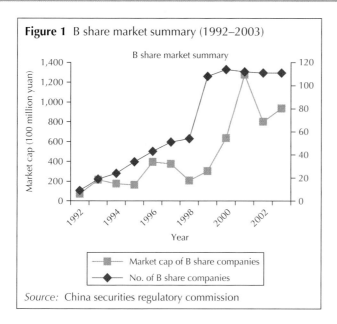

Figure 1 B share market summary (1992–2003)

Source: China securities regulatory commission

with foreign currency accounts were also permitted to invest in the B share market after February 2001.

As a traditional way of investing in China for foreign investors, the B share market will be discussed further in Chapter 2. As new ways to tap into the Chinese stock market continue to emerge, the B share market is gradually losing its appeal. New issues have pretty much dried up and the market size is gradually decreasing (see Figure 1).

Location separations: H and N Shares

In addition to A and B shares, a listed company may also have shares listed on overseas exchanges. For example, H shares are stocks of Chinese companies listed on the Hong Kong Stock Exchange (SEHK), while N shares are those listed on the New York Stock Exchange (NYSE). The trading of these shares is mainly subject to the laws of listing locations rather than Chinese laws.

Compared with the total market capitalisation of listed companies, overseas listings have a much smaller size. According to the China Securities Regulatory Commission (CSRC) statistics, by 2004, the overseas capitalisation was well below 5% of the domestic market capitalisation of A and B shares.

As illustrated by the pie chart below, shares in China's domestic stock market – A shares and nontradable shares – constitute a

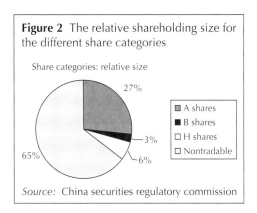

Figure 2 The relative shareholding size for the different share categories

Share categories: relative size

27%

3%

65%

6%

- A shares
- B shares
- H shares
- Nontradable

Source: China securities regulatory commission

Table 4 Summary of share categories in China's stock market

Share category	Descriptions/characters
Individual A shares	Shares of Chinese companies traded on the Shanghai and Shenzhen Stock Exchanges that are denominated in yuan and owned by domestic individuals and institutions, except for limited holdings by foreign investors through the QFII system
Individual B shares	Shares of China companies listed on the Shanghai and Shenzhen Stock Exchanges, which are traded in US$ in Shanghai and HK$ in Shenzhen. Foreign investors are permitted to invest in B shares directly
Legal-person shares	Shares of listed companies that are held by state-controlled domestic institutions. The legal-person shares cannot be traded on the stock market, but can be transferred through private agreement
State shares	Shares of listed companies that are held by local government or state asset management entities. Similar to legal-person shares, state shares cannot be traded on the stock market, but can be transferred through private agreement
H shares	Shares of PRC-registered companies listed in Hong Kong
N shares	Shares of PRC-registered companies listed in New York (NYSE, Nasdaq, etc)

predominant majority interest in the listed companies' capital structure. This book will focus on how foreign investors can explore investment opportunities in the domestic stock market as China carries out an all-dimensional reform of share ownership structures.

ISSUES WITH SEPARATION OF EQUITY OWNERSHIP

The separation of equity ownership has prevented China's stock market from performing the normal capital markets functions. Because the state controls the lion's share of the listed companies, the government has taken on dual roles as shareholder and regulator. In this context, the pursuit for the maximisation of shareholder interests may have a totally different meaning than in developed capital markets.

The controlling state-owned interests have two important features. Firstly, ownership is fragmented and exercised by multiple party and government entities, resulting in "vacancy" of the state as an owner in publicly listed SOEs. Compared to modern corporations in developed markets, the SOEs have no "visible" owners. On the other hand, the "owners" and the company management are closely affiliated, as the personnel, finance and assets are very often not separated between the listed companies and their controlling shareholders.

Secondly, the state-owned interests are not actually traded. This means that the owners of most companies – usually the state or state-controlled institutions – have little direct interest in the performance of the share price, because the public trading price is irrelevant to their equity holdings. As a result, the listed companies are hardly subject to the checks and balances from external public shareholders, and conflict of interests becomes a critical issue. For example, because of the lack of enforcement on fiduciary duty and conflict of interests, controlling shareholders and listed companies frequently enter into unfair related-party transactions that are detrimental to minority shareholders in the public market.

A review of the major market operation and corporate governance problems caused by the separation of equity ownership will be described below.

Excessive speculation by retail investors

The speculation level in China's stock market is extremely high. The most commonly used indicator for market speculation is the "average stock turnover rate", which is defined as:

$$Average\ stock\ turnover\ rate = \frac{Total\ annual\ trading\ value}{Annual\ average\ market\ capitalisation}$$

A higher turnover rate indicates more frequent trading or a shorter average holding period for stocks and is thus an indication of prevalent speculation.

Table 5 Retail *versus* institutional investors – A share trading accounts composition in 2003 (Unit: 10,000)

Total accounts	6835.18
Institutional	32.87
Individual	6802.31
New accounts	138.64
Institutional	1.52
Individual	137.13

Source: China Securities Regulatory Commission

According to a 2002 Dow Jones Indexes report, the annual average turnover for China's A share market during the 1994–2001 period was more than 500%. This can be interpreted as each stock on average being traded five times in a year or, in other words, the average holding period for a single stock was less than two months (one-fifth of a year). By contrast, in developed markets the typical holding period is about two years. The speculation level in China's stock market thus is truly extraordinary.

Although many factors are attributable to this widespread speculation, the segregated share structure definitely plays a significant role. Without sufficient ownership rights to supervise the listed companies, investors in the public market are simply not excited about any long-term investment strategies. Retail investors (currently dominating the market as shown in the table above) in particular focus mainly on speculative profits from frequent trading. Therefore, the market needs more institutional investors to play two important roles: one to act as a counterweight to the controlling shareholders, and the other to make long-term investments to reduce market volatility.

Lack of minority shareholder protection

The separation of equity ownership has created two macro groups of shareholders: the public investors that hold the tradable A shares and the state-controlled entities that hold the nontradable shares. Because on average about two-thirds of the shares in listed companies are nontradable, the nontradable shareholders are usually the controlling shareholders that have the final say during the company's decision-making process.

The interests of the holders of the nontradable shares are not always consistent with those of tradable shares, for example on issues such as corporate financing decisions (see below on excessive equity financing). In extreme cases, those controlling shareholders may enter into transactions where the interests of minority shareholders are blatantly infringed. As an example, the holders of the nontradable shares may organise related-party transactions to transfer assets at submarket prices to firms under their control. To give another example, the controlling shareholders may approve large cash dividends to benefit themselves, because they acquire the nontradable shares at much lower prices than the public investors in the stock market.

Thus for years, the main stock market regulator, the CSRC, has made continued efforts to enforce best practices in listed companies to protect minority shareholder interests. The CSRC has stiffened the penalties for perpetrators of fraud and required companies to follow international accounting standards when disclosing financial performance. In February 2005, the CSRC announced that a protection fund for public stock investors was being created, although it is still unclear how the fund will be used or when it will become operational.

Most notably, the CSRC has created a special voting system that reflects the special characteristics of the shareholding structure in China. In December 2004, the CSRC issued *The Provisions on Strengthening the Protection of Rights & Interests of Public Shareholders*, which created a separate voting right for the holders of the publicly tradable shares in connection with major corporate events. According to the *Provisions*, listed companies' major business decisions, such as rights issues and issuing additional new shares, and equity-for-debt plans, should win majority votes from holders of tradable shares at the general shareholders meeting (this is also known as the "categorised share voting" system).

Despite all the remarkable progress, the segregated shareholding structure in listed companies remains a fundamental barrier to modern corporate governance. For example, the B share market has failed to attract significant interest from foreign investors, which is one clear indication of the suboptimal quality of disclosures and accounting standards of the listed companies, and lack of investor confidence in the corporate governance of those companies. The next step corporate governance reform will require is more institutional investors acting as a counterweight to the controlling shareholders, pushing for more transparency and financial disclosure to meet public (especially foreign) investors' requirements.

Excessive financing in capital markets

The "pecking order" theory in western corporate finance suggests that corporations prefer internal funds whenever possible for new investment projects and they favour issuing debt rather than equity, if external funds are required. An equity or equity-linked offering is typically viewed as a very expensive last resort for corporate finance. The potential dilution in corporate control is the main reason. In other words, common stock or common stock-linked offerings will add new equity investors to the company's ownership structure, thus diluting the share ownership of existing shareholders.

The situation for China's listed companies is completely the opposite. Two important features make equity financing attractive to the controlling shareholders (holders of the nontradable shares) of the listed companies. First, the nontradable shares were acquired at a much lower price than the public A share price. Thus any offering at the public market price brings positive value to the nontradable shareholders. Second, the nontradable share interests in a listed company constitute the predominant controlling stake; thus ownership dilution is not that much of a concern.

The listed companies' preference for equity financing is most evident in their equity-linked financing vehicles such as convertible bonds. Unlike their counterparts in more developed capital markets, Chinese convertible bonds, as discussed in Chapter 3, have been structured to be very "equity like", ie, they are designed to have a very high probability of conversion into the company's common stock upon maturity. Furthermore, Haitong Securities Company concluded, in a 2005 empirical research report, that excessive financing is prevalent in China's listed companies, both for equity and debt financing.

No takeover pressure

Takeovers, especially hostile takeovers, have long been considered an effective corporate governance mechanism to keep corporate management in check. Additionally, researchers have also argued that takeovers help in the allocating of scarce social resources more efficiently, because the takeover process ensures that the resources are managed by the most capable management team, thus maximising shareholder value.

In China, the management of the listed companies is seldom under check for two reasons. The obvious one is that the state as the controlling shareholder, generally speaking, is virtually non-existent with respect to monitoring the management. The more subtle reason is that there is no takeover pressure to contain the management. The majority of the shares of the listed companies are in the form of nontradable shares, which could only be transferred by private agreement. Thus gaining corporate control through public tender offer – the popular takeover form in developed markets – is not typically feasible in China.

As will be discussed in detail in Chapter 9, M&As today have become a common feature in China's stock market, from a virtually unknown term a decade ago. The quick development of the M&A legal framework and the ongoing SOE reform are leading to rapid growth in M&A activities. The increasingly active market for corporate control should foster better corporate governance going forward.

In summary, the above factors make China's listed companies significantly different from listed companies in the US. The differences are summarised in the following table:

Table 6 Major differences between listed companies in China and the US

	Listed companies in China	Listed companies in the US
Ownership structure	❏ Controlling shareholder is usually the state or state-controlled institutions ❏ Controlling portion of the shares are not tradable	❏ Controlling shareholder is the individual(s) or private company that established the firm ❏ All shares are tradable except for shares temporarily restricted from public trading (ie, freely tradable after a restriction period)
Role of institutional investors	❏ Small percentage in total investor composition ❏ Limited enforcement power as minority shareholders	❏ Voting at shareholders' meetings as influential investors ❏ Monitoring performance of companies and promoting best practices in corporate governance
Minority shareholders	❏ Weak protection of minority shareholders' rights	❏ Laws protect minority shareholders, eg supermajority voting, derivative lawsuits

Table 6 (continued)

	Listed companies in China	Listed companies in the US
Corporate finance	❏ Firms mainly rely on banking loan as main financing vehicle ❏ Firms often prefer public equity to debt financing because share offerings do not dilute control and are relatively cheap	❏ "Pecking order" theory suggests that companies prefer debt as a relatively cheap financing method, with equity financing the most expensive
Corporate takeover	❏ Hostile takeover difficult due to limited floating shares in public market ❏ Transfers of nontradable state interests must be authorised by various administrative agencies	❏ Hostile takeovers frequently used to acquire corporate control

NEW TRENDS IN THE TRANSFORMING ERA

Stock market reform in China is centred on the separation of equity ownership. On 1 February, 2004, China's State Council – the supreme executive branch of China – issued the landmark reform guideline, *Several Opinions on Promoting the Reform, Opening up and Stable Development of the Capital Markets*. This guideline from the State Council summed up China's capital market developments over the past decade, and it outlined the directions for future developments. Notably, the State Council officially acknowledged the issue of separation of equity ownership, and it suggested this issue should be "actively and properly solved."

To improve the ownership structure of listed companies, the government has initiated two powerful reforms in recent years. On the one hand, it is promoting a stronger institutional investor base in the A share market, which could potentially become a counterweight to the dominating shareholders of the nontradable shares. On the other hand, it is also taking steps to reduce state ownership through privatisation, which culminated at the most drastic trial in 2005, which aimed to ultimately make all nontradable shares of the listed companies tradable.

Both trends have opened up new investment opportunities for foreign investors. The institutionalisation of the stock market has led to the Qualified Foreign Instructional Investors (QFII) system, which grants qualified foreign investors direct access to China's capital markets. On the nontradable share side, China reopened foreign investors' access to state and legal-person shares, following its accession to the WTO in 2002. As a result, foreign buy-out and private equity firms have been active in M&As or MBO transctions in China.

Institutionalising China's A share stock market

As mentioned earlier in the chapter, speculation is the main theme for the A share market in China, because the momentum of investing by retail investors drives stock market valuations. The government is encouraging more domestic and foreign institutional investors to enter its stock market, as their long-term institutional investments are expected to inject greater stability and rationality into a market that has long been dominated by short-term speculators.

Furthermore, the institutionalisation of the stock market is a vital step towards improved corporate governance in listed companies, because the institutional investor base may serve as a counterweight to the dominating state ownership. For example, in connection with major corporate decision events, institutional investors have participated much more actively than retail investors. Although the CSRC required listed companies to provide on-line voting platforms for shareholders' meetings to facilitate small and medium-sized shareholders, statistics show that those who have voted on-line represent no more than 10% of the tradable shares of the company.

The good news is that China continues to bring more institutional investors to the market, which include securities funds, pension funds, commercial banks, insurance companies and, most relevant to the foreign investors, the QFII. Notably, the recently amended Securities Law removed the previous restrictions on stock trading by state firms and banks, encouraging more sources of funds to participate in the market. According to data from the Shanghai Stock Exchange, stockholdings by institutional investors accounted for a little more than 30% of the tradable share markets as of November 2005.

Investment fund companies

Currently the fund companies are the largest institutional investors in the Chinese market. The CSRC also has allowed foreign firms to participate in the securities and fund management businesses through joint ventures with local firms. These changes will help bring to China sophisticated institutional investors who will be more critical of valuation distortions, and will replace the momentum investing currently driving the domestic markets with more fundamental investments.

Commercial banks
In 2005, Chinese regulators issued rules allowing domestic commercial banks to set up fund-management companies. The commercial banks could potentially become a powerful institutional investor base, as individual and corporate deposits in China's banking system exceeded 25 trillion yuan, or about US$3 trillion, in 2004, according to central bank data.

Retirement funds
In February 2005, detailed guidelines were unveiled to permit retirement funds to invest in the stock market though mutual funds. The regulators have authorised the social-security fund (the retirement fund) to invest 40% of its assets in domestic stocks.

Insurance companies
China's insurance companies are permitted to invest 5% of their total assets in the stock market. Before the October 2004 rule issued jointly by the China Insurance Regulatory Commission (CIRC) and CSRC, insurance companies were only allowed to participate in much less risky investments, such as bank deposits, Treasury bonds, corporate debt and stock funds. In 2005, both domestic and foreign insurance companies were permitted to invest directly in the stock market.

Qualified foreign institutional investors
The new QFII system is a major step for China towards institutionalising the stock market. Introduced in November 2002, the QFII system allows foreign investors, including banks, insurance companies, fund management institutions and any other institution meeting the criteria, to invest directly in China's capital markets. Those qualified investors were given a total US$4 billion quota, with which they could invest in the A shares of listed companies,

Treasury bonds listed on stock exchanges, convertible bonds, corporate bonds and other financial instruments as approved by the CSRC.

The most significant near-term impact of QFII will not be more foreign capital – indeed the Chinese market is full of liquid capital, given the household savings at trillion-dollar level. The investment culture and values of international institutional investors should help develop an institutional investment culture in China, and their relatively long-term investment horizons (as compared to the typical retail investors) should also help reduce market volatility.

Furthermore, QFIIs will accelerate improvements in the standards of corporate governance in China, because Chinese companies will increasingly be benchmarked against their international peers. The opening of the local market will be an important stimulus for Chinese companies to improve corporate governance standards. It is a strong stimulus for improving corporate governance, ushering in a more rational investment philosophy and fostering a closer correlation with the world market.

Deregulation is not only a major step forward for China, but also potentially a huge opportunity for international investors. As will be discussed in detail in Chapter 2, the QFII system has not only given direct market access to a small number of large institutional investors (the QFIIs), but also created a structured product market where smaller foreign investors could gain synthetic exposure to China's A share market from certain QFII brokers/dealers. Coupled with recent financial innovations in China, the QFII system offers foreign investors far more investment alternatives to tap into the Chinese A share market than in recent years, which will be discussed in detail in the next few chapters.

Transfer of nontradable shares

China has been restructuring its ailing SOEs since it started its market economy reform decades ago. In particular, Chinese companies are increasingly facing more and more foreign competition as a result of joining the WTO, and the state has been aggressively looking for foreign investors (as well as domestic ones) during the SOE reform campaign. In its search for foreign technology (both in manufacturing and corporate management), China is looking to increase its competitiveness as its market opens up in full to foreign companies.

This trend is evidenced by a series of new regulations guiding foreign M&A activities in China, in particular, the *"Tentative Provisions on the Use of Foreign Investment to Reorganise State-Owned Enterprises"*, jointly issued by multiple government agencies in January 2003, which acknowledged the goal to invigorate SOEs through foreign equity ownership. What is most significant from recent moves is that foreign investors are being permitted to take controlling stakes in these enterprises. Consequently, a large number of SOEs are becoming available for restructuring or partnering with foreign firms through M&A measures.

Because the publicly tradable shares typically constitute a minority interest in the listed companies, public tender offers are not generally a feasible method for acquiring corporate control in China. Instead, an external investor has to acquire some of the nontradable shares of a listed company to gain a controlling interest in it. For many listed companies, the acquisition of nontradable shares through private negotiation is probably the most direct way of acquiring a controlling or significant interest in them.

Foreign acquisitions of nontradable shares in listed companies first appeared in the 1990s and were quickly prohibited in 1995 by China's State Council. This moratorium was only lifted in 2003, by the *Notice Regarding the Transfer of State-Owned Shares and Legal-Person Shares of Listed Companies to Foreign Parties*. Together with a flurry of other regulatory developments, new foreign investors' access to nontradable shares has created optimism in M&A prospects in China, which will be discussed in detail in Part III.

Sweeping reform in 2005

The QFII system and the M&A market reflect an increase in foreign participation in the two segregated parts of the stock market. On the one hand, the QFII system opens up the domestic stock market to foreign institutional investors with respect to the tradable shares in China. On the other hand, regulatory developments in the M&A market reopened access by foreign investors to the nontradable shares of the listed companies (the state-owned and legal-person shares).

Around mid 2005, Chinese regulators launched the largest scale reform ever in the 15-year history of the Chinese stock market, with the ambitious goal of resolving the "segregated equity owner-ship" issue by making nontradable shares tradable. This reform, as discussed in detail below, brings new twists and simultaneous opportunities to the above-discussed foreign investment regimes.

REFORM ON SEGREGATED EQUITY OWNERSHIP
Overview
Illustrating its complexity and profound implications, the reform on segregated equity ownership is also frequently referred to as the "state-share overhaul reform" and "full-flotation reform." These terms are used interchangeably in China's stock market, and so will be in this book. Each reflects an important aspect of this funda-mental reform in the stock market:

❏ "Reform on segregated equity owner identifies the fundamental issue that reform aims to address.
❏ "State-share overhaul reform" reflect broader context of SOE reform and privatisation, as the reform facilitates the transfer of current state-owned interests to the public market.
❏ "Full-flotation reform" emphasise-marketing trading implica-tion of the reform, as formerly nontradable shares will become tradable, post the reform.

This large reform effort is a powerful and unprecedented new mar-ket force in the Chinese stock market. Making all shares tradable is considered essential for increasing market liquidity, protecting minority investors, making state-owned firms more efficient and resolving all the other issues caused by the separation of equity ownership. In the short term, however, it brings new complications – mixed challenges and opportunities – to investors who trade or transact with the listed companies.

State share overhaul reform – trials and progress
For years, the Chinese government planned to sell most state companies to investors in the public market, but simply pumping a flood of stocks on to the markets proved not to be an effective approach in earlier trials.

The latest attempt at a full flotation occurred in 2001, when the regulators' sudden reform announcement caught investors by surprise. The plan was quickly aborted after key indexes, then at near-record heights, plunged about 30% and spawned a threat of social unrest.

> Instead of making a surprising move as in 2001, regulators unveiled the 2005 full-flotation programme at the start of a weeklong "May 1 holiday", during which the stock exchanges were closed. Apparently, the regulators tried to give investors time to digest the details and prevent a knee-jerk rush to sell on the exchange.
>
> More importantly, the full-flotation programmes in 2005 have followed more capital market rules than one uniform government-imposed scheme. The new campaign is more like a bargaining game between regular investors and the entities holding nontradable shares. The state shareholders must offer cash, shares or other considerations to the public market shareholders to gain shareholder approval to trade their previously nontradable shares. The regulators have chosen to act as a neutral arbiter of others' disputes, which in itself represents a remarkable development for China's stock market.

In May 2005, stock market regulators unveiled the reform measures. Four mid-sized listed companies were chosen for the Phase I experimental programme, and most have had their state-share overhaul plans approved by shareholders. Then in July 2005, Phase II of the trial programme involved an additional 42 companies, representing a broad spectrum of industry sectors and including the largest companies, such as Baoshan Iron & Steel Co. and the China Yangtze Power Company, suggesting an acceleration in the programme to make all equity of listed companies tradable.

The full-flotation reform immediately raised wide public debates and controversies. At the crux of the matter was the level of consideration that should be paid to public investors in exchange for trading the liquidity of nontradable shares. Generally, the share flotation plans involved compensating existing public shareholders with cash or additional stocks in exchange for the public trading liquidity for nontradable shares. Such payments were aimed at cushioning any losses the public shareholders might incur from falling stock prices triggered by the large supply of nontradable shares. As such, proposals to convert the nontradable shares into publicly traded stock required approval from the CSRC and the approval by two-thirds of the holders of the publicly traded stocks.

Considering the sheer number of companies affected and the size of the nontradable shares, the full-flotation reform will surely be a multi-year effort. At the time the pilot programme was launched, nontradable shares represented two-thirds of the US$450 billion stock-market capitalisation in China, and nearly every one of the 1,400 or so listed companies faces the same issue.

So far, the reform has been carried out at an impressively fast pace. Over 300 holdings had already completed the divestment reform by the year-end and another 400–500 are expected to complete the programme by mid 2006. Market sentiment has also rebounded from the original panic and confusions, showing optimism and high expectations. For example, the Mid & Small-Cap Board Index and the New Shanghai Composite Index (see detailed discussions in Chapter 6) – the two existing stock indexes consist solely of companies that have completed the share reform – both closed high with strong trading volumes at their debut.

Trading implications

This ongoing full-flotation reform effort is a powerful and unprecedented new market force in the Chinese stock market. Making all shares tradable is considered essential for increasing market liquidity, protecting minority investors, making state-owned firms more efficient and resolving all the other issues caused by the separation of equity ownership. In the short term, however, it brings new complexities – mixed challenges and opportunities – to foreign investors, as the reform will have a significant impact on investments in the listed companies in many different ways.

New initial public offerings (IPOs)

The IPO offering window has been completely shut down since the share reform launched in mid 2005. The CSRC has suggested that companies that have completed the share reform programme will have priority in raising funds in the stock markets. According to the CSRC guideline, future IPOs will no longer have a nontradable portion.

A share market trading

The full-flotation campaign has cleared the uncertainty for many years around the overhang of nontradable shares, which should be positive in the long run. In the short term, however, the unloading of state shares creates pressure on A share market trading. When the experimental programme kicked off in May 2005, the two stock exchanges fell to a fresh seven-year low in reaction to the public investors' first response, which then modestly rebounded in the summer as the market gradually digested the full-flotation pro-gramme and other new regulatory policies.

To avoid stock price collapses, the regulators have provided strict limits on when and how much can be sold on to the open market. For instance, once a full-flotation plan has been approved, the actual selling of the state-owned shares in such a listed com-pany would be delayed for at least a year by holding periods and other circuit breakers. For big shareholders holding more than 5% ownership, their sale of shares is subject to annual size limits and requires timely public disclosures. In aggregate, the sheer size of the total nontradable shares has created a huge supply and demand puzzle, so it will not be surprising to see further regulatory guidelines on the actual unloading of nontradable shares onto the public market.

Companies with multiple share categories

Existing foreign investors should expect to be affected by the reform programme, as more than 100 Chinese listed companies that also have outstanding H shares (Hong Kong-listed) and B shares (listed in Shanghai and Shenzhen in foreign currency denomination), would also participate. A critical issue arises as to whether H and B shareholders should also receive consideration in connection with the full-flotation reform in their respective companies?

It is debatable as to whether the foreign currency-denominated shareholders (B, H, N shares, etc) are harmed when they are excluded from voting on the reform plan (and consequently, not compensated). For example, some market participants argued that the reform should have no impact on the interest of B and H share-holders for two reasons. Firstly, nontradable shares would be floated in the A share market only. Secondly, the B and H share markets have been completely segregated from the domestic stock market for the past few years because of the non-convertibility of the yuan.

It's a market economy...
How should the B, H, and N shareholders be compensated for the full-flotation reform in China? This topic could easily lead to much academic research in years to come. However, instead of trying to set up a formula for the market, the CSRC in an unusual, yet smart move, decided to let the market decide on the details.

To some extent, this move reflects a new way of thinking at the CSRC and the new regulatory role it intends to take on in the new era. Formerly, the CSRC, as the main supervisory body of the stock market, has been better known for control, supervision and administrative intervention. It probably shows that the CSRC is taking on a more market-economy approach as the stock market transforms into an investor-oriented market.

In its *Guideline for the Reform on the Separation of Equity Ownership in the Listed Companies*, the CSRC concluded that the reform plan to float nontradable shares should be determined by the shareholders in the domestic market, ie, the holders of the nontradable and tradable A shares, which effectively excluded the B, H, and N shareholders from voting on the share float and compensation plan.

However, the CSRC officials, without laying out specific measures, simultaneously stressed that any reform plan by a listed firm that has overseas listings should not in any way harm the legitimate interests of the overseas shareholders. Essentially, the CSRC leaves the issue to the shareholders to work out a reform plan on a case-by-case basis.

Structured investments linked to A shares
Many existing investment products in China reflect the separation of the equity ownership status quo. For instance, convertible bonds in China have been structured to be heavily "equity like". The index calculation methodology for the Shanghai Shenzhen 300 index – the only index that covers both exchanges in China – is another example. The structures for financial products linked to A shares will change significantly once the full-flotation campaign picks up momentum.

Innovation in new investment products
The new full-flotation rules make it clear that the government will leave it to individual companies to negotiate a deal with public

shareholders. The regulators further encourage companies to develop innovative plans and tailored solutions for their share ownership restructuring. For example, as equity options and other derivatives became an effective tool in implementing the full-flotation programme, the option market as discussed in Chapter 4 started from ground zero and quickly became a market of its own within a few months.

At the same time, the regulators are also introducing new measures to support the share reform, such as permitting share buy-back plans among publicly traded companies. In the years to come, the full-flotation campaign will be a strong driving force for the next generation of financial products on China's stock market.

M&A and buy-out transactions

Generally speaking, there are two methods available for external investors to acquire shares of listed companies in order to gain corporate control of them: one is a takeover by public tender offer; the other by private agreement. The tradable shares of listed companies can be accumulated by a public tender offer, whereas the nontradable shares can only be transferred through private negotiation and agreement.

Because the nontradable shares typically constitute the majority interest in listed companies, private negotiation has been the main theme for M&A activities in China. By contrast, successful takeovers through the public market have been few and far between, and they occurred in unique circumstances where the target companies had a very simple ownership structure and few nontradable shares. Once all the shares are tradable, however, a tender offer will become a more feasible approach for M&As in China, and external investors will be able to gain a controlling interest in listed companies through capital market transactions.

CONCLUSION

For the past few years, one of the biggest bets and hottest topics in global markets has been China's economic growth. China has enjoyed near double-digit economic growth for more than a decade, and its outflow of exports and inflow of foreign direct investments (FDI) are ever-increasing. In the coming years, as the world expects, China will also create the largest demand in the international economy with its more than 1 billion consumers.

Despite this, investors hoping to participate in China's economic miracles have experienced a different story in their stock investments in China. China's stock market, having grown at a tremendous pace under a mostly state-oriented framework, reached a critical transition point in the new millennium. In early 2005, the market indexes reached an eight-year low, amid uncertainties about the next phase in the Chinese stock market.

Still, investors may find grounds for optimism in China's stock market by focusing on its long-term potential. In the coming years, China will increasingly rely on its stock market to fuel its economic growth. The market, however, will drift away from its earliest mission to provide alternative financing to the troubled SOEs. Instead, it will promote share ownership reform in listed companies and provide financing solutions to one of the most dynamic, fastest-growing economies in the world.

Two fundamental themes underlying China's current share reform have opened up tremendous opportunities for foreign investment. The effort to institutionalise the stock market has led to the QFII system, which has continued to attract global money managers and securities firms. The privatisation of the ailing SOE sector has led to increasingly active foreign M&A activities in China. In the new era, foreign investors have many new investment vehicles available to invest in China, and China's stock market performance is poised to converge with its economic growth in the near future.

2

Emerging Access to China's Stock Market

China's stock market could be confusing to many foreign investors. The unusual uncertainty and complexity of the market give both bulls and bears good cases. There are plenty of enthusiastic research reports bullish on "China's Wild Ride" or "The Great Leap Forward". But from time to time, some more cautious commentary articles also pop up with eye-catching titles, such as "The Best China Investment Strategy: Forget About It".

All these conundrums boil down to one fundamental question – for investors interested in one of the world's fastest-growing economies, what is the best way to gain the desired exposure? The answer is, of course, it depends.

There are a few investment vehicles that investors are relatively familiar with – such as B shares, H shares, N shares, exchange-traded funds (ETFs) linked to the China index, and mutual funds focusing on China or China-related stocks. Following its WTO accession in December 2001, however, China's stock market has started to open up the yuan-denominated local A share market to foreign investors. As a result, new channels to invest in China's stock market have become available to foreign investors of late, and the market is generally optimistic that this welcome trend should continue in the future.

For example, the new QFII scheme permits qualified investors to invest in China's listed A share market directly, and it leads to a structured products market where smaller investors may gain synthetic exposure to the A share market. Separately, the more developed M&A regulatory framework in China also permits foreign investors to acquire nontradable state shares to pursue a controlling stake in Chinese companies.

This chapter will examine a broad spectrum of investment vehicles for China's stock market – some are more familiar options and some are new breakthroughs on the rise. The new addition of investment products will be discussed in detail in Part II and Part III of this book. For a particular investor – retail, institutional, hedge fund, or venture fund investor – the appropriate investment choice largely depends on such investor's risk preference and financial sophistication.

TRADITIONAL WAYS TO INVEST
H shares or N shares

Up until now, most foreign investors have concentrated on a small number of Chinese stocks that trade on US exchanges (the N shares) or the stock markets in Hong Kong (the H shares), where the bulk of Chinese companies listed outside the mainland are traded. That is because for many investors, Chinese equity markets still remain something of an unknown and unquantifiable risk. Overseas listed shares are convenient investment vehicles for investors because they are denominated in local currencies and their trading activities are mainly subject to the laws of listing locations rather than Chinese laws. Therefore, the issue of corporate governance or market manipulation is not as significant as in China's local stock markets.

However, the H and N shares have their limitations. Firstly, as mentioned in Chapter 1, overseas capitalisation of Chinese companies is well below 5% of the domestic market capitalisation of A shares and B shares. The foreign listed shares, therefore, could serve as an easy way to gain some Chinese exposure, but may not be an efficient way to participate in China's broad economic growth.

Secondly, pricing discrepancies between overseas shares and locally listed A shares of the same company could be significant. For example, there are several Chinese companies that list both A shares and H shares. Because the two share types are not fungible and trade in different currencies, there are no pure arbitrage mechanisms to make pricing consistent. As a result, the same company may trade at different P/E multiples on different markets. This kind of price discrepancy presents both a risk and an opportunity for foreign investors.

Thirdly, the structure of some H share companies can be confusing for investors. For example, "red-chips" refer to shares of Chinese companies that are registered overseas and listed abroad (mostly in Hong Kong). Red-chip companies typically have substantial interests in China and are controlled by a parent company that is affiliated with or controlled by the Chinese government. What the parent lists as an H share company may be just a minority portion of a subset of its activities. The value of the H share company, therefore, has a lot to do with its transactions and arrangements with the parent company.

Finally, the Chinese government historically has allowed only a few chosen firms – mostly large, strategically important and relatively better-performing, state-owned enterprises (SOEs) – access to overseas capital markets. As a result, in the past decade, Hong Kong has been the main destination for the country's biggest state-owned companies in search of capital, followed by New York and London. But this trend may change soon.

Of late, the Shanghai and Shenzhen Stock Exchanges have been seeking a bigger piece of the global fundraising pie, in part to revive confidence among domestic investors as well as to attract interest among foreign institutions that are being allowed to buy limited amounts of domestic equity through the QFII system. Chinese domestic investors, prohibited from buying shares from overseas, due to the inconvertibility of the yuan, have also argued that China needs to give local investors the same access to high-quality Chinese stocks that trade only in Hong Kong and/or New York, otherwise China's domestic stock market may be "marginalised". Following this trend, overseas listings may become less frequent for Chinese companies in the future.

American Depositary Receipts

For Chinese companies not listed in the US exchange, the American Depositary Receipt (ADR) mechanism provides US investors with a convenient way to invest in such non-US securities. An ADR is a US$-denominated equity ownership in such a non-US-listed Chinese company that is issued by a US bank serving as a depositary and custodian bank. ADRs listed on the New York Stock Exchange (NYSE) and Nasdaq are relatively easy to buy and sell.

Those that are listed must abide by US generally accepted accounting principles (GAAP).

The ADRs represent the local shares of the company held on deposit by the custodian bank in the company's home country (in other words, the ADRs are "backed" by corresponding local shares), and they typically offer the same corporate and economic benefits enjoyed by the domestic shareholders of the non-US-listed Chinese company.

Theoretically, the ADR should be a "mirror image" of the shares traded in the issuer's home market, because arbitrage traders in the two markets will make any price difference disappear. In the case of Chinese ADRs, however, the market frequently observes a significant difference between the prices of the ADR and the underlying stock on its home exchange. The non-convertibility of the yuan and the US dollar is partly the reason, because there is no perfect arbitrage mechanism to make the prices converge. Supply and demand is another important factor: only a small fraction of China's listed companies have ADR listings; therefore, investors are likely to bid up the ADRs when demand is high .

B shares

Compared to H shares, N shares and ADRs, B shares are a much more direct approach to investing in China. They are listed on the exchanges in China and they are denominated in yuan, like A shares, but they are bought and sold in foreign currencies and foreigners are allowed to buy them directly. Dividends and other distributions on B shares are also paid in foreign currencies, though calculated and declared in yuan. The B share market was specifically created for foreign investors at its inception in 1991, but Chinese individuals with foreign currency accounts have also been permitted to invest in the B share market since February 2001.

Many Chinese companies have issued both A and B shares. These shares are for the same listed company and traded on the same exchanges, but their prices are always different, sometimes even by a significant degree. It's very easy to see why.

Firstly, A shares are traded in yuan, whereas B shares are traded in Hong Kong dollars or US dollars (depending on which exchange the B share is listed). Currently, the yuan is not freely convertible to either foreign currency so A and B shares are traded in isolated markets. Secondly, the two share systems are unlikely to merge in the near future (which will ultimately converge the prices), even though there have been many proposals for such a consolidation. This is because a merger of the two categories of shares would give foreign investors unrestricted access to the A share market, which currently has foreign ownership restrictions.

One distinctive trading behaviour of the B share is that sometimes it is traded at a significant discount to A shares of the same company. The B shares' lack of trading liquidity was generally believed to be the reason. Additionally, the excess domestic demand for A shares was also an important factor before Chinese individuals were permitted to invest in B shares in 2001. In other words, the local investors had very limited investment alternatives besides the A share market, and their active trading apparently put upside pressure on A shares. Finally, some analysts have attributed the discount to the fluctuations in foreign currencies and the uncertainties in foreign currencies' potential convertibility into yuan. This B share discount, however, has narrowed since the government changed its policy in 2001 to permit Chinese individuals to invest in both A and B shares.

Needless to say, investing in B shares has a distinctive risk in contrast to shares trading in Hong Kong (H shares) and the US (N shares or ADRs). Although priced in Hong Kong and US dollars, B shares are not subject to the same degree of regulatory supervision seen in the Hong Kong and US stock markets. Generally speaking, the issuers' financial reporting is subject to more lax accounting standards, and there may not be ample transparent disclosure about issuing companies.

Another significant risk is the poor trading liquidity. Trading in B shares is often cumbersome and unloading underperforming stocks may be even more difficult. For funds with not-insignificant exposure to B shares, the fund managers reportedly rely on Hong Kong-listed shares for liquidity, in the event that they suddenly need to liquidate share positions to meet investors' redemption requests.

Hampered by the liquidity and quality issues of listed companies, B share new issuance declined in the 1990s and slowly dried up in the new century. The CSRC statistics showed that in the years following the end of 2001, B share issuance was few and far between. Today, B shares represent only a small percentage of the companies listed on the exchanges. In addition, the B share market is further marginalised by the QFII system, which permits foreign qualified investors to invest directly in the A share market. Therefore, B shares may become a less relevant investment option for foreign investors in the future.

China-focused mutual funds, ETFs and hedge funds

Although foreign investors are able to invest directly in the various categories of Chinese shares described above, many investors prefer a China-focused fund for important advantages, including diversification, liquidity, convenience and professional management.

The China-focused mutual funds typically own broad baskets of Chinese stocks, thus offering investors diversity and thereby mitigating the company-specific risks of individual stocks. Most actively managed funds own a mixture of ADRs, Hong Kong-listed Chinese companies, and sometimes a smaller percentage of B shares. The other side of the equation, of course, is that when a portfolio is broadly diversified, a big price jump in an individual growing company would not lead to significant appreciation of a large portfolio. Though actively managed funds often underperform stock indexes in more efficient western markets, many believe that active management may locate excessive returns in a segmented and inefficient market like China.

China-focused ETFs, on the other hand, typically track an index of overseas-listed Chinese companies or China-related stocks. An ETF is an index-tracking mutual fund or unit trust traded on an exchange. It invests in the constituent securities of the underlying index like an index mutual fund, but it is priced continuously and can be bought and sold on the exchange throughout the trading day like a single stock.

The iShares FTSE/Xinhua China 25 Index ETF is one example. The FTSE/Xinhua China 25 Index consists of 25 of the largest and most liquid companies. Those constituent shares in the index trade on the Hong Kong Stock Exchange and are denominated in Hong Kong dollars. The ETFs invest in their corresponding ADRs and the fund is denominated in US dollars, giving international investors easy access to the Chinese market.

Table 1 Summary of traditional investment vehicles

Investment vehicle	Description and character
H shares and N shares	Shares of individual Chinese companies listed on exchanges in Hong Kong or New York. Denominated in foreign currencies and regulated by foreign exchanges
ADRs	Stocks listed on the US exchanges and "backed" by the shares of individual Chinese companies. Traded in US dollars
B shares	Shares of individual Chinese companies listed on exchanges in China and traded in US dollars or Hong Kong dollars
Mutual funds	Investment in a basket of Chinese companies or China-related stocks. Risks and returns are more diversified
ETFs	Basket of investments that can be traded on exchanges. ETFs typically track an index of H shares or ADRs
Hedge funds	Less regulated funds pursuing dynamic investment strategies. Typically attract sophisticated investors with high net-worth

Additionally, there are hedge funds that are subject to lighter regulation. As such, they could pursue more dynamic and risky strategies, offering a more high-risk, high-return investment approach. However, they are mainly available to high net-worth investors only and the investment return will be subject to fund management fees and performance fees.

QUALIFIED FOREIGN INSTITUTIONAL INVESTOR (QFII) PROGRAMME

Since its accession to the WTO in December 2001, China has gradually opened up to foreign investors its domestic stock market – the A share market and the nontradable state-owned and legal-person shares. As discussed in Chapter 1, among all the tradable shares of Chinese companies, the yuan-denominated A share is the dominating component; additionally the nontradable shares (ie, the state and legal-person shares) are approximately twice the size of total tradable shares. Thus post-WTO market deregulation and privatisation is not only a major step forward for China, but also potentially a huge opportunity for international investors.

In particular, the QFII scheme was introduced in late 2002 to permit foreign qualified institutional investors to invest in China's domestic capital market directly. Separately, foreign acquisition of nontradable state and legal-person shares has been clarified and activated through new M&A regulations since 2002. All these developments could result in more foreign involvements, restructurings and, potentially, takeovers for China's listed companies.

Thus a few new alternatives for investing in China are on the rise. Firstly, the large institutional investors may invest in Chinese A shares and other financial products directly through the QFII scheme and small investment funds may make similar investments via the facilitation from the QFIIs. Secondly, the QFII system enables investment banks (whether qualified QFIIs themselves or through the QFIIs) to offer capital market investors various access products and structured derivatives that are linked to China's A shares. Thirdly, foreign private equity and hedge fund investors may acquire state and/or legal-person shares of the listed companies through M&As or management buy-outs (MBOs).

QFII programme overview

In November 2002, the CSRC and the People's Bank of China (PBOC) jointly introduced China's QFII system. The QFII system allows foreign investors, including banks, insurance companies, fund management institutions and other institutions meeting the criteria, to invest in China's capital markets directly. The funds from the QFIIs will be exchanged into yuan and kept in a special account managed by the PBOC. The QFIIs will then be permitted to buy and sell A shares and other financial instruments directly within certain limits.

Compared to the QFII systems in other Asian regions, China's QFII scheme set rather high standards with respect to minimum asset size, capital adequacy and operating history. (See Table 2 for a summary of QFII criteria.)

The QFIIs could invest in a wide variety of financial products, including yuan-denominated shares listed on China's stock exchanges, ie, A Shares (notably, the nontradable shares are off-limits to QFIIs), Treasury bonds, convertible bonds and corporate bonds listed on the stock exchanges. In addition, QFIIs may invest in closed or open-ended funds approved by the CSRC. The QFIIs'

Table 2 QFII eligibility

Type of institution	Operating history	Paid-in capital	Securities assets under management in the last fiscal year
Funds	> 5 years	N/A	Total assets ≥ US$10 billion
Insurance companies	> 30 years	≥ US$1 billion	≥ US$10 billion
Securities firms	> 30 years	≥ US$1 billion	≥ US$10 billion
Commercial banks	N/A	Total assets ranked in the top 100 globally	≥ US$10 billion

Source: *"Provisional Measures on Administration of Domestic Securities Investments of Qualified Foreign Institutional Investors (QFII)"* by CSRC and PBOC. Full text in Appendix 2A

trading activities, however, are subject to strict size limitation and foreign-exchange control.

Investment size limitation

The CSRC's QFII rules set percentage limits on QFII's potential investments in Chinese listed companies. Each QFII cannot own more than 10% of the total outstanding shares of a single listed company and all QFIIs' ownership in aggregation of a listed company cannot exceed 20%. The Shanghai and Shenzhen Stock Exchanges further issued the implementing rules to set forth the relevant procedures on the trading limits. For example, in instances where the 20% limit has been exceeded, the exchanges will notify the QFIIs that they have to divest their holdings within five trading days, using a last-purchase, first-sale method.

These limitations are apparently intended to prevent QFIIs dominating A share trading – 20% of total outstanding shares actually represents a large percentage of a listed company's A shares, which trade on the exchanges, because on average, only one-third of a listed company's shares are tradable on the market. However, these strict size limitations may have unintended impacts on share trading.

For one thing, the possibility of forced divestment will be an important factor when institutional investors make investment decisions, especially when the QFII has already acquired a significant position in such stocks. Since the stock exchanges notify QFIIs that the 20% threshold has been exceeded only after the close of the trading day, QFIIs have difficulty in figuring out whether a purchase will cause the 20% threshold to be exceeded (in which case they would have to sell that position within five trading days). This uncertainty will be priced in as a discount to QFII's otherwise bid price for the stock. For another, a strict ownership limitation may cause excess volatility in stock trading where QFII ownership is nearing the limit, because QFIIs may incidentally purchase a large amount of shares when their holdings are already close to the limit and then will be forced to sell securities that are over the limit.

Capital repatriation control

The Chinese QFII system has strict control on the inflow and outflow of foreign capital. Each QFII may only apply to remit an amount within the quota assigned by the State Administration of Foreign Exchange (SAFE). For capital outflow, the rules require that the principal investment shall stay in China for three years with respect to closed-end fund QFIIs and one year for other QFIIs. Even then, repatriation must be approved by SAFE and must be carried out in instalments. These provisions force investors to stay in the market for a considerable time, which apparently is to deter the potential burst of international "hot money".

These repatriation restrictions reduce the liquidity of QFII investments in the Chinese markets. Take a US mutual fund QFII for example. The proceeds from the sale of its A share investments cannot be readily converted into US dollars and be used to satisfy redemption requests. Furthermore, the repatriation restrictions limit the investment manager's ability to adjust their portfolios when they deem it economically appropriate or, under more extreme circumstances, to liquidate the fund for regulatory reasons.

Momentum in the QFII programme

Despite the high standards and trading restrictions, the QFII system offers foreign investors unprecedented investment opportunities. For the first time since the inception of the Chinese stock market, foreign investors are permitted to participate in the A share market, which represents the lion's share of tradable shares of listed companies. As China continues its financial reform and capital account liberalisation, there is reason to be optimistic that the QFII system in the near future will give foreign investors more freedom in investment alternatives, trading size and foreign currency repatriation.

The global financial institutions and money managers not surprisingly responded immediately to the potential opportunities in

Table 3 Current QFIIs and their respective investment quotas

	QFII name	Approval date	Quota, US$ million
1	UBS	23 May, 2003	800
2	Nomura Securities	23 May, 2003	50
3	Citigroup Global Markets	5 June, 2003	400
4	Morgan Stanley	5 June, 2003	400
5	Goldman Sachs	4 July, 2003	50
6	Deutsche Bank	30 July, 2003	200
7	HSBC	4 August, 2003	200
8	ING Bank	10 September, 2003	50
9	JPMorgan Chase	30 September, 2003	50
10	Credit Suisse First Boston	24 October, 2003	50
11	Nikko Asset Management	11 December, 2003	250
12	Standard Chartered Bank	11 December, 2003	75
13	Merrill Lynch International	30 April, 2004	75
14	Daiwa Securities	10 May, 2004	50
15	Hang Seng Bank	10 May, 2004	50
16	Lehman Brothers	6 July, 2004	75
17	Bill & Melinda Gates Foundation	19 July, 2004	75
18	Invesco Asset Management	4 August, 2004	450
19	ABN Amro	2 September, 2004	75
20	Société General	2 September, 2004	50
21	Dresdner Bank	15 September, 2004	75
22	Barclays	21 September, 2004	75
23	Franklin Templeton	26 September, 2004	*
24	Fortis	11 October, 2004	100
25	BNP Paribas	11 October, 2004	75
26	CALYON S.A.	10 January, 2005	75
27	Power Corporation of Canada	21 October, 2004	50
28	GS Asset Management	25 November, 2005	200
29	Government of Singapore Investment	16 November, 2005	100
30	Martin Currie	30 November, 2005	120
31	Temasek Fullerton	12 December, 2005	100
32	AIGIG	12 December, 2005	50
33	JF Asset Management	29 December, 2005	*
34	Dai-Ichi Mutual Life	29 December, 2005	*
	Total		5,645

*Awaiting investment quota from CSRC.
Source: China Asset Management Co. www.chinaamc.com as of 6 January, 2006

the QFII system. The initial US$4 billion investment quota was fully subscribed by April 2005. Quickly responding to the huge demand for QFII status, the regulators decided in July to expand the total QFII quota from US$4 billion to US$10 billion, which triggered a new round of investment quota applications and approvals. (See Table 3 for the current QFIIs and their respective quotas.)

NEW INVESTMENT OPPORTUNITIES WITH QFII

The market impact of the QFII schemes goes way beyond the QFIIs themselves. In addition to making investments for their own accounts, the QFIIs could offer structured financial products to their clients with synthetic exposure to Chinese markets. Therefore, the QFII leads to a broad array of investment opportunities to the general foreign investor base, even though only the largest financial institutions may qualify for the high QFII standards.

With their access to China's capital markets, the QFIIs could potentially participate in three major trading activities. Firstly, a QFII could invite other foreign fund management companies to invest in A shares through its QFII quota. Secondly, a QFII could buy investment securities in the Chinese markets and then use a simple arrangement to transfer the exposure (which is known as access products) to investors. Thirdly, a QFII could offer investors structured investments with tailored exposure to China's capital markets, and manage the risk through trading dynamically in the QFII market.

Investment quota sharing

The majority of investment funds are not in a financial position to meet the QFII criteria. Accordingly, a market practice is for an investment manager to enter into an arrangement with a QFII whereby the QFII sets aside a portion of its quota for the use of the investment fund manager. Such an arrangement gives the investment fund some desirable exposure to the Chinese market without fully becoming a QFII.

Under the terms of a facility agreement, the QFII agrees to procure the execution of purchases and sales of A shares on behalf of such investment managers. Essentially, the QFII acts as a facilitator between the investment manager and the custodian bank/broker and ultimately the underlying Chinese stock. For investors, this means many investment funds could potentially add in exposure to China's domestic capital markets through cooperation with the QFIIs.

Synthetic exposure through access products

Since the QFII scheme was launched in 2003, firms have been offering clients market-access products linked to A shares and A share indexes. For example, a QFII could first purchase A shares in the Chinese market, then issue to offshore investors the access products (such as zero-strike warrants) linked to such A shares. The access products essentially replicate the economic exposure of the underlying A shares. The structure is illustrated as follows:

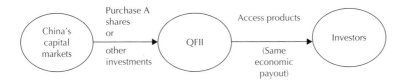

QFII access products could go well beyond exposure to pure A shares. Recent financial innovations in China have brought to market a wide range of investment products, which will be discussed in detail in Part II of this book. A few QFII investment banks have reportedly offered access products linked to a variety of investment products in the Chinese market, which include, among other things:

Convertible bonds

Chinese convertible bonds have been popular among the QFIIs since the inception of the QFII scheme. They have special features that reflect the unique shareholding structure in China's listed companies, making them interesting investment alternatives to Chinese stocks.

Corporate warrants and options

Corporate warrants and exchange-listed options were brought back to the market in 2005, a decade after options/warrants trading was banned (shortly after its inception) in the early 1990s, because of overspeculation in the market. They offer investors a leveraged investment on the underlying stocks or indexes.

ETFs

ETFs offer an efficient way for investors to invest in a broad market index. The Shanghai Stock Exchange in 2004 introduced the first A share-based ETF – the Shanghai ETF50 – and the Shenzhen Stock Exchange around the same time introduced a similar innovative fund product – the listed open-end funds (LOFs).

Index products

Index-linked products are gradually gaining popularity in China, although speculation is still the dominant theme in the market. Following the introduction of the first unified index that covers both the Shanghai and Shenzhen Stock Exchanges in 2005, the market should see more index funds and index-linked products in the near future.

Principal-protected funds

Principal-protected investments are popular globally, and they are attracting investors in China because of the multi-year bear market. Principal protected funds have distinctive Chinese characteristics, as China's debt and derivatives markets are still in the early development process.

Structured investments supported by dynamic trading in QFII

Finally, investors could seek specific exposure from QFII investment banks through more structured investments. In that case, the QFII would purchase the base shares or investments underlying the offered structured investment and then dynamically trade in the QFII market to hedge its risk exposure. The structure is illustrated below.

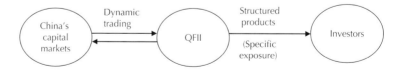

Take iShares' FTSE/Xinhua A50 China Tracker for example. It is an exchange-traded fund that tracks the performance of the FTSE/Xinhua China A50 Index, which includes 50 major A shares on the Shanghai Shenzhen Stock Exchange. It was launched before the Shanghai Stock Exchange introduced the first ETF in China – the SSE50 ETF. Its offering illustrates that an investment bank could acquire A shares through the QFII programme and then offer foreign investors specific investment exposures, which cannot be offered through the simpler access products.

Interestingly, the offering of iShares' FTSE/Xinhua A50 involves some access products in the process. For this offering, Barclays Global Investors (BGI) (the offering investment bank) has teamed up with Citigroup Global Markets, which has a QFII licence and issues Chinese A shares Access Products (CAAPS). The access product reportedly is a form of zero-strike warrant on A shares, which replicates the economic interests of the underlying A shares. Citigroup Global Markets also serves as the market-maker to process the creation and redemption requests by the market investor.

Although structured products and derivatives could offer investors more tailored investment exposures, sometimes they may involve high structuring costs. Because individual banks create them for specific investors, they are not the focus of this book.

"SECOND QFII SYSTEM"
Nontradable share acquisition versus QFII
The QFII scheme should not be seen as a stand-alone piece of stock market reform. Instead, it is a part of the full-scale campaign by China's stock market regulators to increase foreign participation in the troubled stock market and listed companies.

Around the same time that the QFII system was introduced, a flurry of important new regulations were also issued by the major regulators of China's M&A market. Most notably, acquisition of state-owned equity interests (the nontradable shares) was made available again to foreign investors after the moratorium a decade ago.

These important new developments included:

❑ "*Issues Relevant to the Transfer of State Shares and Legal Person Shares in Listed Companies to Foreign Investors Circular*", November 2002, lifting the 1995 moratorium on foreign investors purchasing nontradable shares from China's listed companies;
❑ "*Using Foreign Investment to Reorganise State-Owned Enterprises Tentative Provisions*", January 2003, acknowledging the goal to invigorate SOEs through foreign equity ownership; and

❏ *"Provisional Rules on Mergers and Acquisitions of Domestic Enterprises by Foreign Investors"*, March 2003, establishing transaction guidelines for foreign investment in state-owned enterprises.

Therefore, in addition to adopting the QFII system to bring foreign institutional investors into the tradable A share stock market, China is simultaneously uplifting its regulatory framework on the acquisition of nontradable shares of listed companies by foreign investors. These two groundbreaking reforms boost foreign participation in every share category of listed companies' ownership structure.

The access to nontradable shares is an important complement to the QFII system, because the nontradable shares typically constitute the controlling stake in listed companies and they are off-limits to the QFIIs under the current QFII rules.

The investment mechanism in the nontradable share world is also very different from the A share/QFII world. The nontradable shares are typically acquired via private negotiation, instead of open-market transactions as in the QFII world. In many cases, the transfer price for nontradable shares is significantly less than the trading price for the corresponding tradable A shares. Part III of this book will discuss investments in nontradable shares through M&A and related-investment structures such as MBOs.

Post share reform: "Second QFII system"

The 2005 reform on the segregated equity ownership of listed companies adds a new twist to the foreign investment framework. As discussed above, foreign investors not holding QFII status used to be able to acquire a stake in listed companies by purchasing nontradable shares through private agreement. The issue arises because following the share structure reform, nontradable shares in listed companies will become fungible with the tradable A shares in the secondary market.

In other words, with the proportion of nontradable shares in listed companies decreasing, previously acquirable nontradable shares will suddenly be placed out of the reach of foreign investors not holding QFII status. Apparently intending to ensure that listed companies remain reachable to those investors, five government bureaus issued a joint rule at the beginning of 2006 to allow non-QFII foreign investors to purchase strategic stakes in tradable shares from companies that have completed the share-reform programme.

Many market players view the rule as a parallel paradigm to the QFII system. Under this rule, qualified investors – essentially those with at least US$100 million total capital or US$500 million under management – could purchase stocks from existing shareholders or new shares issued by those companies. With the ability to sell their stakes in the open market, foreign investors would enjoy more liquidity in their investments than in the traditional nontradable share acquisition framework, although the rule imposes a minimum deal size of 10% of the listed company and a three-year holding period. While detailed rules are to be issued, the transaction mechanism most likely would be similar to the traditional acquisition of the nontradable shares.

The following table summarises the emerging investment strategies in China's stock market.

Table 4 China: emerging investment strategies

Emerging strategies	Description and character
Qualified Foreign Institutional Investors (QFII) scheme	QFIIs can invest directly in A shares, listed government bonds, convertible bonds, corporate bonds and other financial instruments as approved by the CSRC
Access products	Investment products that provide investors with synthetic exposure to Chinese A shares or A share-related instruments that the QFIIs could invest in, such as convertible bonds, stock funds, etc
Structured products linked to A shares	Structured investment products offered by the QFIIs that are linked to the A share market and provide structured payout for investor's specific needs
Foreign acquisition of state and legal person shares through M&A	New rules have reopened the acquisition of the nontradable shares (which typically constitute the controlling interests in listed companies) by foreign investors
Management buy-out (MBO)	Foreign investors team up with corporate management to acquire nontradable shares for corporate control in listed companies
Foreign acquisition of strategic stake in post-reform companies	New rule permits qualified strategic investors to purchase strategic stakes in post-reform companies with minimum size and holding period requirements

CONCLUSION

For many years, foreign investors interested in China could only access limited investment alternatives in the offshore market, such as Chinese companies listed on the Hong Kong Exchange or their ADRs traded in New York. Now, following decades of free market reforms in China, its domestic stock market is increasingly open to foreign capital investments.

The new QFII system and M&A regulatory framework have opened up unprecedented opportunities for foreign investors – institutional or retail – to gain exposure to China either directly or indirectly. The multi-year bear market in China, in an unintentional way, has made the domestic stock market valuation much closer to the international norms. Foreign investors are clearly developing an appetite for Chinese securities, as illustrated by the ever-increasing QFII quota and the active foreign M&A market in China. The following chapters will discuss in detail the emerging investment alternatives in China's stock market.

APPENDIX 2A: QFII RULE – UNOFFICIAL TRANSLATION
Decree of China Securities Regulatory Commission and the People's Bank of China
No. 12:   The "Provisional Measures on Administration of Domestic Securities Investments of Qualified Foreign Institutional Investors (QFII)", which will come into effect from 1 December, 2002, is hereby promulgated.

Chairman of CSRC: Zhou Xiaochuan

Governor of People's Bank of China: Dai Xianglong

5 November, 2002

Provisional Measures on Administration of Domestic Securities Investments of Qualified Foreign Institutional Investors (QFII)
Chapter I General Provisions

Article 1 Based upon China's relevant laws and administrative regulations, these Measures are promulgated for the purpose of governing Qualified Foreign Institutional Investors' investments in China's securities market and promoting developments of China's securities market.

Article 2 Qualified Foreign Institutional Investors (hereafter referred to as QFII which can be a single or a plural, as the case may be) are defined in these Measures as overseas fund management institutions, insurance companies, securities companies and other assets management institutions which have been approved by China Securities Regulatory Commission (hereafter referred to as CSRC) to invest in China's securities market and granted investment quotas by State Administration of Foreign Exchange (hereafter referred to as SAFE).

Article 3 The QFII should mandate domestic commercial banks as custodians and domestic securities companies as brokers for their domestic securities trading.

Article 4 The QFII should comply with laws, regulations and other relevant rules in China.

Article 5 CSRC and SAFE shall, in accordance with the laws, supervise and govern the securities investing activities undertaken by the QFII within the jurisdiction of China.

Chapter II Qualifications, Criteria and Approval Procedures
Article 6 A QFII applicant should fall within the following criteria:

(1) The applicant should be in sound financial and credit status, should meet the requirements set by CSRC on assets size and other factors; and its risk control indicators should meet the requirements set by laws and securities authorities under its home jurisdiction;
(2) Employees of the applicant should meet the requirements on professional qualifications set by its home country/region;
(3) The applicant should have a sound management structure and internal control systems, should conduct business in accordance with the relevant regulations and should not have received any substantial penalties by regulators in its home country/region over the last three years prior to application;
(4) The home country/region of the applicant should have a sound legal and regulatory system, and its securities regulator must have signed the Memorandum of Understanding with CSRC and maintained an efficient regulatory and cooperative relationship;
(5) Other criteria as stipulated by CSRC based on prudent regulatory principles.

Article 7 The criteria of assets scale and other factors as referred to in the aforesaid article are: For fund management institutions: having operated a fund business for more than five years and managing assets of not less than US$10 billion in the most recent accounting year; for insurance companies: having operated an insurance business for more than 30 years with paid-in capital of not less than US$1 billion and managing securities assets of not less than US$10 billion in the most recent accounting year; for securities companies: having operated a securities business for more than 30 years with paid-in capital of not less than US$1 billion and managing securities assets of not less than US$10 billion in the most recent accounting year; for commercial banks: ranking among the top 100 of the world in total assets for the most recent accounting year and managing securities assets of not less than US$10 billion. CSRC may adjust the aforesaid requirements subject to the development of the securities market.

Article 8 To apply for QFII qualification and an investment quota, an applicant should submit the following documents to CSRC and SAFE, respectively, through its custodian:

(1) Application forms (including basic information on the applicant, investment quota applied for and investment plan, etc);
(2) Documents to verify that the applicant meets the requirements set out in Article 6;
(3) Draft custody agreement signed by its expected custodian;
(4) Audited financial reports for the three most recent years;
(5) Statement on sources of the funds, and letter of undertaking promising not to withdraw funds during the approved period;
(6) Letter of authorisation by the applicant;
(7) Other documents as required by CSRC and SAFE. All the aforesaid documents, if written in languages other than Chinese, must be accompanied by their Chinese translations or Chinese extracts.

Article 9 The CSRC shall, within 15 working days from the date the full set of application documents is received, determine whether to grant approval or not. Securities Investment Licences will be issued to those applicants whose applications have been approved whereas written notices will be given to those applicants whose applications have been rejected.

Article 10 Applicants shall apply to SAFE through their custodians for investment quotas after obtaining the Securities Investment Licences. SAFE shall, within 15 working days from the date the full set of application documents is received, determine whether to grant approval or not. Applicants whose applications have been approved will be notified in writing of their permitted investment quotas and Foreign Exchange Registration Certificates will be issued. Written notices will be given to those applicants whose applications have been rejected. The Securities Investment Licence will automatically become void if an applicant is unable to obtain the Foreign Exchange Registration Certificate within one year after the Securities Investment Licence is granted.

Article 11 In order to encourage medium and long-term investments, preference will be given to the institutions managing closed-end Chinese funds subject to the requirements of Article 6 or pension funds, insurance funds and mutual funds with good investment records in other markets.

Chapter III Custody, Registration and Settlement
Article 12 A custodian should meet the following requirements:

(1) Has a specific fund custody department;
(2) With paid-in capital of no less than 8 billion yuan;
(3) Has sufficient professionals who are familiar with custody business;
(4) Can manage the entire assets of the fund safely;
(5) Has safe and efficient ability of liquidation and completion of a business transaction;
(6) Has qualifications to conduct foreign exchange and yuan business;
(7) No material breach of foreign exchange regulations for the three most recent years. Domestic branches of foreign-invested commercial banks with more than three years of continual operation are eligible to apply for the custodian qualification. Their paid-in capital eligibility shall be based on their overseas headquarter's capital.

Article 13 Approvals from CSRC, People's Bank of China (hereafter referred to as PBOC) and SAFE are required for custodian status.

Article 14 Domestic commercial banks should submit the following documents to CSRC, PBOC and SAFE to apply for custodian status:

(1) Application forms;
(2) Copy of its financial business licence;
(3) Management system in relation to its custody business;
(4) Documents verifying that it has efficient information and technology systems;
(5) Other documents as required by CSRC, PBOC and SAFE. CSRC, together with PBOC and SAFE, will review application documents and decide whether to approve the applications or not.

Article 15 A custodian shall perform the following duties:

(1) Safekeeping all the assets that the QFII places under its custody;

(2) Conducting all QFII-related foreign exchange settlements, sales, receipts, payments and yuan-settlement businesses;

(3) Supervising the investment activities of the QFII, and reporting to CSRC and SAFE in case QFII investment orders are found to have violated laws or regulations;

(4) Reporting to SAFE about foreign exchange remittance and repatriation of the QFII, within two working days after the QFII remits/repatriates its principal/proceeds;

(5) Reporting to CSRC and SAFE about the status of the QFII's special yuan account, within five working days of the end of each month;

(6) Compiling an annual financial report on the QFII's domestic securities investment activities in the previous year and sending it to CSRC and SAFE within three months of the end of each accounting year;

(7) Keep the records and other related materials on the QFII's fund remittance, repatriation, conversion, receipt and payment for no less than 15 years;

(8) Other responsibilities as defined by CSRC, PBOC and SAFE based on prudent supervision principles.

Article 16 A custodian should strictly separate its own assets from those under its custody. A custodian should set up different accounts for different QFII, and manage those accounts separately. Each QFII can only mandate one custodian.

Article 17 The QFII should mandate its custodian to apply for a securities account on its behalf with the securities registration and settlement institution. When applying for a securities account on behalf of the QFII, a custodian should bring the QFII's mandate and its Securities Investment Licence and other valid documents, and file with CSRC the relevant situation within five working days of opening a securities account. QFII should mandate its custodian to open a yuan settlement account on its behalf with the securities registration and settlement institution. The custodian shall be responsible for the settlement of the QFII's domestic securities investment, and shall file with CSRC and SAFE the relevant situation within five working days of opening a yuan settlement account.

Chapter IV Investment Operations

Article 18 Subject to the approved investment quota, a QFII can invest in the following yuan financial instruments:

(1) Shares listed on China's stock exchanges (excluding B shares);
(2) Treasuries listed on China's stock exchanges;
(3) Convertible bonds and enterprise bonds listed on China's stock exchanges;
(4) Other financial instruments as approved by CSRC.

Article 19 A QFII may mandate domestically registered securities companies to manage their domestic securities investments. Each QFII can only mandate one investment institution.

Article 20 For domestic securities investments, a QFII should observe the following requirements:

(1) Shares held by each QFII in one listed company should not exceed 10% of the total outstanding shares of the company;
(2) Total shares held by all QFII in one listed company should not exceed 20% of the total outstanding shares of the company. CSRC may adjust the above percentages based on the development of the securities market.

Article 21 The QFII's domestic securities investment activities should comply with the requirements as set out in the Guidance for Foreign Investments in Various Industries.

Article 22 Securities firms should preserve the trading and transaction records of a QFII for at least 15 years.

Chapter V Fund Management

Article 23 Upon the approval of SAFE, a QFII should open a special yuan account with its custodian. Within five working days of the opening of the special yuan account, the custodian should report to CSRC and SAFE for filing.

Article 24 Revenue articles in the special yuan account shall include: settlement of funds (foreign exchange funds from overseas and accumulated settlements of foreign exchange should not exceed the approved investment quota), proceeds from the disposal of securities, cash dividends, interests from current deposits and bonds. Expense articles in the special yuan account shall include: cost of purchasing securities (including stamp tax and commission charges), domestic custodian fee and management fee, and payment for purchasing foreign exchange (to be used to repatriate principals and proceeds). The capital of the special yuan account shall not be used for money lending or guarantee.

Article 25 Within three months of receiving its Securities Investment Licence from CSRC, the QFII should remit principals from outside into China and directly transfer them into special yuan accounts after full settlement of foreign exchange. The currency of the principals from QFII should be exchangeable currency approved by SAFE and the amount of the principal should not exceed the approved quota. If the QFII has not fully remitted the principals within three months of receiving its Foreign Exchange Registration Certificate, the actual amount remitted will be deemed as the approved quota; thereafter the difference between the approved quota and the actual amount shall not be remitted inward prior to the obtaining of a newly approved investment quota.

Article 26 In the case that a QFII is a closed-end Chinese fund management company, it can mandate its custodian, with the submission of required documents to SAFE to apply for purchase of foreign exchange for the repatriation of principals by stages and by batches three years after its remittance of the principals. The amount of each batch of principal repatriation should not exceed 20% of the total principals, and the interval between two repatriations should not be shorter than one month. Other types of QFII can mandate their custodians, with the submission of required documents, to apply to SAFE to repatriate the principals by stages and by batches one year after their remittance of the principals. The amount of each batch of principal repatriation should not exceed 20% of the total principals, and the interval between two repatriations should not be shorter than three months. The overseas receivers of the above-mentioned repatriation should be the QFII themselves.

Article 27 A QFII whose principal of approved investment quota is remitted to China for less than one year but more than three months, after the submission of a transfer application form and transfer contract and upon approval of CSRC and SAFE, may transfer the approved investment quota to other QFII or other applicants who have fulfilled the requirements of Article 6. After receiving its Securities Investment Licence from CSRC and investment quota from SAFE, the transferee can remit the difference as its principals if the value of the transferred assets is lower than the investment quota approved by SAFE.

Article 28 If the QFII intends to remit principals inwards again after it partially or fully repatriates its principals, it should re-apply for an investment quota.

Article 29 If the QFII needs to purchase foreign exchange to repatriate its post-tax profits of the previous accounting year which have been audited by Chinese CPA, the QFII should mandate its custodian to apply to SAFE 15 days prior to repatriation, together with the following documents:

(1) Repatriation application form;
(2) Financial reports of the accounting year in which the profits are generated;
(3) Auditor's report issued by Chinese CPA;
(4) Profits distribution resolutions or other effective legal documents;
(5) Tax payment certificates;
(6) Other documents as required by SAFE. The overseas receivers of the above-mentioned repatriation should be the QFII itself.

Article 30 SAFE may adjust the timeframe required for the QFII to repatriate its principal and proceeds, subject to the needs of China's foreign exchange balance.

Chapter VI Regulatory Issues
Article 31 CSRC and SAFE should annually review the QFII's Securities Investment Licence and Foreign Exchange Registration Certificate.

Article 32 CSRC, PBOC and SAFE may require the QFII, custodians, securities companies, stock exchanges, and securities registration and settlement institutions to provide information on the QFII's domestic investment activities, and may conduct on-site inspections if necessary.

Article 33 Stock exchanges and securities registration and settlement institutions may enact new operation rules or revise previous operation rules on the QFII's domestic securities investments, the implementation of which will be effective upon approval of CSRC.

Article 34 In the event of any of the following, the QFII should file with CSRC, PBOC and SAFE within five working days:

(1) Change of custodian;
(2) Change of legal representatives;
(3) Change of controlling shareholders;
(4) Adjustment of registered capital;
(5) Litigations and other material events;
(6) Having substantial penalties imposed overseas;
(7) Other circumstances as stipulated by CSRC and SAFE.

Article 35 In the event of any of the following, the QFII should re-apply for its Securities Investment Licence:

(1) Change of business name;
(2) Acquisition by or merger with other institution(s);
(3) Other circumstances as stipulated by CSRC and SAFE.

Article 36 In the event of any of the following, the QFII should surrender its Securities Investment Licence and Foreign Exchange Registration Certificate to CSRC and SAFE respectively:

(1) Having repatriated all its principals;
(2) Having transferred its investment quota;
(3) Dispersion of authorised entities, entering into bankruptcy procedures, or assets being taken over by receivers;
(4) Other circumstances as stipulated by CSRC and SAFE. If the QFII fails to pass the annual review on Securities Investment Licences and Foreign Exchange Registration Certificates, as mentioned in Article 31, the Licences/Certificates will automatically be invalid and the QFII should return these Licences/Certificates as required by the aforesaid Article.

Article 37 In accordance with their respective authorities, CSRC, PBOC and SAFE will give warnings or penalties to the QFII, custodians and securities companies, etc who violate these Measures. The same breach, however, should not be subject to two administrative penalties or more.

Chapter VII Supplementary Provisions
Article 38 These Measures are also applicable to institutional investors from Hong Kong Special Administrative Region, Macao Special Administrative Region and Taiwan Region, who conduct securities investment businesses in Mainland China.

Article 39 These Measures will enter into force as of 1 December, 2002.

Promulgated by China Securities Regulatory Commission and the People's Bank of China on 5 November, 2002

Part II

Financial Innovations and New Offerings

The newly adopted QFII system and the latest financial innovations in China have opened up interesting opportunities for foreign investors. This welcome trend should continue as China further implements its WTO commitments. Learning from the western markets, China's stock market has adopted innovative financing and investment products, providing foreign investors with many new investment vehicles with which to participate in China's economic growth.

These new investment vehicles, however, exhibit important Chinese characteristics because of the existing economic and regulatory infrastructure and, in particular, the unique segregated equity ownership structure in Chinese listed companies. It is critical for foreign investors, therefore, to understand the subtle nuances of investment products in China, even though they appear similar to their counterparts in the more developed markets.

Meanwhile, in mid 2005 China launched what were indisputably the biggest ever reforms in the history of China's stock market, the so called "full-flotation" reform, which aims to resolve the segregated equity ownership issue completely. This fundamental reform has profound implications for the future valuation and trading behaviour of existing financial instruments and it is leading to fast-paced financial innovations in the post-reform era.

Part II will examine the cutting-edge financial products that represent a broad spectrum of investment styles and risk/reward profiles. These range from aggressive investments such as warrants and options, index-related investments such as exchange-traded funds, investments with downside protection such as convertible bonds and capital-protected funds, and finally, potential short selling trades. Combined with QFII access and the continued financial innovation, China is offering foreign investors far more investment alternatives to tap into its stock market than only a few years ago.

3

China's Convertible Bonds

Since China launched the QFII system in 2003, the approved foreign institutions have actively participated in trading yuan-denominated stocks and bonds in China. The QFIIs have shown great interest in Chinese convertible bonds (CBs) as a means of achieving potentially attractive returns. In addition, QFIIs have reportedly started to offer structured products to provide investors the synthetic exposure to Chinese CBs.

As a result, Chinese CBs have recently become popular among Chinese issuers and foreign investors. They offer unique features such as low-conversion premiums, an annual reset of the conversion price and commercial bank-guaranteed payments. These features reflect the different objectives of Chinese issuers as well as the unique character of China's stock market, making them interesting investment alternatives to Chinese A share stocks.

BACKGROUND: CB ECONOMICS

Convertible bonds are classic examples of hybrid instruments, ie, instruments with both equity and fixed-income (debt) features. A CB is a debt instrument with an attached conversion feature, which allows the holder to exchange the CB into a specified number of the underlying common stock, at or before maturity. By adjusting the various structural parameters, a CB can be designed to be strongly "equity-like", or strongly "debt-like", or a mixture of the two.

A CB is a very complex instrument in that it has various embedded options. In addition to the obvious option to convert the bond into stock, a CB typically also includes the CB issuer's option to call the bond from bondholders before maturity, the bondholder's option to put the bond back to the CB issuer before maturity, and further in many Chinese CB cases, the CB issuer's option to adjust the conversion price of the conversion option. Below is a list of the key CB market terms that will be used in this chapter.

CB market terminology

Convertible bond:	A debt instrument whereby the bondholder has the right, over a specific time period, to exchange the debt security for a predetermined number of stocks (also referred to as the "underlying stock") at the conversion price
Conversion price:	The equity price per share at which convertible bondholders could convert the debt into the underlying stocks. Convertible bondholders typically convert when the stock price is above the conversion price
Conversion ratio:	The number of stocks to be received upon conversion of a CB. It can be derived by dividing the issue price of the CB by its conversion price
Conversion premium:	The amount by which the conversion price of a CB exceeds the stock price on the day the CB is issued. A higher conversion premium means the stock price needs to rise considerably higher after the CB is issued before it is economically sensible to convert the CB into the underlying stocks, and vice versa
Coupon:	The annual rate of interest on the CB's face value that is paid by the issuer to the bondholder
Call price:	The price at which the issuer of a CB has the right to redeem the bonds before maturity
Put price:	The predetermined price at which the bonds can be tendered by the convertible bondholders to the issuer before maturity
Maturity date:	The date at which the issuer must repay the entire principal value of the bond to the bondholders
Yield to maturity:	Also referred to as "effective yield". The total return to the investor taking into account the interest rate on the bond, its current price, and the time remaining on its maturity date

Conceptually, a CB could be viewed as a corporate bond plus an equity call option on the underlying stock. As such, the hybrid feature of a CB could be illustrated as follows:

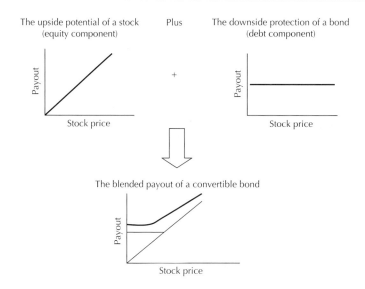

As illustrated above, a CB exhibits the characteristics of both debt and equity during its life, depending on the stock price movements, the company's credit rating profile, and other market conditions. The general theme of CB investments is that the debt portion produces a predictable stream of cashflow income, whereas the conversion feature gives the convertible bondholders the upside potential if the stock goes higher. Hedge funds and large institutional investors, however, may pursue different trading strategies with CBs, which will be discussed at the end of this chapter.

CHINESE CBS: STOCK OFFERING EQUIVALENT

China's CBs demonstrate strong equity features, so they are very equity-like instruments. In other words, the CBs are structured to have a high probability of conversion into equity stocks. The major reason for this structural preference, not surprisingly, is the segregated ownership structure in China's listed companies.

Controlling shareholder preference

As discussed in Part I, for historical reasons, around one-third of the total shares of China's listed companies trade on the exchange and the rest of the shares are held by one or more state-owned investors whose shares are nontradable. The largest shareholders are not as sensitive to share price and ownership dilution as are smaller stockholders of the listed shares and they have the ability to vote in bigger blocks to approve CB offers.

Listed companies in China, therefore, favour much more equity financing (such as stock, rights, or other equity-linked instruments offerings) over debt financing (such as corporate debt offering). By contrast, the western corporate finance theory suggests that an equity or equity-like financing constitutes a negative market signal on the issuer's stock price (see box for a description of the so called "pecking order" theory). This equity offering preference in China is reinforced by a similar trading preference by the Chinese stock market investors as described below.

Market investors preference

In China, a 2005 research report by a member securities firm of the Shenzhen Stock Exchange found a unique phenomenon in China's CB market.

Comparing the price movements of Chinese CBs and their under-lying stocks, the research found that stock price movement is posi-tively correlated with the equity-likeness of the CB being offered. In other words, the more equity-like a new CB offering is, the more upside movement for its trading price upon offering, and vice versa. This is drastically different from the pecking order capital structure theory and what has been observed in developed markets.

The research attributes this paradox mainly to the special trad-ing behaviour in China's stock market. Chinese stock investors mainly make profits from active trading, ie, through the price fluc-tuations in the financial instruments. For any financial instrument, the more equity-like it is and the more volatile its price movement, the better it fits investors' high-risk/high-return preference. Thus CBs with strong equity features are welcomed by the market with positive trading reactions.

Capital structure theory – pecking order
The pecking order theory is generally attributed to SC Myers in "The Capital Structure Puzzle", *Journal of Finance*, **39** (July 1984). In the pecking order model, an equity offering is typically regarded as a very expensive last resort for corporate finance, and market reaction to new equity offerings is typically negative.

But why would the stock market feel reluctant to accept new equity offerings? More specifically, why is a follow-on equity offering for a listed company typically considered a negative market signal on its stock price?

This negative market response is typically explained by the "asymmetric information" about the company between the corporate management and the external investors. Because the corporate management is believed to have more accurate information about the company, investors could rationally interpret a new equity offering as a sign that the company is overvalued (the implied premise, notably, is that managers would avoid issuing securities, particularly equity, when the company is undervalued).

Therefore, if a company is bullish on company prospects, and thus considers its stock undervalued, it should favour debt financing instead of equity financing. This way, it can avoid dilution of share ownership and keep future stock price appreciation exclusive to the company and existing external shareholders.

CB *versus* rights and follow-on equity offerings

It is quite clear, so far, that CB offerings in China are in some way "backdoor equity offerings" by the listed companies. But why not straight equity or rights offerings up front, if the ultimate goal is to convert the CB into underlying stocks?

Apparently, the principal-protection feature offered by the debt side of a CB makes two substantial differences. Firstly, with the stock market trading at a multiple-year low, investors are wary about new equity offerings, so a CB that offers both strong equity features (to be discussed in details below) and debt-like cashflows seems to be the perfect solution. For investment banks, the investor participation interest also means fewer underwriting risks compared with common stock offerings.

Secondly, the bond payment obligations create issuer discipline over cashflow management and corporate governance as a whole. As such, in China, CBs are treated like "debt" from a regulatory point of view. Compared with equity offerings, which are always subject to a complex and time-consuming regulatory approval process, some Chinese companies have reportedly found that CBs were easier to launch than stock-purchase rights or follow-on stock offerings from a regulatory point of view.

CB STRUCTURE FEATURES

As discussed above, the CBs in China are designed to be very equity-like instruments to make them popular with retail investors. This is reflected in a few structural features, such as a low conversion premium, conversion price anti-dilution adjustment and conversion price annual reset.

Low conversion premium/conversion price

The low conversion premium in Chinese CBs illustrates the stock offering's essence. The *Implementing Measures for Convertible Bond Offerings by Listed Companies* issued by the CSRC provides that the conversion price shall be the average trading price of the stock for the 30-day period prior to the offering, plus a "certain premium".

With full discretion to set the pricing terms, Chinese issuers and underwriters have typically set the conversion premium at or around 0.1%. Furthermore, the *Provisional Measures on Administration of Corporate Convertible Bonds*, approved by China's State Council in 1997, permits issuers to set the conversion price at a discount to the spot stock price, if the issuer is a major SOE.

As a result, most convertible bonds in China have a conversion price that is only slightly higher than the stock price was at the date of issue. For CB investors, the stock price does not need to appreciate much before it becomes economic to convert. By contrast, many US issuers look for structures to achieve a high-conversion premium to limit potential dilution. They intentionally issue convertible instruments that are similar to debt, with features like "contingent conversion" to make conversion very unlikely. Furthermore, many US issuers have been purchasing call spreads concurrently with convertible offerings to increase the effective conversion premium and to reduce dilution.

Conversion premium in the US CB market: a comparison

Unlike the rules in China that vaguely require a "certain conversion premium" for CB offerings, the US securities laws and tax laws all have specific provisions addressing the conversion premium:

Securities Law – many CB issues are offered in the Rule 144A market, and the SEC's 144A rule requires the effective conversion premium to be no less than 10% in order for the CB not to be fungible with underlying equity for regulatory reasons.

Tax – the US Tax Code Section 163(l) denies interest deduction on "equity settled debt instruments". As such, Section 163(l) would deny the interest deduction if a CB "is reasonably expected to result" in conversion of the principal amount into issuer stock. However, the legislative history of Section 163(l) indicates that the provision was not expected to be applied to a CB where the conversion price is "significantly higher" than the stock price on the CB issue date.

As a result, CBs in the US market typically have a not-insignificant conversion premium when they are issued.

Conversion price adjustment for future equity offerings

The anti-dilution adjustment formula used in some Chinese CBs further reveals its equivalent nature to equity offerings. In particular, the conversion price (and the conversion rate) will be adjusted upon the issuing company's future equity offerings. If a CB issuer offers new common shares at a later time, the conversion price will be adjusted as follows:

$$P1 = (P0 + A * K) / (1+K)$$

Where:

$P1$ = new conversion price after anti-dilution adjustment

$P0$ = current conversion price

A = offering price of new shares

K = % of new shares on current outstanding shares

Following such an anti-dilution adjustment, if additional shares are issued and priced higher than the bond's conversion price (ie, $A > P0$), the conversion price will be increased accordingly. Similarly, if new shares are offered at a lower price ($A < P0$), the conversion price will be adjusted to a lower price. In other words, the conversion price, the price at which the issuer sells stocks in the future if the bond is converted into shares, changes in accordance with the current value of the common stock price on the stock.

In the US CB market, conversion price/conversion rate adjustments for future new stock offerings are uncommon. Even with respect to those corporate events that are covered by bond indenture for anti-dilution adjustments, the bond indenture typically has a general provision to avoid any possible negative impact to the convertible bondholders. Such a provision would probably read:

> If, however, the application of the foregoing [conversion price/conversion rate adjustments] formula would result in a decrease in the conversion rate, no adjustment to the conversion rate will be made.

By contrast, according to some Chinese CB prospectuses, if additional shares are issued and priced higher than the CB's conversion price, the conversion price will be reset to a higher level, which means the conversion rate will drop. This will be a real issue to investors if the company issued the CB when stock price was low (hence a relatively low-conversion price) and later issued new common stocks when the stock price is high (which will be used to reset the conversion price higher).

Conversion price annual reset

In addition, many of the CB issues in China have empowered the issuers to reset the conversion price downward, annually, if the price of shares falls significantly. This reset feature offers investors more shares if the stock price declines, with the goal of keeping the bond's conversion value at par.

A typical reset provision will read as follows (the numbers in brackets vary among different offerings):

> During the term of this convertible bond, if the closing price of the issuer's common stock is less than or equal to [90%] of the then applicable conversion price for at least 20 trading days in any period of 30 consecutive trading days, the Board of Directors of the issuer may reduce the applicable conversion price by no more than [10%], provided that the conversion price after such adjustment shall not be less than the per share book value of the common stock. The Board of Directors should not exercise this conversion price reset right more than once in any [12] months.

This feature is similar to the reset CBs that were popular in Japan in the mid 1990s, when, due to their large real-estates exposure, Japanese banks were considered a risky investment. As the stock market was depressed, equity issuance was not an option to raise capital. The reset feature in Japan's CBs was included to give investors insurance against the decline of the bank's stock. Similarly, the reset feature in China protects investors against a significant drop in the stock price, as it aims to keep the conversion option in-the-money when the stock price declines significantly.

On the issuer's side, the right to reset the conversion price is also important. CBs typically have contingent put options for the investor. If the stock prices go below a certain level (say 70% of the conversion price), bondholders can put the bonds back to the company for the par value in cash. Because the stock price trigger for resets is higher than for contingent puts, the issuers could potentially reset the CB to avoid the contingent puts. In other words, when the stock price starts falling, the issuers could reset the CB before the stock price falls further to trigger investor's put rights.

The reset feature is very valuable to investors. However, due to stock price fluctuations, this feature is difficult to value because the reset conversion price is also determined by the past history of stock price; hence, it is "path dependent". In other words, a later reset of the conversion price depends on the conversion price set on the immediately preceding reset date, which in turn depends on the conversion price set at an even earlier date. Further complicating the valuation, the issuer determines the date to reset the conversion price annually, instead of at a fixed reset date.

But in the case of China's CBs, pricing difficulty may give way to non-economic considerations, namely, that many CB offerings are intended to result in the issuance of the underlying common stocks. Thus it is critical for issuers to have the reset feature to avoid investors exercising those contingency puts. In fact, because the short selling mechanism is not currently available in China (to be discussed in more detail later in this chapter), those typical CB pricing models in developed markets that are based on no-arbitrage assumptions are not directly applicable in China anyway.

Together, a low conversion premium at the original issuance and the issuer's ability to reset the conversion price over time, lead to the extremely high likelihood that CBs will be converted into shares through the bond life. For example, when a Chinese corporation won approval for a record 10 billion yuan (US$1.2 billion) CB sale (equivalent to a fifth of its market value), minority shareholders strongly protested about the potential dilution impact. Consequently, the issuer agreed to mollify the minority shareholders by reducing the convertible offering size and pledging not to lower the conversion price for three years.

FINANCIAL INNOVATION DISCOUNT

Convertible bonds are still new to China's stock markets and Chinese investors so there are a few features designed to provide investors additional comfort to invest in them, which in a sense is a form of "financial innovation discount".

Coupon compensation for non-conversion

At maturity, if CBs have not been converted into shares, most CBs will provide investors with extra coupon compensation. The typical extra interest formula is:

Extra interest = X% ∗ term − sum of interests received during CB term

The $X\%$ is set when the CB is issued, and obviously it is set at a higher level than the actual coupon rates on the CB. Such coupon compensation at maturity is similar to the premium put feature (ie, the holder could require the issuer to repurchase the CB at a price above the principal amount of the CB) seen in other Asian regions. That is, if conversion is not economically feasible due to stock price drops or other reasons, investors are still able to realise a high yield-to-maturity.

High issuing company standard

The rules concerning China's CB offerings require a higher return on equity (ROE) and earnings strength for convertible offerings than normal common stock or debt offerings. The *Provisional Measures on Administration of Corporate Convertible Bonds*, approved by China's State Council in 1997, specifically require corporate performance for issuer companies to qualify for CB offering, including:

❏ The company makes a profit for the most recent three consecutive years, with ROE greater than 10% (the threshold may be lower than utility, raw materials and infrastructure companies, but should be no less than 7%).
❏ The debt-to-asset ratio of the company will be no greater than 70% after the planned CB offering is issued.

For investors, these requirements obviously are the first layer of protection to the issuer company's credit risk. By contrast, the disclosure-based US market does not impose substantive requirements for issuers from the regulatory body such as ROE or debt-to-asset (D/A) ratio. In addition, the US CB market traditionally has been a major financing alternative for start-up and early-stage companies, which may or may not have reached profitability when they seek CB financing.

Commercial bank credit support

Furthermore, both the coupon and principal repayments are usually guaranteed by commercial banks. The guarantees are typically "joint and several" so that if the issuer is in default on paying the coupon and/or the principal amount, the investors could pursue the guaranteeing bank directly. (By contrast, if they are "general guarantee", the investors could only pursue the bank after they have claimed against the issuer.)

The bank guarantee provides important value to CB investors. The principal repayment is only relevant if the company's stock price has dropped significantly so that it is not economical to convert the bond into shares. But, typically, the company's credit would be deteriorating when its stock price is falling (indicating the company's financial condition is worsening). Therefore, the external credit support from commercial banks kicks in when it is most needed.

It is worth noting, however, that there are significant credit differences between the banks in China. Furthermore, it is impossible to hedge out the credit risks of these CBs completely, because a credit default swap (CDS) market for Chinese domestic companies is essentially nonexistent. If the credit guarantee is provided by a large government-owned bank – making the credit of the CB effectively the credit of the government-owned bank – buying CDS protection on Chinese sovereign debt could be a close proxy hedge for the credit risk.

The additional credit support via external guarantee is typically used to enhance the credit profile of convertible issues and hence to lower coupons or increase the conversion premium. However, that is not the case in China. Instead, the commercial bank's guarantee, a higher ROE requirement and the extra coupon compensation are all a form of "financial innovation discount". They provide additional incentives for investors to feel comfortable investing in CBs, a relatively unfamiliar investment vehicle in China.

In summary, the major structural differences between Chinese and US CBs are listed below:

	Chinese CB	US CB
Initial conversion premium	Low	High
Conversion price adjustment for future equity offering	Common	Not common
Annual reset of conversion price	Common	Not common
Issuer's ROE and earning strength	High	No regulatory requirements
Extra coupon for non-conversion	Common	Not common
Bank credit support	Common	Not common

CONVERTIBLE ARBITRAGE TRADING

Convertible arbitrage trading is a popular strategy for many US hedge funds. The strategy basically involves two major components. The major part is to short sell underlying stocks to hedge out any stock price risk and trade on the implied volatility of the embedded call options in CBs. The other part is to hedge out the credit and interest rate risks on the CBs, which typically involves a combination of purchasing equity put options, shorting the underlying stock and/or purchasing credit protection in the CDS market.

While leaving details to a more specific CB trading book, this so-called "dynamic arbitrage trading" strategy, like any other financial derivatives trading, is dependent on two major factors: firstly, the nonlinear price profiles of financial instruments (which feature CBs definitely have – as shown in the price profile chart earlier in this chapter); secondly, the ability to adjust the short position of the underlying stocks from time to time to keep the trading portfolio (long positions in CBs and short positions in stocks) "delta hedged".

Unfortunately, short selling remains illegal in China's stock market. Chinese securities laws have yet to permit domestic or foreign investors to borrow stock. As a result, when investing in Chinese CBs, foreign investors cannot use short selling to manage risk or to lock in trading profits. A more subtle implication is that western valuation models do not apply directly to the Chinese CB market, because the "no-arbitrage" assumption for those valuation models may not hold in a market without a short selling mechanism.

> **Short selling in China**
>
> Stock short selling had been strictly banned by China's Securities Law when it was initially formulated in 1998. Most parts of south-eastern and eastern Asia were going through the Asian financial crisis then, and the legislators naturally placed the prevention of financial risks above concerns for liquidity and efficiency of the market.
>
> As market linearisation continues, short selling mechanisms are emerging in various areas of the financial markets. The emerging ETF and options markets have led to "synthetic" short sale mechanisms under certain circumstances; the newly introduced buy-out repo in the T-bond market has made short selling officially possible in the fixed-income market.
>
> The sweeping amendments to the Securities Law in late 2005 officially lifted the ban on stock lending and shorting transactions. The system for direct stock short selling is on the horizon. See the detailed discussion in Chapter 8.

Nevertheless, China's domestic stock market is poised to embrace stock or index short selling in the near future. As China gradually opens its capital markets in line with international standards, the introduction of short selling is a natural next step and encouraging developments have gradually emerged (see box). Once stock short selling is officially introduced to the market, the economic terms and trading behaviour of stocks and structured products such as CBs may change dramatically as arbitrage trading strategies emerge.

PROSPECT: CB IN FULL-FLOATING ERA

CBs have been popular among issuing companies and investors in China. In 2003, CBs surpassed follow-on stock offerings and rights offerings to become the No. 1 financing choice for listed companies for the first time. The major driving force behind this trend is the unique shareholding structure in listed companies, and the corresponding preference for equity form financing tools as discussed in detail in Chapter 1. As such, the current reform on segregated equity ownership structure will have a significant impact on existing CBs as well as the CB market's future developments.

Existing CBs

The full-flotation campaign intends to make the nontradable shares of the listed companies tradable in the A share market. Generally, the share floating plans involve compensating existing public shareholders with cash or additional stocks. Such payments are aimed at cushioning any losses the public shareholders might incur from falling stock prices triggered by the large supply of nontradable shares. Thus for existing CBs, the single most important question is, should CB holders also receive value compensation?

So far among the companies that have launched the full-flotation reform, very few have had an outstanding CB. With respect to the limited precedents, the CB holders unfortunately did not receive special value compensation, nor was the conversion rate (price) adjusted.

For example, the JingNiu Energy CB was the first occasion that the CB market met the share reform. The company did not provide special compensation (either a one-off payment or an adjustment to the conversion terms) to CB holders. Instead, the CB holders were permitted to convert the bond into stocks within a 19-day window period. Upon conversion into shares, the CB holders were entitled to the full-flotation consideration as normal public stockholders.

The mechanism in JingNiu's CB issue is more like a "forced conversion" than "value compensation". From a valuation perspective, CB holders were not necessarily "fairly" compensated. In real trading, however, many CB holders decided to convert into shares to participate in the reform (ie, receiving a compensation package from the reforming company as common stockholders), because the CB would not receive any compensation and they faced the risk of the CB price falling should the stock price come under pressure, post the share reform.

Although the segregated equity ownership and the corresponding reform is a unique Chinese phenomenon, it is comparable (in a very loose sense) to an issuer company's distribution to existing common stockholders, which in more developed CB markets would result in an anti-dilution adjustment to the CB terms to preserve CB investors' interests. It remains to be seen whether reforming companies will compensate the existing Chinese CB investors ever and how new CBs issued by companies not yet having completed the reform will address this issue in their offering prospectus.

FUTURE OFFERINGS

In future CB offerings, the adjustment mechanism for full-flotation will definitely be an important deal term. But even more significantly, future CB structures may be very different from the existing issues once the equity ownership reform is fully implemented.

Once the shares of the listed companies are fully tradable in the public market, the controlling shareholders will become more sensitive to potential ownership dilution when considering equity-linked offerings. As such, future CBs are likely to be more debt-like and less equity-like, and they may become more comparable to their US counterparts structurally. Finally, for new issuing companies that have not yet completed the share reform, they will have to develop a mechanism in the CB that addresses the potential share reform's impact on the bond's valuation.

CONCLUSION

Convertible bonds in China have unique features that reflect the character of China's regulatory system and stock market. They are more akin to equity offerings as the low-conversion premium and annual reset of the conversion price make it highly likely that the CBs will be converted into shares. Additional investor-friendly features, such as the extra coupon compensation and the commercial bank guarantee, are added to encourage investor participation in this new investment system in China.

Combining the low-conversion price and solid bond floor, China's CBs provide an alternative approach for investors seeking exposure to Chinese stocks. Because a short selling mechanism is not yet available, specific trading strategy and risk management should be developed in accordance with the Chinese CBs' distinctive financial terms. The current reform on the listed companies shareholding structure should have a significant impact on the existing CB issues as well as future offerings.

4

Warrants and Options

Warrants and options retuned to China's stock market in late 2005 after regulators had prohibited derivatives trading for nearly a decade. The debut of the warrants on Bao Steel Co. stock in August 2005 was the first official acknowledgement of equity derivatives in China.

After being awaited by stock exchanges and securities firms for years, warrants and options were initially brought into the market to facilitate the 2005 state-share overhaul reform. But it was soon becoming an important trading market of its own. As early as 6 December, 2005, the trading volume of the then six existing options exceeded the total share trading on the two stock exchanges.

Although the young option market is currently characterised by excessive speculative trading, it is poised to become one of the biggest option trading markets in the world. The growth of the option market would further lead to increased activities in other parts of the A share market such as exchange-traded funds (ETFs) and index-linked products. As the building blocks for complex derivatives products, the emerging option market should also provide a catalyst for continuing financial innovation in China's stock market.

BACKGROUND ON OPTION TRADING

Options are among the most common form of financial derivatives. The word "derivative" originates from mathematics and refers to a variable, which has been derived from another variable. The same is true for financial derivatives: they derive their value from the value of some other asset, which is known as the underlying asset.

For example, an equity option on the stock of XYZ Company will derive its value from the share price of the XYZ stock.

Thus it naturally follows that the value of a derivative should not exceed that of the underlying asset. After all, the value of the derivative is derived from such an underlying asset. However, early in China's equity derivatives history (a decade ago, more precisely), the market saw situations where options on a stock were traded at a higher price to the underlying stock. That was a blatant violation of any pricing theory for derivatives, but probably a clear manifestation of the Chinese stock market at its nascent development stage.

There are two basic types of options. A call option (sometimes referred to as a warrant) gives the investor the right to purchase the underlying stock by a certain date for a certain price. A put option gives the investor the right to sell the underlying stock by a certain date for a certain price. The options distinguish themselves from financial forwards and futures in one important aspect. Options give the investor the right to buy or sell the underlying stock, but the investor is not obligated to do so as in the case of forwards and futures.

Below is a list of the key option market terms that will be used in this chapter.

Option market terminology

Call	An option contract giving the holder the right to buy the underlying security at a specified price for a fixed period of time (before the option contract's expiration date)
Put	An option contract giving the holder the right to sell the underlying security at a specified price for a fixed period of time (before the option contract's expiration date)
American-style option	An option contract that can be exercised at any time between the date of purchase and the date of expiration
European-style option	An option contract that can only be exercised at the date of expiration
Exercise	To implement the right under which the holder of an option is entitled to buy (in the case of a call) or sell (in the case of a put) the underlying security

Option market terminology (continued)

Expiration date	The date when an option and the right to exercise it terminates
Strike price	The stated price per share at which the option holder can buy or sell the underlying security
At-the-money	The current market value of the underlying security is the same as the exercise price of the option
In-the-money	A call option is said to be in-the-money if the current market value is above the option's exercise price. A put option is in-the-money if the current market value of the underlying security is below the exercise price
Out-of-the-money	A call option is out-of-the-money if the strike price is greater than the market price of the underlying security. A put option is out-of-the-money if the strike price is less than the market price of the underlying security
Premium (option price)	Purchase price of the option. The premium is factored by the current marketplace conditions of the underlying stock, such as stock price and volatility
Intrinsic value	Intrinsic value is the in-the-money portion of an option's premium
Time value	The portion of the option premium that is attributable to the amount of time remaining until the expiration of the option contract. Time value is whatever value the option has in addition to its intrinsic value
Premium	This is the price that the buyer of the option pays to the option writer (seller). The premium is factored by the current marketplace conditions of the underlying stock, such as volatility, time value and volume
Volatility	A measure of the fluctuation in the market price of the underlying security. Mathematically, volatility is the annualised standard deviation of returns
Hedge	A trading strategy used to limit investment loss by making a transaction that will offset a current option position

OPTIONS/WARRANTS IN CHINA: HISTORICAL OVERVIEW
SRC rights

The earliest form of option-like security in China was the Subscription Rights Certificate (SRC). The SRC was created in the early 1990s when a few state-owned companies were restructured into listed companies in order to have their shares trading on the stock exchanges. The market demand for those IPO shares was so huge that investors first had to buy the SRCs to qualify them to participate in a lottery for the right to purchase IPO shares.

As would be expected in a brand new stock market, the IPO shares all had a significant first day jump in prices so that the initial costs for SRC and IPO share purchase prices looked like a sure bargain. As a result, a black market for SRCs quickly sprang up in 1992 as retail investors aggressively sought these certificates. Signalling the explosive interest in the stock market, many SRCs were traded at ten times their original issue price.

However, this (unofficial) SRC trading quickly faded away in 1993 as increasing numbers of companies issued shares and the demand for shares was weakened by some short-term market corrections. The SRC market disappeared shortly after, as a bank account-based IPO subscription system was introduced to completely replace the SRC system.

Transferable pre-emptive rights

Compared to the SRC, the transferable pre-emptive right (TPR) was much closer to a true option instrument in modern capital markets, yet its appearance in the Chinese stock market was similarly brief.

The first TPR came to the Chinese market in 1992. A few listed companies issued TPRs in connection with their follow-on stock offering, which gives the existing shareholders the right to purchase new shares to maintain their percentage ownership in those companies. Considering existing shareholders may be unwilling – or unable – to purchase new shares, the exchanges made such rights transferable and tradable on the exchanges.

This new trading product soon proved to be a magnet for volatile trading. For example, the TPRs in many cases were traded at a higher price to the underlying stock, a blatant violation of any pricing theory for derivatives. The most extreme situation involved a TPR trading at a premium to the underlying stock for more than a month with the premium as high as 30% on certain trading days in that period. (This, of course, had to do with the lack of the stock short selling mechanism to be discussed in Chapter 8.) As a result, the market regulator moved quickly to ban the trading in 1996 following rampant speculation.

Warrants and options

China's stock exchanges and securities firms have been pushing for an options market for years. For one thing, they hoped that options on stocks as a basic financial derivative could lead to more structured financial instruments such as options on ETFs (see Chapter 5 on ETFs) or index futures (see Chapter 6 on Index Products). For another, Chinese securities firms desperately looked for new sources of brokerage fees as the Chinese stock market continued to make new lows in the last few years.

Meanwhile, retail investors have demonstrated a strong demand for new trading instruments as well. Many of them have lost interest in the A share market as they struggle with the multi-year bear market. Warrants and options are particularly attractive to them because they are traditionally more interested in speculative trading than long-term investment, as they provide investors with leveraged exposure to stocks (see box). From the regulators' perspective, the investors, after many years experience with the A share stock market, should have a better understanding of the inherent risks and could manage the potential speculative trading better this time when options are reintroduced to the market.

Option leverage: investment gain/loss multiplier

To start, let us look at some numerical examples. Suppose an investor has US$1,000 to invest and is bullish on ABC stock, which is trading at US$100 per share. Obviously, the investor can buy 10 ABC shares at the spot price directly. Alternatively, the investor may make the same investment via at-the-money call options (strike price at US$100) on ABC shares. Assuming a one-year investment horizon, the risk-free rate $r = 1\%$, stock volatility $\sigma = 30\%$, and no dividend paying, the price for the at-the-money European call option, based on the Black-Scholes pricing formula, is US$12.37.

Because at maturity, the option holder will gain one-for-one for any price move above the original stock price of US$100, the investor could invest in 10 at-the-money options for 12.37 * 10 = US$123.70 and gain the same exposure for stock gains as if he invests US$1,000 in 10 shares. In other words, for the same US$1,000 capital, the investor can invest in 1,000/12.37 = 80 options, giving himself eight times of gain/loss exposure (80/10) than the equivalent stock position.

Therefore, an option position can give investors the same exposure in a stock position with less initial investment. This ratio of the
underlying stock price over the corresponding option premium, often
referred to as "gearing" (stock price/option premium), provides investors
with one measure of option leverage. For a given rate of return on an
underlying security, an investor can increase those returns by applying
the leverage of options.

However, the leveraging power of options, which can magnify profits, can also magnify losses if the underlying security moves in the
opposite direction. This illustrates the classic financial trade-off
between risk and reward. In the above example, if the stock price ends
up at US$99 at maturity, the stock position will have a modest 1%
loss, while the option position will suffer a 100% loss: with stock price
drops below the strike price, all options expire worthless.

Finally, the 2005 stock market reform regarding the separation of
equity ownership (also known as the full-flotation reform) has provided an additional catalyst. As discussed in the next subsection,
warrants have proved to be an effective financial tool to facilitate the
government's campaign to make state-owned nontradable shares
tradable. Their application in the full-flotation reform, together with
the broad market demand, has successfully brought warrant/option
trading back to China's stock market.

As a quick aside, in the context of this state-share overhaul
reform, the warrants received by the A share investors are actually
issued by the large nontradable shareholders. Strictly speaking,
they are not warrants in the traditional corporate finance sense.
Typically, the "option" is issued by an independent third party
other than the issuer of the underlying stock, while the "warrant"
is issued and guaranteed by the corporate issuer itself.

In the Chinese market, the two exchanges have made a similar
distinction, for example in the *Tentative Measures for Administration
of Warrants* that serves as the main options trading rules of the
exchanges. However, investors generally refer to the call options
received in the share reform as "warrants", even though strictly
speaking they are issued by the nontradable shareholders, not the
listed company itself. Therefore this chapter will also use the term
"warrants" for that purpose, whereas "options" are used to refer to
those created by the securities firms.

THE RETURN OF WARRANTS
Attractive tool for full-flotation reform

As discussed in detail in Chapter 1, the full-flotation reform focuses on the dichotomy of tradable and nontradable shares of the listed companies. The primary goal is to transform the nontradable shares into tradable shares, hence the notion of full flotation. Because the potential new supply of tradable shares may dilute existing shareholders' ownership and put pressure on the A share trading price, the nontradable shareholders are required to provide compensation to the public investors for the right to float.

Warrants soon become an attractive alternative to free shares and cash, as the listed companies, the tradable shareholders, and the nontradable shareholders balance their respective interests in determining the appropriate compensation package. The warrant's flexibility in structuring, the lack of immediate price pressure on the corresponding A shares, and the high trading value that the market assigns to them have effectively created a win-win situation among the major players in the share reform.

No immediate stock price pressure

For years, the Chinese government has planned to unload the enormous state-owned nontradable shares without flooding the market. But its early attempts all inevitably led to sharp stock price declines and had to be retracted quickly. The concern that when the nontradable shares become tradable they will overwhelm the market demand, causing share prices to slump dramatically, has weighed on the A share market for a long time.

To facilitate the latest full-flotation reform efforts, the regulators have encouraged financial innovations that stabilise stock prices. For example, in connection with the share reform, the CSRC in early 2005 for the first time authorised the listed companies to buy back their shares on the open A share market, as the share buyback mechanism provides listed companies with another alternative to support the stock prices when they are under pressure from the full-flotation reform.

The warrants are effective for two major reasons. Firstly, when the tradable shareholders receive warrants as compensation, they could cash in by selling the warrant itself, without any direct impact on the A share stock price. By contrast, where free shares are paid to public A share investors as reform compensation, many investors would choose to sell those shares to lock in profits, thereby depressing the stock price in the A share market. Secondly, when securities firms issue similar options, they would be accumulating the underlying shares to hedge and collateralise their positions, which actually gives stocks upward momentum.

Structuring flexibility

Warrants could be flexibly structured to fit the specific situations of the listed companies. For example, specific nontradable shareholders could award the public investors warrants on their stock holdings, whereby the underlying shares become tradable upon exercise of the warrants. Alternatively, warrants could also be used as the consideration in the flotation of all nontradable shares in the listed company.

In some cases, warrants (or other forms of option instruments) are the only feasible consideration form to implement the share reform. For example, China Vanke Co., a Shenzhen-listed company, has only one large holder of nontradable shares, which holds a mere 12.89% of Vanke's total shares. There was little room for this nontradable shareholder to give free shares to A share investors as compensation, and put options on Vanke stock were eventually used to execute the share structure reform.

Legal reform to facilitate

The debut of the warrants on Bao Steel Co. stock in August 2005 was the first official acknowledgement of equity derivatives in China. This groundbreaking development was supported by a broad relaxation in the securities regulatory framework.

Securities law amendment

The long-awaited amendments to China's 1998 Securities Law was finally approved by the Standing Committee of the National People's Congress in October 2005. Through the new amendments, Chinese lawmakers sought to address many of the Chinese market's structural problems such as disclosure requirements, financial products innovation, and shareholder protection.

One of the most important aspects, however, is that the new securities law clears the way for the development of a derivatives market. For years, the investment community argued that a lack of hedging tools such as futures and options had made investors unable to manage their risks effectively, a key barrier for the next-stage development of the stock markets.

The new Securities Law has explicitly legalised derivatives products, and it empowers the State Council to enact detailed rules in the near future to regulate the derivatives industry and promote its development. In addition, the new law no longer insists that securities must be traded in spot transactions (ie, physically owned shares), which opens the door for potential stock lending and short sales, which are critical for the further growth of many derivative securities markets such as warrants.

Green light for investment funds

To promote the warrants market, the CSRC also released a circular to broaden the business scope of domestic fund management companies to cover warrants. Previously, domestic funds were only allowed to invest in stocks and bonds. As most funds are large tradable shareholders of the listed companies, they receive a substantial amount of warrants when the companies issue warrants in connection with their share reform.

The CSRC circular clarifies that fund managers are allowed to hold, sell or exercise warrants that are received in the share reform, as before that there were no rules in China regarding whether investment funds could invest in derivative products. More importantly, the CRSC rule empowers the funds to actively invest in warrants trading in the A share market within a certain volume limitation, adding some institutional investors base to the burgeoning warrant market.

T + 0 trading mechanism

In another move to facilitate warrant trading, the market regulators permit warrants trading on a "T + 0" basis. As a result, warrants in China can be bought and sold an unlimited number of times in one day, leading to heavy trading volume and volatility. So far, the A share stock market implements a "T + 1" system; thus a newly bought share can only be sold on the next trading day.

Chinese stock market record from warrant T + 0 trading

On 8 December, 2005 the put option on China Vanke Co. traded extremely actively on the Shenzhen Stock Exchange. Its trading volume, 4.66 billion, set a record for single-day trading volume for any investment product in China's stock market history.

The outstanding Vanke options are 2.14 billion units. Thanks to the T + 0 trading system, the Vanke option reached an unprecedented trading volume with a 217.6% daily turnover rate on ber 8.

By contrast, in the A share market, China United Telecommunications Co. has the largest tradable share amount of 6 billion shares. With the T + 1 trading system in the A share market, it is virtually impossible to reach a 70% daily turnover to have a trading volume comparable to the Vanke record. In the near future, this record would probably only be challengeable by further active trading in the warrants/options market.

Source: Bloomberg

Is T + 0 trading a violation of the Securities Law? To dampen then-excessive speculation, the Shanghai and Shenzhen Stock Exchanges in 1996 changed A share securities trading from T + 0 to T + 1 settlement, which was further formally incorporated into the Securities Law when it was promulgated in 1998. The Bao Steel warrants trading started T + 0 trading in August 2005 but the Securities Law amendment was only adopted in October 2005.

Apparently the Bao Steel warrants T + 0 trading did not violate the Securities Law either before or after the amendment. On the one hand, the existing Securities Law before amendment, although it prohibits T + 0 trading, only covered straight equity stocks – thus, strictly speaking, derivatives such as warrants did not fall within the old Securities Law framework. On the other hand, in the amended Securities Law the concept of "securities" was broadened to cover derivatives instruments such as warrants and options, but the T + 0 trading prohibition was also removed.

Requirements for an issuing company

The *Tentative Measures for Administration of Warrants* issued by both the Shanghai and Shenzhen Stock Exchanges on 18 July, 2005 is the first specific regulation on equity derivatives in China. The Tentative Measure set fairly high qualifications for listed companies to list their warrants (and other options) on the exchanges:

❑ The market value of tradable shares for the most recent 20 trading days must be no less than 3 billion yuan*;

❑ The cumulative turnover ration for the most recent 60 trading days must be above 25%;

❑ Outstanding tradable shares must number no less than 300 million shares.

*approximately US$1 = 8.1 yuan.

These requirements aim to ensure that the underlying shares have sufficient liquidity, because the price correlation between the warrants and the underlying shares would lead to much more trading activity in the shares once warrants are listed. If the shares are thinly traded, the risk of excessive volatility and price manipulation will be exacerbated.

Nevertheless, the warrant market showed extraordinary volatility from day one. As discussed in later sections, the regulators then moved quickly to try to reduce market volatility/speculation from a different angle, ie to permit securities firms to issue similar warrants to increase the supply of warrants in the market.

BAO STEEL: FIRST LISTED WARRANT IN CHINA

The warrants on Bao Steel Co. stock were the first to be listed in China after regulators prohibited derivatives trading in the early 1990s. Shanghai Bao Steel Group, parent of Baoshan Steel Co. (the listed company), offered 387.7 million warrants (one warrant for every 10 tradable shares) free to A share shareholders in exchange for the right to float the company's nontradable shares.

The terms of the warrants are as follows:

Bao Steel warrant terms

Warrant	Bao Steel (GTB1 580000)
Underlying stock	Bao Steel Co. (G 600019)
Issue Date	22 August, 2005
Call/Put	Call
Strike price (yuan)	4.50
Stock price at issuance (yuan)	4.63
Maturity date	30 August, 2006
American/European option	European
Exercise ratio	1:1
Settlement method	Physical

Source: Bloomberg

Dramatic price rises

The Bao Steel warrants closed at 1.263 yuan at their debut, 84% higher than the opening price of 0.688 yuan, which is a reference price set by the Shanghai Stock Exchange based on the commonly used Black-Scholes option valuation method. The warrant's price jump on heavy volume indicated investors' intense interest in the new product but at the same time raised concerns about speculation and inaccurate pricing.

For example, the warrant price reached 1.8 yuan following a few days trading sessions. With the Bao Steel A share trading at around 4.5 yuan, the warrant price implied a volatility of 100% or so for the Bao Steel stock, which is an incredible number for such a blue-chip stock.

One major reason for these abnormal trading prices is the T + 0 trading system for options. As mentioned earlier, new rules were put in place to permit warrants trading on a T + 0 basis, whereby the warrants can be bought and sold multiple times in one day. The

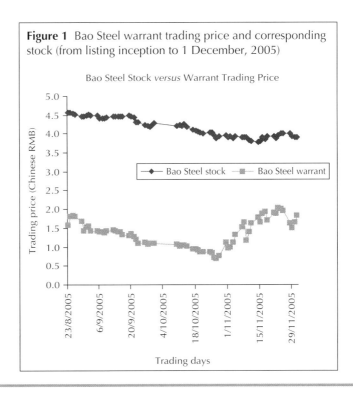

Figure 1 Bao Steel warrant trading price and corresponding stock (from listing inception to 1 December, 2005)

T + 0 trading system has led to many trading days where the daily turnover rate of the listed options far exceeded 100%, leading to their extremely volatile trading prices.

Additionally, the special price limits for options trading also contribute to drastic trading price movements. The A share market has a daily 10% limit on up and down price movements; the up/down limits for warrant trading are a lot wider. According to the exchange rules:

$Warrant\ up\ limit = W_{(T-1)} + (S_{(T)} - S_{(T-1)}) * 125\% * Exercise\ ratio$
$Warrant\ down\ limit = W_{(T-1)} - (S_{(T-1)} - S_{(T)}) * 125\% * Exercise\ ratio$

Where:

$W_{(T-1)}$ – warrant closing price on the previous trading day

$S_{(T)}$ – stock closing price on the day in question

$S_{(T-1)}$ – stock closing price on the previous trading day

Exercise ratio = how many shares a warrant can be converted into (typically 1:1)

For example, if:

❑ On T − 1 day, the warrant closing price is US$1, and the stock closing price is US$10
❑ On T day, the stock reaches the upper limit, US$11

Then the warrant upper limit price is:

$$W_{(T)} = 1 + (11 - 10) * 125\% = 2.25$$

That is, for the warrant trading price to reach the upper limit, it needs to appreciate $(2.25 - 1)/1 = 125\%$ from its previous day closing price.

Winner's curse

The problem of the winner's curse occurs during any auction process when bidders must estimate the true or final value of a desired good. Because of incomplete information, emotions or any other number of factors regarding the item being auctioned, bidders can have a difficult time determining the item's intrinsic value. As a result, the winning bid typically overestimates the item's true value.

In Behaviour Finance studies, the winner's curse is likely to occur in financial markets when the following factors exist: lack of supply (scarcity), insufficient information (difficult to value), and excess liquidity. All these factors existed in the Bao Steel warrant situation. So it is not surprising that Bao Steel warrants traded at prices much higher than the fair value suggested by the standard derivatives valuation model.

The key reason for the warrant's high trading price, however, is probably due to supply and demand. Combining the limited supply of tradable warrants in the market and the pent-up demand for new trading instruments in the A share market, the sharply rising prices for the Bao Steel warrants is a classic winner's curse phenomenon in behaviour finance terms (see box). All the key factors existed in China's warrant market, particularly during the first three months following the Bao Steel warrant's debut.

Firstly, Bao Steel warrants were the first and only listed warrants in China to start trading. Secondly, warrants were new financial instruments in China so investors were learning to value these complex products. Finally, with A shares in a multi-year bear market, investors rushed to invest in warrants as the next big thing because they feared being left behind. The dramatic rise of Bao Steel warrants provides a perfect case for behaviour finance research.

Market manipulation investigation

Most illustrative of the speculative trading nature, Figure 2 shows that the stock and warrant trading diverged completely in the two weeks around 31 October, 2005 – although derivatives pricing theories suggest they should move up or down in the same direction. During that period, the stock price was drifting around 4 yuan per share and slowly moving downward, yet the warrant trading price moved up strongly from its all time low. The daily trading price of the warrants in that period is shown in the following chart.

31 October, 2005 was a critical trading day. Before that, the Bao Steel warrants tumbled in a few trading sessions and closed at 0.765 yuan per warrant on Friday, 28 October. On Monday, 31 October, however, the price of the warrants surged 46.54% to close at 1.123 yuan, with a trading volume of 1.658 billion yuan – more than double the 494 million yuan on the previous trading day.

The Shanghai Stock Exchange quickly reacted to this abnormal trading pattern and launched an investigation into potential price manipulation. In an official statement, the Exchange declared that it had identified irregular trading in the warrants. Without identifying the names, it ordered a few securities firms' branches to suspend their trading in Bao Steel warrants, as they were found to be lax with risk control. In addition, the Exchange urged member

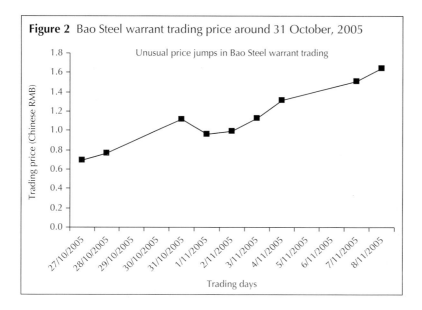

Figure 2 Bao Steel warrant trading price around 31 October, 2005

brokerage houses to conduct a self-inspection on risk management in warrants trading to help maintain "normal market
order."

However, despite the investigation into potential market
manipulation, the warrant trading was not brought to a complete
halt either by the exchanges or regulatory bodies. There are two
possible reasons. Firstly, warrants have quickly become an important trading instrument and also a necessary tool for the ongoing
stock market reform. It is in everyone's interest to maintain a successful warrant trading market. Secondly and probably more
importantly, although the large movements were clearly a result of
intense speculation, it would be hard to prove manipulation: the
dramatic intra-day trading could well have been driven purely by
excessive speculation in the market.

As an interesting aside, the warrants dropped only modestly
when the Shanghai Stock Exchange issued the investigation report
on 1 November. They then continued to climb higher in later
trading days, shrugging off the penalty decisions issued by the
Exchange (as shown in Figure 2 above).

But the volatile trading in Bao Steel warrants drove the exchange and regulatory agencies to take additional actions. They moved quickly to permit securities firms (the dealers) to issue options with substantially similar terms, in the hope that an increased supply of warrants could rein in the rampant speculation in the market. This mechanism was immediately applied to the Wuhan Steel warrant, the second listed warrant in China.

WUHAN STEEL: FIRST LISTED PUT, FIRST DEALER CREATION
Wuhan steel: first put option

Following Bao Steel, China's Wuhan Iron & Steel Co. (Wuhan Steel) listed both warrants and put options on the Shanghai Stock Exchange on 23 November, 2005, becoming the first listed company to issue put options (and the second to issue warrants). The put option was another major breakthrough because in a market without a short selling mechanism, put options enable investors to express their bearish view on a stock (or an index).

In connection with the share reform, Wuhan Steel Group, the parent of the listed company Wuhan Steel, provided a compensation package to A shareholders in exchange for the flotation of the nontradable shares they held. The compensation package included, for every 10 A shares, 2.3 shares of stock, 1.5 put options and 1.5 warrants on Wuhan Steel stock. Because the warrants and put options had substantially the same terms except for different exercise prices, investors refered to the combination of the Wuhan warrant and put option as a "butterfly" position in derivatives terminology.

Terms of the warrants:

Wuhan Steel warrant terms

Warrant	Wuhan Steel (JTB1 580001)
Underlying stock	Wuhan Steel Co. (G. 600005)
Issue date	23 November, 2005
Call/put	Call
Strike price (yuan)	2.90
Stock price at issuance (yuan)	2.77
Maturity date	22 November, 2006
American/European option	European
Exercise ratio	1:1
Settlement method	Physical

Terms of the put options:

Wuhan Steel put option terms

Option	Wuhan Steel (JTP1 580999)
Underlying stock	Wuhan Steel Co. (G. 600005)
Issue date	23 November, 2005
Call/put	Put
Strike price (yuan)	3.13
Stock price at issuance (yuan)	2.77
Maturity date	22 November, 2006
American/European option	European
Exercise ratio	1:1
Settlement method	Physical

Source: Bloomberg

Concerned about the rampant speculation in the option market, both Wuhan Steel and the Shanghai Stock Exchange took action. In its public notice disclosing the warrant and put compensation package used for the share reform, Wuhan Steel warned investors that China's stock market "lacks experience in warrants trading" so that investors should "be fully aware that the warrants market may be highly speculative."

The Shanghai Stock Exchange, on the other hand, attempted to curb the extreme speculation in the warrant market by increasing the supply of warrants. Days before the official launch of the Wuhan Steel warrants and put options, the Exchange officially authorised qualified securities companies to issue warrants and put options on Wuhan Steel stocks with the same terms. The securities firms issued the first batch of dealer-created options in China shortly after the Wuhan Steel options made their debut on 23 November, 2005.

Warrants/options created by securities firms

The re-introduction of warrants to China's stock market was initially intended to be restricted to the full-flotation reform, that is, warrants used by listed companies to make nontradable shares become tradable. Financial institutions issuing options on listed companies was expected to be a second-phase initiative. However, because rampant speculation characterised the first warrant listing, the exchanges and regulatory agencies, in an attempt to force warrant prices to trade at normal levels, moved quickly to roll out mechanisms for securities brokerages to issue similar options.

On 21 November, 2005 – two days before the Wuhan Steel options officially started trading – the Shanghai Stock Exchange issued a notice to permit qualified securities firms to continuously create new warrants and put options on Wuhan Steel stock. These dealer-created warrants and put options have the same terms as those issued in connection with the full-flotation reform, and they trade under the same code on the Exchange.

According to the Exchange trading rule, the *Tentative Measures for Administration of Warrants*, financial institutions must deposit a performance guarantee (in the form of shares or cash) when they issue options on listed companies based on the following formula:

Share deposits to guarantee call options issued:
Number of shares to deposit
   = *Number of options * Exercise ratio * Guarantee ratio*

Cash deposits to guarantee put options issued:

Number of shares to deposit
   = *Number of options * Exercise price * Exercise ratio * Guarantee ratio*

The guarantee ratio is determined by the Exchange and can be adjusted from time to time. In the notice authorising brokerage firms to issue Wuhan Steel warrants and put options, the Shanghai Stock Exchange require firms to provide full-amount contract performance guarantees (ie, the guarantee ratio = 1).

As a result, securities firms must purchase the same number of Wuhan Steel shares as collateral when they issue the call options (warrants). Similarly they need to deposit the full cash amount equal to the strike price when they issue the put options. Therefore, the maximum number of warrants to be created is constrained by the 2.37 billion existing tradable shares in the A share market. On the other hand, the number of put options to be created is theoretically unlimited, as long as the securities firms find sufficient cash to satisfy guarantee requirements.

Wuhan warrant and put option trading

Since their debut on 23 November, 2005, Wuhan Steel's call warrants and put options closed at their daily upper limits for three consecutive trading days. Then, on 28 November, 10 brokerages began selling put options on Wuhan Steel, which had a significant impact on the trading of Wuhan Steel put options as well as on the stock itself. The regulators imposed the three-day gap between warrants issued for share reform and option created by securities firms, apparently giving A shareholders time to realise value from the share reform compensation payment before being affected by the new supply of options from securities firms.

It is worth noting that the trading behaviour of Wuhan Steel's warrants and put options exhibited a violation of option pricing theory. For the first three straight trading sessions, the Wuhan Steel warrants surged by more than 10% each day, and curiously, so did the put options. Because warrants and put options give investors the opposite rights with respect to the underlying stock, their prices in theory should move in opposite directions. This abnormal price relationship between Wuhan Steel's warrants and put options clearly showed some investors' frenzied exuberance over option trading.

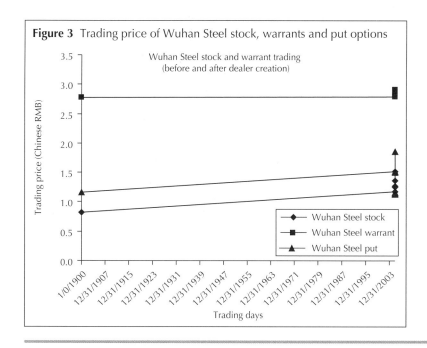

Figure 3 Trading price of Wuhan Steel stock, warrants and put options

Put option trading

Because the guarantee mechanism is simpler for put options (cash collateral) than call warrants (share collateral), the securities firms launched put options on Wuhan Steel first.

The first batch of qualified securities houses issued a total of 1.127 billion additional put-option warrants on Wuhan Steel on 28 November, thus raising the total number of Wuhan Steel's put warrants traded on the market to 1.601 billion on Monday, 28 November from the 474 million issued in connection with the full-flotation reform.

The option market reacted immediately and strongly to the massive number of new Wuhan put options created by the dealers. On the same day, the put option tumbled to its daily low price limit. Although no call options were created, the Wuhan Steel warrants dropped 10.12% and Bao Steel warrants 17.45%, as the market expected similar warrant creations to be in the pipeline. In the following trading days, the large amount of put options created by securities firms led to further price drops in Wuhan Steel put options, bringing its trading to more a "rational level" (see Figure 3 above).

Call warrants trading

Warrants created by securities firms quickly followed suit. On 29 November, a number of securities firms issued 157 million call options on Wuhan Steel. Because the physical shares purchased as call option issuance guarantees would create additional market risk to the securities firms, the number of call warrants created was much smaller than the put options created (12.9% of the 1.127 billion Wuhan put options issued). Consequently the pressure on Wuhan warrants trading was relatively milder – as the above figure shows, the warrant trading price fluctuated modestly after the brokerage houses started to issue call options on Wuhan Steel.

It is interesting to note that the stock trading side was also affected by the dealer creation mechanism. Dealers have to purchase Wuhan stocks as the performance collateral for the call options they issue. This mechanism thus drives issuers (securities firms) to purchase shares on the open market, giving the stock upward momentum. As the above figure shows, the stock price of Wuhan Steel increased significantly on 25 November, a day before the securities firms launched their options.

OPTIONS ON SHENZHEN STOCK EXCHANGE
New listings
Both Bao Steel and Wuhan Steel trade on the Shanghai Stock Exchange. At the beginning of December 2005 the Shenzhen Stock Exchange listed its first three options. The three options started trading on the same day, as the Exchange apparently attempted to dampen trading speculation by concentrating on the supply of options.

Nevertheless, all three options soared on their debut. The put options of Panzhihua New Steel & Vanadium Co. Ltd, the put options of China Vanke Co. Ltd, and the call warrants of Angang New Steel Co. Ltd, all reached their daily price upper limit within a few hours of trading, illustrating the strong interest from options investors. However, these new additions help investors better appreciate the risk involved in option trading. The total six options on the exchanges present a more balanced picture with mixed ups and downs, reminding investors that warrants trading has more than one "up" direction in which to go.

Terms of put options of Panzhihua New Steel & Vanadium Co. Ltd:

New Steel & Vanadium put option terms

Option	New Steel & Vanadium Co. (PGP1 038001)
Underlying stock	New Steel & Vanadium Co. (G. 000629)
Issue date	5 December, 2005
Call/put	Put
Strike price (yuan)	4.85
Stock price at issuance (yuan)	3.30
Maturity date	3 May, 2007
American/European option	European
Exercise ratio	1:1
Settlement method	Physical

Terms of put options of China Vanke Co. Ltd:

China Vanke put option terms

Option	Vanke (HRP1 038002)
Underlying stock	China Vanke Co. (G. 000002)
Issue date	5 December, 2005
Call/put	Put
Strike price (yuan)	3.73

Terms of put options of China Vanke Co. Ltd: (continued)

China Vanke put option terms

Stock price at issuance (yuan)	3.78
Maturity date	4 September, 2006
American/European option	European
Exercise ratio	1:1
Settlement method	Physical

Terms of call warrants of Angang New Steel Co. Ltd:

Angang New Steel warrant terms

Option	Angang (JTC1 030001)
Underlying stock	Angang New Steel Co. (G. 000898)
Issue date	5 December, 2005
Call/put	Call
Strike price (yuan)	3.60
Stock price at issuance (yuan)	4.21
Maturity date	5 December, 2006
American/European option	European
Exercise ratio	1:1
Settlement method	Physical

Source: Bloomberg

Option creation mechanism on Shenzhen exchange

Probably concerned about speculation in the options market, the Shenzhen Stock Exchange moved slowly and carefully on the option creation by securities firms front. In the option creation rule issued in December 2005, the Shenzhen Exchange indicated its own principles, which included a few major differences to those of the Shanghai Stock Exchange.

Firstly, the number of options to be created is limited on a daily basis. If the number of options initially issued (ie, the warrants issued in connection with the full-flotation reform) is below 600 million units, the maximum number of options to be issued on each day should be fewer than 300 million; if above 600 million, fewer than 50% of the initial issuance number.

Secondly, the total number of outstanding options is also limited. The notice provided that the number of underlying shares of the total outstanding options (issued either by full-flotation reform or by securities firms) should not exceed the number of the freely tradable shares of such listed company. This aims to avoid potential share delivery difficulty at settlement time, because so far all the options in the market are physically settled at maturity.

Thirdly, the Exchange created more response time for investors. Options created on day T must be disclosed on the web on the same day, and such options can only be sold out on day T + 2. This provides investors with sufficient time to re-evaluate their trading strategy.

Fourthly, the Notice led to more information disclosure. In addition to the issuing securities firm's disclosure on the web regarding their potential option issuance, the Exchange would also, after the close of each trading day, announce on its official website the daily creation and redemption of options by securities firms, option intra-day trading information, and the options potentially issuable on the next trading day.

In general, all these new measures are designed to provide more transparency in the warrant market and to regulate the option issuance by the securities firms. The actual outcome, however, can only be tested by future option issuance by securities firms once the detailed issuance rule has been set.

DEALER OPTIONS MARKET: CHALLENGES AND OPPORTUNITIES

As China experiments with options trading, the dealer options creation mechanism has so far been mainly used to increase the supply of tradable options to dampen speculation. Meanwhile, the upcoming dealer options issuance mechanism – options issuance independent of the full-flotation reform – is probably even more important for the future development of China's options market.

This is because the warrants and put options issued in connection with the full-flotation reform (eg, the Wuhan Steel warrants and put options) will soon disappear in a year or two – the exchanges and regulators are expecting to substantially complete the reform in 2006 and the warrants and put options issued in the reform typically have a maturity term of approximately one year.

Thus the next-stage option market – a market from a pure sales and trading perspective (as compared with the warrant market that emerged from the full-flotation reform) – will rely exclusively on the options issued by securities firms. Aside from options trading on the exchanges, an over-the-counter (OTC) derivatives market would also emerge from the process, as investors seek customised exposure to the stock market from the securities firms.

The market is expecting the exchange to issue detailed rules in the near future regarding options issuing mechanisms by securities firms. Once promulgated, options issuing mechanisms would, of course, provide the Chinese securities firms with a new business line with promising revenue prospects. Nevertheless, the firms will also face a few major challenges.

Pricing

When dealers are mainly mimicking the warrants/options issued by listed companies that are implementing the full-flotation reform, they take a free ride with the inflated trading price of the existing option trading (eg, in the case of the Wuhan Steel warrants and put options analysed earlier this chapter). However, option pricing will be the primary difficulty when dealers issue options on their own, as there is a lack of comparable derivative products on China's stock market.

In derivatives terminology, the pricing issue means dealers need to determine at which level of "stock price volatility" to issue options. Typically, securities firms resort to using historical volatility (ie, stock price volatility in the past) as an indicator of future volatility in pricing when there are no comparable products available for reference. However in the post-full-flotation era, the A share market's historical data would prove irrelevant, because the stock market since the full-flotation reform has taken on a new look in the magnitude of tradable shares, liquidity and trading dynamics.

Dynamic delta hedging

The secondary difficulty is how to hedge the risks involved in the options issued. There are multiple levels of risks to be taken care of (see box). For a start, "delta hedging" involves dynamically selling and buying the underlying stock to offset the price fluctuation in an option's value caused by stock price movements.

In financial derivatives terms, the delta for a securities firm is "positive" when it issues call options, meaning the securities firm needs to maintain a long position on the underlying stock. Symmetrically, the delta is "negative" when a put option is issued, whereby the securities firm needs to maintain a short position to hedge the stock price movement risk.

One problem with delta hedging is the inefficiency due to the frequent rebalancing necessary every time the market moves significantly. This can be costly in terms of the high transaction costs involved in the rebalancing or of the risk the issuer is exposed to if no action is taken. In China's options market the effect of frequent rebalancing is particularly relevant, as the A share market is characterised by high volatility and dramatic short-term movements.

The more critical issue is the lack of a short mechanism. The issuing dealer needs to short stocks (ie, a negative delta) when it issues put options. Call options with a positive delta typically involve buying instead of shorting for hedging purposes. However, because the securities firms are currently required to purchase the full number of underlying shares as performance collateral, they would also need to short to determine the right delta hedging (in derivatives, the full number of underlying shares purchased by the securities firms overhedges their stock price risk). Thus, short selling will be crucial for both call and put option issuances by the securities firms.

The current legal framework in China does not permit stock borrowing and short selling. Without a short mechanism, the dealer's ability to issue options is significantly constrained. As will be discussed in detail in Chapter 8, China's capital markets have made substantial progress in short trading in many respects, and the stock market is poised to embrace a direct short trading mechanism in the near future.

Greeks for options trading

Many terminologies for options trading are referred to as "Greeks", for example:

❑ Delta – the rate of change of the option price with respect to the price of the underlying stock. In the case of a call option, a delta of 80% means the option issuer needs to buy 80% of the underlying stocks to hedge out the stock price risk (and vice versa for put options).
❑ Gamma – the rate of change of the portfolio's delta with respect to the price of the underlying stock.
❑ Vega – the rate of change of the value of the portfolio with respect to the volatility of the underlying stock.

A particular option portfolio is hedged when it is set up in such a way that the value of the portfolio remains approximately the same for a small change in stock price or its volatility. Then the portfolio is considered to be delta-neutral, gamma-neutral, and/or vega-neutral.

Gamma and vega hedging

Traders can only hedge their portfolio's gamma through the use of other options, which also has implications for vega hedging which, like gamma hedging, involves the use of other options. This is made difficult by the fact that the lack of an equity derivatives market means that only delta hedging with a long position is possible.

Thus, to develop the options market, the Chinese regulators would also have to help create an OTC market in stock options, by which the issuers of exchange-traded options could hedge their exposure through the OTC market via trades with other institutional players. At this stage, securities firms are only authorised to issue options with the same terms as the warrants/put options distributed in connection with the share reform. It will be some time before an OTC market can take place.

Share delivery at maturity

As reported, the exchanges and the securities firms have been holding discussions on securities firms creating cash-settled options. These are directly related to the potential settlement issues with respect to the existing options, which are all physically settled (see box). Securities firms would need the cash settlement alternative to have sufficient flexibility in option issuance and settlement, which is particularly true for options on an index or other baskets of

---

Where to find shares?

On 7 December, 2005, the number of outstanding Wuhan Steel created warrants reached 1.13 billion units and the put options 1.57 billion, following a few days of aggressive options creation by the securities firms.

However, the total tradable A shares of Wuhan Steel were only 2.37 billion. Because securities firms need to purchase the same number of A shares as collateral when they create the call options, the number of actual tradable A shares available in the market was reduced to 1.24 billion.

Therefore, the outstanding put options theoretically are not fully covered. When investors exercise their put options, they would need to purchase the A shares and deliver them to securities firms for the put exercise price in cash. Because the number of A shares available in the market was reduced to 1.24 billion following the call option creation, they are not sufficient to fully cover the put options when they are exercised on the maturity date.

Source: China Securities Newspaper, 7 December, 2005

---

stocks where physical delivery of the underlying securities could become very complex.

PROSPECT

With less than half a year's existence, the options market in China has shown strong momentum and tremendous growth potential. It is growing quickly both in size and rationality. More related financial innovations are expected to follow in the near future, and new trading strategies are also on the rise.

Options: a new market

The growth of trading activity on the options market has been truly phenomenal. Shortly after its inception, the trading volume on the options market quickly became comparable to that of the A share market. On 6 December, 2005 – slightly more than 3 months after the debut of the Bao Steel warrant in August, the trading volume of the then-existing six options exceeded that of the combined A and B share trading on both the Shanghai and Shenzhen Stock Exchanges for the first time.

As share reforms and dealer options creation mechanisms continue to unfold, listed companies and securities firms will issue more new options. This young market will keep growing and it has the potential to become one of the biggest options markets in the world.

More rationality

Many market players believe that the rampant speculation in the current options market is caused by the imbalance of supply and

Table 1 China's options market trading exceeds stock market volume on 6 December, 2005

6 December, 2006	Trading volume (billion yuan)
Options on Shanghai Exchange	7.366
Options on Shanghai Exchange	2.813
Total option trading	**10.179**
A, B shares on Shanghai Exchange	5.255
A, B shares on Shanghai Exchange	3.275
Total A, B share trading	**8.530**

Source: ZhongHua Industry & Commerce Times, 6 December, 2005

demand, ie, the strong demand for options trading from investors and the limited supply of available options so far.

The supply side should improve quickly. Firstly, more and more listed companies plan to use warrants or put options in their share reform. Secondly, securities firms will continue to issue options through the options creation mechanism as a new revenue line. Thirdly, aside from the full-flotation reform, listed companies may also look into warrant issuance as an attractive financing alternative.

The demand side should also become more rational as China makes an effort to increase the institutional investor base in the stock market. The speculation in warrants trading is no different from the general speculative nature of China's stock market. As institutional investors tend to be more rational in pricing securities and derivatives, the increased participation by institutional investors should help stabilise both the stock and options markets. For example, the CSRC has authorised investment funds to invest in options warrant within certain volume and value limits.

In summary, China's options market should reach a better equilibrium of supply and demand in the future. This will dampen speculation in the market and make the options more "investable."

Continued innovation

The market will host a huge variety of options instruments in 2006. As the market becomes comfortable about warrants and put options as compensation for the full-flotation reform, the listed companies are designing new forms of options to suit their specific situations.

For example, the put option of Guangzhou Baiyun International Airport Co., which debuted on 23 December, 2005, was a Bermuda-style option, which gives the option holders the right to exercise on a few pre-specified dates before the maturity date.

More innovations will probably come from the securities firms when they are permitted to issue options on their own. The options issued by securities firms are likely to go beyond individual stocks to a basket of stocks or a broad market index (eg, options on ETFs). The option's economic payout similarly would have more variety than the plain vanilla European call and put options. The innovations in the options market should further lead to more structured financial instruments such as capital-protected products which will be discussed in Chapter 7.

More trading strategies

New trading strategies are emerging as the growing options market interacts with other financial innovations in China. For example, China Vanke Co. had a CB outstanding and it also issued put options for its state share reform. From the economical payout point of view, a CB position (with its Chinese characteristics examined in Chapter 3) is equivalent to the combined position of a stock and a put option. As a result, traders could trade, on a relative value basis, between the CB market and the stock market.

Furthermore, arbitrage trading opportunities are also arising between the stock market and the options market. For the call and put options on the same stock and with the same strike price and same maturity, the following relationship exists (the so-called "put-call parity"):

$$P + S = C + PV(K)$$

Where:

P = Put option (European-style) price
S = Stock price
C = Call option (European-style) price
PV(K) = present value of strike price

If the above equation does not hold, that means that some instrument (the call, put and/or stock) is mispriced, and consequently arbitrage opportunities exist. For example, if the put is overpriced, an investor could sell puts and stocks and buy calls to lock in profit, and vice versa.

In Wuhan Steel's case, it has both call and put options outstanding and their price relationship may lead to a potential arbitrage trading strategy. Of course, Wuhan Steel's warrant and put options have slightly different strike prices so a relative trade between the two would not be a completely risk-free arbitrage. But as the options market continues to expand, arbitrage trading should definitely arise and it should help keep options trading prices at a reasonable level.

CONCLUSION

The return of warrants and options is a major part of the continuing market liberalisation in China. It is creating a new fast-growing trading market for A share investors and is steering the way for the future introduction of more derivative products. Although this young market is characterised by extremely volatile trading due to the T + 0 trading system, higher daily price limits and scarcity of tradable options, it has the potential to become one of the biggest and most important options markets in the world.

Options are useful investment tools providing investors with leveraged exposure to stocks or stock indexes. In the near term, options in China's domestic market are mostly suitable for day-trading products and may only be used for a short-term, momentum-trading-based strategy. In the longer term, however, an improved balance in supply and demand, as well as a potential short selling mechanism, should bring rationality to the market and options should become an important alternative for accessing China's stock market.

The dealer's OTC options market will also emerge once securities firms are permitted to issue options on their own. Although faced with many trading issues, the OTC market has huge growth potential and will enable investors to achieve a variety of exposure to the stocks or indexes. Continued innovation in the options market will also lead to new trading strategies and innovative investment products in the Chinese stock market.

5

Exchange-Traded Funds

Researching individual stocks in China is a daunting task for individual investors unfamiliar with the Chinese corporate governance and reporting system. Even global financial institutions can face significant costs in researching the relatively opaque Chinese market. Thus for investors mainly focused on long-term investment objectives, China-related exchange-traded funds (ETF) products are attractive investment tools.

In the Hong Kong and US markets, there are China-related ETFs that mostly attempt to track the shares of Chinese firms listed in Hong Kong or the US. Following the recent introduction of the QFII system, foreign investment banks were also able to offer ETFs linked to China A shares. Most recently, the Shanghai Stock Exchange (SSE) introduced the SSE50 ETF, the first A share ETF traded on China's stock exchanges, which is expected to lead to additional ETFs linked to other A share indexes as well as structured products linked to the SSE50 ETF.

ETFs are very different from individual stock picking or actively managed mutual funds, as they intend to passively track a given sector or index that relates to the broad Chinese stock market. The ETF products that are linked to Chinese A shares provide investors with more direct access to China's broad economic growth and they can be a valuable tool for portfolio diversification. This chapter will explain the various ETF products in China as well as a similar, yet different, fund product called "listed open-ended funds" (LOFs).

BACKGROUND OF ETF ECONOMICS

An ETF is a listed security intended to track the performance of an established index or predetermined basket of securities. It combines some of the characteristics of an ordinary share with those of an index-tracking investment fund. Like an index fund, an ETF is a passive investment vehicle on the underlying index or specified basket of securities.

Primary and secondary markets for ETFs

ETFs involve a primary market for ongoing unit creation and redemption operating in conjunction with a secondary market, which is traded on the exchange.

Primary market: ETF units are subscribed (creation) and redeemed (redemption) on the primary market. New units of an ETF are created when investors deliver a creation basket of constituent stocks (plus any cash component) of the underlying index to the fund manager of ETF. On the other hand, on redemption of ETF units, investors will present a number of ETF units to the fund manager of the ETF in exchange for the constituent stocks of the underlying index and cash component.

Secondary market: once ETF units have been created, investors can buy and sell the ETF units on the stock exchange (ie, the secondary market).

See Figure 1 for an illustration of ETF creation and redemption in the primary and secondary markets.

The difference is that an ETF is bought and sold like a share – with the price moving continuously through the day. By contrast, traditional mutual funds can only be traded once a day at a fixed price related to a closing net asset value. That makes ETFs not just a very simple way to invest, but also a far more flexible and efficient tool than traditional funds. This hybrid feature of ETFs is achieved by the interaction of the two markets (primary and secondary) involved in ETF trading.

CHINA-FOCUSED ETFS ON OVERSEAS EXCHANGES

Prior to the SSE50 ETF on the Shanghai Stock Exchange, existing China-focused ETFs mostly attempted to track the shares of Chinese firms listed in Hong Kong or the US. The PowerShares Golden Dragon Halter USX China Portfolio, for example, tracks an index

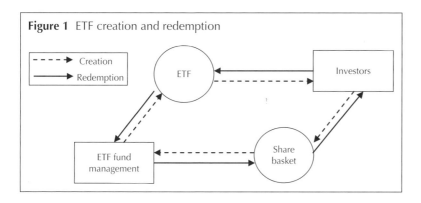

Figure 1 ETF creation and redemption

Table 1 Different types of China-focused ETFs on overseas exchanges

Shares being tracked	Example	Listing exchange
Index of US-listed Chinese companies (N shares) or US companies with a "China concept"	PowerShares Golden Dragon Halter USX China Portfolio	American Stock Exchange (US)
Index of Hong Kong-listed Chinese companies (H shares) and/or their ADRs	iShares FTSE/Xinhua China 25 Index ETF	London Stock Exchange and New York Stock Exchange
Index of China domestic A shares	iShares FTSE/Xinhua A50 China Tracker	Hong Kong Stock Exchange

Source: Bloomberg

comprising US-listed Chinese stocks. The iShares FTSE/Xinhua China 25 Index ETF, on the other hand, tracks an index of the 25 largest and most liquid companies that trade on the Hong Kong Exchanges.

Following the introduction of the QFII system, foreign investors started to have access to ETFs linked to China A shares. On the one hand, investment banks have created ETF products linked to the China A share basket through trading the underlying shares through the QFII scheme. On the other hand, China's domestic stock exchanges have also introduced ETF products linked to the exchange-created A share stock index, such as the SSE50 ETF.

OFFSHORE A SHARE ETFS

The recent QFII system has made it possible for foreign investment banks to offer A share-based ETF products on overseas exchanges.

The iShares FTSE/Xinhua A50 China Tracker, for example, is an ETF that invests in Chinese A shares, through the corresponding Chinese A shares Access Products (CAAPs) issued by a connected person or QFII, as the underlying investments.

For ordinary foreign investors, they could simply place orders with local brokers to buy and sell the iShares ETF on the Hong Kong Stock Exchange (SEHK). The behind-the-scenes structure as illustrated below, however, is somewhat more complex.

To offer the iSharesXinhua/FTSE A50 China Tracker, Barclays Global Investors (BGI) needs to make corresponding investments in China A shares. BGI has thus teamed up with Citigroup, a QFII with direct access to the China A share market. Citigroup reportedly purchases A shares and then issues zero-strike warrants called CAAPs to replicate the economic interests of the underlying A shares. Therefore, the ETF essentially invests in the synthetic exposure of the A shares (the CAAPs) as opposed to the underlying A shares directly. Citigroup, naturally, also serves as the market-maker to facilitate the ETF creation and redemption process.

These QFII-trading-based ETF products, such as the FTSE/Xinhua A50 Index ETF, have a few structural disadvantages when compared to the ETFs supported by China's domestic stock exchanges, such as the SSE50 ETF (discussed in detail below). Firstly, the exchange has no extra costs related to the QFII's quota arrangement, such as the one between BGI and Citigroup. Secondly, ETFs on the Shanghai Stock Exchange have better economies of

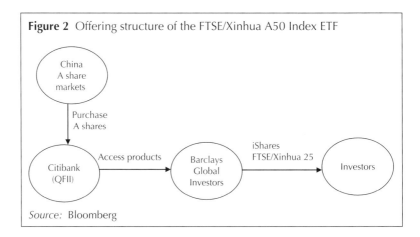

Figure 2 Offering structure of the FTSE/Xinhua A50 Index ETF

Source: Bloomberg

scale to achieve cost efficiency in custodian and administration costs. When the bank with the QFII licence serves as the market-maker to manage the creation and redemption process, the available QFII quota is the natural limitation of the offering size. The domestic stock exchange, by contrast, has no such limitation.

THE SSE50 ETF

The SSE50 ETF started trading on the Shanghai Stock Exchange in February 2005 and is the first local ETF based solely on local yuan-denominated A shares in China. It tracks the Shanghai 50 Index (hence the name "SSE50"), which consists of mostly blue-chip A shares listed on the Shanghai Stock Exchange.

According to statistical research by the Shanghai Stock Exchange, the SSE 50 Index covers approximately 25% of the trading volume and capitalisation of the stocks traded on the exchange. The index performance demonstrates a 97% correlation to that of the Shanghai Composite Index, which consists of all the A and B shares on the exchange. The SSE50 ETF is thus designed to link the most liquid blue-chip A shares and provide a close representation of the broad stock market.

Arbitrage trading and small ETF premium/discount

Since its inception, the SSE50 ETF trading price has exhibited a very small discount or premium (generally less than 0.5%) to the NAV of the underlying index portfolio. In comparison, the exchange-traded closed-end funds in China generally demonstrate significant discounts and – in some cases – premiums to their NAVs, as do the closed-end funds in many foreign markets. This is achieved by the T + 0 arbitrage trading mechanism between the primary and secondary markets for the SSE50 ETF.

The SSE50 ETF trading rule permits T + 0 trading between ETF creation/redemption (the primary market) and ETF unit trading (the secondary market). This means that on the same trading day, an investor could deliver shares to subscribe to an ETF from primary dealers and then sell the ETF unit in the secondary market, or buy an ETF unit in the secondary market and then redeem it from primary dealers for the basket of shares to be sold in the stock market. This T + 0 infrastructure facilitates arbitrage trades between stock baskets and ETF units, which is illustrated in the figure below.

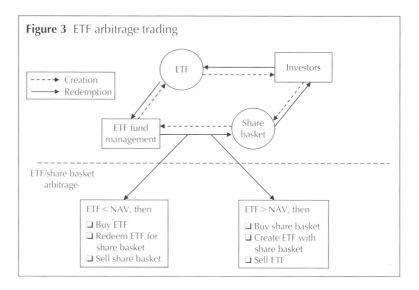

Figure 3 ETF arbitrage trading

Such arbitrage trading prevents the SSE50 ETF trading price from deviating substantially from its NAV (in other words, a very small discount or premium to the underlying index). When certain constituent stocks in the SSE 50 Index were selected to participate in the full-flotation share reform, however, the SSE50 ETF at times demonstrated an extraordinary premium. This unusual pheno-menon will be discussed in detail later in this chapter.

ETFs participate in extraordinary market moves

In addition to conventional ETF benefits such as low cost, trading flexibility and liquidity, the SSE50 ETFs also attract Chinese retail investors because they are a new way of trading the index. Because they offer real-time pricing, ETFs allow active traders to take advantage of extraordinary market moves.

ETFs have a big advantage over index funds in capturing poten-tial sudden market movements, which have not been uncommon in China's stock market history. This is because an ETF is a real-time purchase allowing the investor to gain market exposure instantaneously, whereas the value of an index fund is generally calculated each day only after closing. Such a difference is import-ant to investors in the Chinese market because historically, individ-ual trading sessions also play a similarly decisive role in an investor's portfolio performance, as shown in the table below.

Table 2 10 biggest up and down days in the Chinese market
(1994–2001)

	Date	% gain	Date	% loss
1	1 August, 1994	34.20	23 May, 1995	−17.20
2	18 May, 1995	28.57	5 October, 1994	−12.27
3	3 August, 1994	19.18	9 August, 1994	−10.73
4	5 August, 1994	16.59	16 December, 1996	−9.95
5	10 August, 1994	16.44	17 December, 1996	−9.86
6	5 September, 1994	15.93	14 October, 1994	−9.36
7	19 September, 1995	11.37	18 December, 1997	−9.28
8	7 October, 1994	10.91	22 May, 1997	−8.97
9	26 April, 1996	10.24	29 September, 1994	−8.42
10	22 February, 1995	10.04	16 May, 1997	−8.28
Avg		**17.35**		**−10.43**

Source: Dow Jones Indexes. From 31 December, 1993 to 31 December, 2001

As the Dow Jones Indexes report further points out, if an investor missed all the 10 best days in Table 2, he would have suffered a 65% loss over the past eight-year period, even if he was in the market on all other days including during the best year – 1996. Therefore, these 10 best days determined much of the positive performance of the investor's portfolio.

The two most volatile years, 1994 and 1995, contain nine of the 10 largest "up" days and five of the 10 largest "down" days. This concentration might be due in part to the fact that 10% circuit breaker was not implemented until December 1996. Separately, empirical research sponsored by the Shanghai Stock Exchange in 2000 suggested that market regulatory changes by government agencies are the major reason for those extraordinary movements on the big board in China.

Interestingly, two of the most recent big daily movements involved share reform in each case. On 24 June, 2002, the Shanghai Stock Composite Index experienced a huge 9.25% jump on the news that the State Council decided to stop its plan to reduce state-ownership of the listed companies. On 8 June, 2005 there was a strong rebound after the market hit an eight-year low. The Shanghai Composite Index surged 8.2%, the biggest single-day rise in three years, on speculation that the government could soon launch various market-supportive measures in connection with its second full-flotation reform plan.

As China continues its capital markets reforms, it is likely to see more dramatic intra-day movements in the near future as the stock market undergoes fundamental changes. The real-time pricing feature of ETF products provides investors with an effective tool to capture those opportunities.

Flexible creation

One important innovation regarding the SSE50 ETF is its flexible creation process. ETFs are typically created by assembling baskets of shares that represent the index underlying the ETF. The SSE50 ETF, however, could be created with a basket of SSE50 index constituent stocks, or be created with a number of single constituent stocks. This ETF creation flexibility is reportedly the first time this has happened in the history of ETFs. As such, the SSE50 ETF provides a valuable risk-management and diversification alternative for Chinese investors with concentrated stock positions.

In addition, the SSE50 ETF can be subscribed to with cash or a combination of cash and stocks. That is, investors can use certain amounts of cash to replace the stocks they are lacking to create the index basket (the so-called "cash in lieu" mechanism). There are three types of cash in lieu mechanism:

1. *Restricted* cash in lieu: for creation and redemption transactions, certain constituent stocks are not allowed to be substituted by cash.
2. *Optional* cash in lieu: when subscribing to fund units, investors are allowed to use cash to replace all or part of the constituent stocks. However, when redeeming units investors are restricted from using a cash replacement.
3. *Compulsory* cash in lieu: for certain constituent stocks, investors must use cash to make creations and redemptions.

The optional and compulsory cash in lieu mechanisms are particularly important for SSE50 ETF trading during the full-flotation reform. When a company starts its full-flotation effort to seek A shareholders' approval, the stock trading is suspended and trading cannot resume until the company's full-flotation plan is approved by the shareholder meeting or implementation of the full-flotation plan starts. Whereas trading of certain constituent stocks was suspended for the full-flotation reform, the cash in lieu mechanism in the SSE50 ETF has managed to keep the ETF redemption and creation processes functioning smoothly.

ETF trading during full-flotation pilot programme

On 20 June, 2005, the stock exchanges suspended all trading of the 42 companies that were selected for phase II of the full-flotation pilot programme (the "full-flotation trial companies"). Those stocks resumed trading only after the companies publicly announced their full-flotation programme details, which included, most importantly, how the public A shareholders would be compensated.

Although seven constituent stocks of the SSE50 ETF were among the 42 full-flotation trial companies, the SSE50 ETF traded extremely actively on 20 June, 2005. Its trading volume almost doubled from the previous trading session, and it closed at a 1.35% premium to the SSE 50 Index value on that day.

Because of the market's bullish expectation of the stock price of the full-flotation trial companies, there was a temporary imbalance between the ETF trading price and NAV. On the one hand, the index NAV was calculated based on the closing price of the trial companies before trading suspension. On the other hand, many investors with a bullish view expected the trial companies' stock price to rise significantly once they resumed trading upon the announcement of their full-flotation details. Thus the arbitrage traders could contemplate a trade strategy as follows:

At time T	At time T'
❏ Certain companies selected for full-flotation pilot programme (including some SSE50 constituent stocks)	❏ Full-flotation pilot companies announce detailed plans
❏ Corresponding stock trading suspended	❏ Stock trading resumed
❏ NAV of ETF calculated based on stock price before trading suspension	❏ Corresponding stock prices **expected to jump from the stock price before trading suspension**
❏ **Trade: purchase SSE50 ETF, which is linked to stock prices before trading suspension**	❏ **Trade: 1) redeem SSE50 ETF for the share basket and 2) sell share basket at the new, higher (as expected) stock price when trading resumes**

Obviously, this is not a typical arbitrage trade in the sense it is not a truly risk-free arbitrage. This trading strategy is based on the assumption that the stock price of the full-flotation trial companies will jump once trading resumes. If at time T' the stock price does not jump as much as expected or actually drops lower, the trade may result in a less than expected profit or even a loss.

ETF premium – market bullish sentiment on full-flotation programme

On the day of the full-flotation programme announcement, the SSE50 ETF trading premium reflected the market expectation that the stock price of those companies involved would jump once they resumed trading.

The expected price jump of those trial companies could be calculated from the SSE50 ETF premium. Because the SSE 50 Index is an adjusted market capitalisation weighted index (see more detailed discussion on China's stock index in Chapter 6), the ETF premium could be expressed as:

% premium of SSE50 ETF =
        Trial companies' weight in SSE 50 $\times$ expected % price jump

The seven constituent companies constitute approximately 30% weight in the SSE 50 Index, and the SSE50 ETF reportedly closed at a 1.35% premium to the underlying index. Thus:

Expected % price jump when trading resumes = 1.35%/30% = **4.5%**

Therefore from the SSE50 ETF trading on 20 June, 2005, it could be inferred that the broad market viewed the full-flotation programme as very positive for the stock performance of those chosen companies.

Data from *ZhenQuanShiBao* (Securities Newspaper in Shanghai, China), 7 July, 2005.

PROSPECTS: TWO EXCHANGES, MULTIPLE ETFS

The SSE50 ETF has attracted wide investor interest and traded actively since its inception at the beginning of 2005. Because of its great trading liquidity, many financial institutions in China have started contemplating structured products linked to the SSE50 ETF, such as exchange-listed call options on the SSE50 ETF. In addition, both exchanges are also working on introducing new ETFs linked to other A share indexes.

There are a few new ETFs reportedly in the pipeline, linking to the various indexes on the two exchanges:

❑ Shanghai Stock Exchange 180 Index
❑ Shanghai Stock Exchange Dividend Index
❑ Shenzhen Mid & Small Cap Board Index
❑ Shenzhen Stock Exchange 100 Index
❑ An unofficial index developed by a securities firm.

The upcoming wide variety of ETF products would greatly enrich index investments in China in three major ways.

Firstly, some new ETFs will offer investors broader exposure to the Chinese market than the existing SSE50 ETF. As will be discussed in Chapter 6, China's stock indexes do not have a core of blue-chip companies, unlike more established indexes. As such, the stock indexes in China need a large number of constituent stocks to make them representative of the broad market. The SSE50 Index at its inception covered approximately 25% of the trading volume and capitalisation of the stocks on the Shanghai Stock Exchange. The ETFs linked to the SSE180 Index or potentially the Shanghai Shenzhen 300 Index (see detailed discussion in Chapter 6) should be investment products more closely linked to the overall A share market.

Where is the hedge?

In developed markets, ETFs and index futures are closely related to each other. The index futures are an important hedging tool for ETF trading, which facilitates the pricing discovery in futures trading. As such, many foreign markets introduce the two index-linked products – ETF and index futures – at the same time.

In China, the index futures lag behind the progress in ETF trading. As the new ETF trading on the Shanghai Stock Exchange matures, the market could expect the exchanges in China to offer ETF and index futures linked to broad market indexes, such as the Shanghai Shenzhen 300 Index, the new Unified Index of the two exchanges.

Secondly, more ETFs will cover specific industry sectors or stock groups. For example, the Shanghai Stock Exchange Dividend Index focuses on stocks with stable cash dividend distribution records, whereas the Mid & Small Cap Board Index (see detailed discussion in Chapter 6) exclusively covers the medium and small capitalised companies listed on the Shenzhen Stock Exchange. The different ETFs to some extent also reflect the different focus of the two exchanges: the Shanghai Exchange is poised to become the "main board" in China with respect to the core blue-chip stocks whereas the Shenzhen Exchange with its up and running Mid & Small Cap Board Index may emphasise a growth-focused market modelled on Nasdaq.

Finally, the new ETFs will lead to new arbitrage trading strategies. Take, for example, the SSE180 ETF which was expected to launch by the end of 2006. As reported, the ETF for the SSE180 index will not completely replicate the index, but rather take 120 stocks from the index as its constituent stocks. As a result, the corresponding arbitrage trading will have additional complexity and variety. Furthermore, with a larger number of constituent stocks in the SSE180 ETF, there will be more opportunities to have event-driven arbitrage trading such as the one related to full-flotation reform as discussed above. Finally, when there are two or more ETFs trading in the market, investors could further arbitrage trading among the different ETFs.

LISTED OPEN-ENDED FUNDS

Around the same time that the Shanghai Stock Exchange started trading the SSE50 ETF, the Shenzhen Stock Exchange introduced to the market listed open-ended funds (LOFs). LOFs and ETFs sound similar to many investors, and they both share similar creation, redemption and trading features. There are, however, certain fundamental differences between the two financial products.

Two trading systems in LOF

Before LOFs, closed-end and open-ended funds in China have had two separate issuing and custody systems and the two types of fund are traded in two separate markets. Closed-end funds and ETFs are traded on the exchange, while open-ended funds are purchased or redeemed through fund companies, banks and securities companies. A LOF is an open-ended fund that is listed and transacted on a stock exchange. LOFs are expected to make mutual funds more attractive to investors by adding in the liquidity of exchange trading.

Once approved by the Shenzhen Stock Exchange, the unit interests of the mutual fund can be issued through the trading system of the bourse and become listed as a LOF. The first LOF became listed on the Shenzhen Stock Exchange on 20 December, 2004. Investors can either trade a LOF like a regular stock on the exchange, or redeem a LOF as in the case of a regular mutual fund.

As the stock market is trading around its multiple-year low, Chinese retail investors are becoming more interested in principal-protected investments (see detailed discussion in Chapter 6) and they are putting substantial redemption pressure on mutual funds. Turning a mutual fund into a LOF gives investors another alternative way to redeem their investment, which potentially reduces the redemption pressure on the fund itself.

Primary participating dealers = quasi market-makers?
There are designated "primary participating dealers" at the exchange to ensure the liquidity of LOF trading. Those dealers are similar to the market-makers in developed markets, but with one major difference.

The market-makers typically provide both bid and asking prices to manage the trading flow, whereas the primary participating dealers in China would provide a bid price only. Furthermore, offering a bid price is not a continuous obligation. According to the exchange rules, the primary participating dealers are only obligated to provide a bid price when there is no "reasonable" bid price in the market for "a certain period of time".

Additionally, a LOF, like an ETF, allows investors to modify their asset allocation more quickly, because the commission for trading a LOF is substantially lower than the subscription and redemption fees for the equivalent funds. Therefore, investors do not necessarily take a long-term view on the underlying mutual funds when they invest in LOFs.

Arbitrage trading with LOFs

LOFs offer similar arbitrage opportunities to the SSE50 ETF. However, LOFs in their early days involve two trading systems and two depositary systems, and the conversion between a LOF unit and the underlying mutual fund interest requires T + 2 settlements to cross the two systems. In other words, it takes two days to purchase a mutual fund and then convert it into a LOF unit, or alternatively, to purchase a LOF unit and convert it into a mutual fund interest to be redeemed. As such, there is a two-day risk in arbitraging a LOF and the underlying mutual fund.

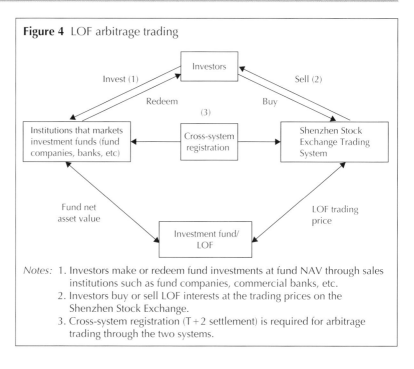

Figure 4 LOF arbitrage trading

Investors

Invest (1)   Sell (2)

Redeem   Buy
(3)

Institutions that markets investment funds (fund companies, banks, etc)   Cross-system registration   Shenzhen Stock Exchange Trading System

Fund net asset value   LOF trading price

Investment fund/ LOF

Notes: 1. Investors make or redeem fund investments at fund NAV through sales institutions such as fund companies, commercial banks, etc.
2. Investors buy or sell LOF interests at the trading prices on the Shenzhen Stock Exchange.
3. Cross-system registration (T + 2 settlement) is required for arbitrage trading through the two systems.

The Shenzhen Stock Exchange has recently introduced a fund investment and redemption mechanism at the exchange, which enables investors to make or redeem mutual fund interests through the exchange instead of the traditional sale institutions such as commercial banks or securities firms. As such, the LOF arbitrage trading can be executed without the need for cross-system registration (because both legs of trading can be done through the exchange). This new mechanism should make LOF trading much more active in the future and thus keep the LOF trading price close to the underlying mutual fund NAV (ie, no substantial premium or discount in trading).

Comparison of ETFs and LOFs
The SSE50 ETF and LOFs are similar financial innovations, but with some key differences. Firstly, the SSE50 ETF is a new product for investors to trade the SSE50 Index whereas LOFs offers investors an alternative way of redeeming their mutual fund investments. Secondly, the SSE50 ETF is typically created from and redeemed as a basket of shares, whereas LOFs are created from and settled in cash.

Thirdly, the SSE50 ETF tracks an index, so it is effectively a passive investment strategy, whereas LOFs have no constraints on investment strategies, so the mutual fund underlying a LOF could follow either an actively managed or a passively managed strategy. Finally, they used to have different potential arbitrage trading risks because their settlement and depositary systems differ, although the cross-system registration was recently eliminated from LOF trading.

Will the growing number of ETFs in China's stock market marginalise the LOFs? The answer should be no, at least in the near term. Firstly, the Shenzhen Stock Exchange has set up a mechanism to facilitate the fund subscription and redemption through the exchange itself. This process has eliminated the cross-system registration required in current LOF arbitrage trading, thus making the LOF trade much more efficiently.

Secondly, investments in ETFs are essentially passive investments in index tracking funds. By contrast, the mutual fund underlying a LOF could follow either an actively managed or a passively managed strategy. Many investors believe that in an emerging economy such as China's, investing in an index-linked fund has some drawbacks. For one thing, active management may locate excessive

Table 3 Summary of differences between LOFs and ETFs

	SSE50 ETF	LOFs
Investment tool	SSE50 ETF is a new product for investors to trade the SSE50 Index	LOFs offers investors an alternative way of redeeming their mutual fund investments
Creation/redemption mechanism	SSE50 ETF is typically created from and redeemed as a basket of shares	LOFs are created from and settled in cash
Passive/active strategy	SSE50 ETF tracks an index, so it is effectively a passive investment strategy	LOFs have no constraints on investment strategies, so the mutual fund underlying a LOF could follow either an actively managed or a passively managed strategy
Arbitrage trading mechanism	Arbitrage trading T + 0	Arbitrage trading T + 0 (T + 2 before cross-system registration was eliminated)

returns in a segmented and inefficient market such as China. For another, the high trading volatility in the stock market makes it important for the fund manager to have the ability to adjust his or her portfolio as conditions warrant. By contrast, the composition of a major index usually changes only annually or semi-annually, and not necessarily in a desirable direction when it actually happens.

CONCLUSION

China's growth story is enticing, but individual stock picking in this fast-developing and ever-changing market is a challenging task for normal investors. Therefore, index-based ETFs are attractive investment alternatives as they provide investors with exposure to a given sector or index that relates to the broad Chinese stock market, while preserving the trading liquidity as a single stock.

Through the QFII system, large investment banks have been able to offer A share-linked ETFs to provide investors with more direct access to China's broad economic growth. At the same time, the Shanghai and Shenzhen Stock Exchanges have initiated a series of A share-based ETFs (including the SSE50 ETF that is already trading), which in turn drives financial institutions to develop derivatives investments linked to those ETFs. Foreign investors could expect to find a wide variety of A share-based ETF products and their related derivatives products available for them in the near future.

The LOFs are similar to the ETFs, but with some key differences. The major difference is that the funds underlying the ETFs are index tracking funds, thus effectively a passive investment strategy, whereas the underlying funds in the LOFs could follow either an actively managed or a passively managed strategy. As corporate reporting and disclosure in China is still developing, active fund management is sometimes believed to add value vis-à-vis pure index tracking. Therefore, the LOFs should also be as attractive an investment alternative in the near future as the ETFs.

China's Stock Index and Index Products

In efficient markets such as the US, index investments have almost conclusively demonstrated their superiority over actively managed investment funds, both in academic theory and real world practice. Historically, most professional managers failed to outperform the appropriate market indexes, and those who managed to do so occasionally could rarely repeat such success in a consistent manner.

The Chinese stock market, of course, is far from efficient. The corporate reporting and disclosure system is still in the early stages of development; only a small percentage of the listed companies are covered in detail by the equity research professionals in securities firms (and even fewer presented in English); and, finally, security mispricings could exist in the market for a long time because there is no sufficient trading mechanism (for example, stock short selling) available for investors to take advantage of them.

Can you beat the index?

The theory that underlies index investing can be summarised as follows: investors as a group cannot outperform the market, because they themselves are the market.

It follows that the investors as a group must underperform the market, because the friction costs – namely the operating expenses, advisory fees and portfolio transaction costs – constitute a direct deduction from the market's return. Compared with actively managed funds, index funds pay no advisory fees and have limited portfolio turnover, thus keeping these costs to a minimum. This cost-saving advantage

---

> explains why index funds have provided superior long-term returns compared with actively managed funds.
>
> In a highly efficient market such as the US, there is abundant market evidence to support the above index investment theory. However, the theory is challenged in less efficient markets, as many believe that professional managers may be able to reap excess returns through superior research and better trading skills.

Therefore, many people believe that active management could add value when investing in China, at least in the near term. However, as China continues its effort to increase the institutional investors' base and simultaneously reduce the speculation level in the stock market, index investments should soon gain in popularity in China, as in more developed markets.

This chapter will review the special issues related to the stock indexes in China and specifically, the Shanghai Shenzhen 300 index, which is the only index that tracks the overall stock markets in China. It will then discuss how the share ownership reform – the full-flotation campaign – has an impact on the stock indexes' behaviour and what index products to expect in the near future.

STOCK INDEXES ON CHINA'S STOCKS

Since its inception in 1990, China's stock market has expanded from eight listed stocks to more than 1,300 listed stocks. The Shanghai Shenzhen 300 index (the so-called "Unified Index") issued by the Shanghai Stock Exchange and Shenzhen Stock Exchange in April 2005 is, however, the first stock index in China that tracks its overall stock markets. Historically, investors mostly considered the Shanghai Composite Index, which tracks all A and B shares listed on the Shanghai Stock Exchange, to be the national benchmark for China's stock market.

> **A tale of two exchanges**
> One unusual feature of China's stock market is the two-exchange system. Namely, the stock market consists of two exchanges of similar size co-existing side by side; by contrast, many developed markets that had a multiple-exchange system in the earlier days have migrated into a single-exchange system through industry consolidation.

Furthermore, the stocks on the Shanghai and Shenzhen Stock Exchanges perform quite differently. According to research data by the Dow Jones Indexes, the stocks on the two exchanges had a difference in return exceeding 5% during the eight years from 1993 to 2001. As such, it is not surprising that for a long time, the two exchanges have maintained separate indexes for the stocks on each exchange.

For years, many investors and analysts have called for a consolidation of the two exchanges to simplify market trading and analysis. The Unified Index may be a test step in that direction. Separately, many have speculated that the regulators may some day move all Shenzhen-traded companies to the Shanghai bourse while turning the Shenzhen exchange into a growth-focused market modelled on Nasdaq.

Before the Shanghai Shenzhen 300 index, there were three major categories of stock indexes for China's domestic stock market. First, the exchanges each had a series of indexes to track their respectively listed stocks, eg, the Shanghai Stock Exchange 50 Index that supports the SSE50 ETF discussed in the previous chapter.

Table 1 Major stock indexes on China stocks

Index name	Description
Shanghai Shenzhen 300 Index	Tracks 300 most representative A share stocks listed on the Shanghai and Shenzhen Stock Exchanges
Shanghai Composite Index	Tracks all the A and B shares listed on the Shanghai Stock Exchange
Shenzhen Composite Index	Tracks all the A and B shares listed on the Shenzhen Stock Exchange
Shanghai Stock Exchange 50 A share Index (SSE50 Index)	Tracks the 50 most representative A shares listed on the Shanghai Stock Exchange, which is the underlying index for the SSE50 ETF
Shanghai Stock Exchange 180 A share Index (SSE180 Index)	Tracks the 180 most representative A shares listed on the Shanghai Stock Exchange. The SSE expects to launch a new ETF on the SSE180 Index
S&P/CITIC 300 index (CSSP300 Index)	Tracks the 300 largest, most liquid A shares on China's stock exchanges
FTSE/Xinhua China A-50 Index	Tracks the 50 largest A share companies on China's stock exchanges
Dow-China Total Market Index	Represents 95% of shares traded on the Shanghai and Shenzhen exchanges
FTSE/Xinhua China 25 Index	Tracks the top 25 Chinese companies by total market capitalisation. Stocks are weighted by B, H, or red-chip share cap as appropriate

Source: Bloomberg

Secondly, a number of securities firms developed their own brand indexes that tracked stocks in both exchanges, for example the S&P/CITIC 300 index, FTSE/Xinhua China A50 Index, and Dow-China Total Market Index. Thirdly, some overseas institutions also created separate indexes to track the B, H and red-chip shares (shares of foreign-incorporated yet China-affiliated companies), such as the FTSE/Xinhua China 25 Index.

Joint index efforts

In September, the Shanghai and Shenzhen stock exchanges set up China Stock Index Limited, a company designed to provide underlying indexes for investors in the planned stock index futures products.

SPECIAL ISSUERS IN CHINA'S STOCK INDEXES

The Dow Jones Indexes company's 2002 research report identified many unique challenges that the Chinese stock indexes face. Those challenges include the tremendous volatility in the market, irregular expansion through IPOs, incredible speculation, disappointing earnings of the companies, and the low dividend yield on the stocks.

Above all these, there are two major factors that limit the "investability" of China's stock indexes. One is the lack of a core of true blue-chip companies in the market, which implies that the index needs a large number of constituent stocks to make it representative of the broad market. More importantly, it makes the index composite unstable, ie the indexes have high turnover rates as the constituent stocks slide in and out of the indexes because of fluctuations in their economic performance.

The other is the segregated share-ownership structure, particularly the substantial state ownership in the listed companies. The low free-float ratio (percentage of shares freely tradable in the market) raises the question as to whether the float market value or the total market capitalisation or something else is the appropriate weight for the constituent stocks in the index. These two issues are discussed in detail below and are reflected in the indexing methodology for the SSE300 Index.

Lack of blue-chip core

At the core of each mature market, there is a group of blue-chip companies that could easily represent the broad market or dominate the benchmark index's movement. By contrast, the numerous small-cap companies at the bottom are relatively insignificant. According to Dow Jones Indexes, these core blue-chip companies usually share four key characteristics: large market value, low volatility, high liquidity and a solid shareholder base. With such a stable blue-chip core in the index, any adjustments of the component stocks typically involves only smaller stocks that are not part of the core.

China's stock market is very different. The history of China's market economy is short and most of China's largest, better-performing companies are listed on the foreign exchanges (mostly in Hong Kong and New York) instead of the domestic exchanges. China's stock markets thus do not have a group of true blue-chip stocks with long histories of stable performance.

Because there is no blue-chip core, the stock indexes in China need a large number of constituent stocks to make them representative of the broad market. For example, the SSE300 Index uses 300 constituent stocks to cover about 65% of the total market capitalisation of the two exchanges (at inception). For another, the 50 component stocks in the SSE50 Index (the underlying index for the SSE50 ETF discussed in Chapter 5), only covers at inception approximately 25% of the trading volume and floating capitalisation of the stocks on the Shanghai Stock Exchange.

Furthermore, the lack of a blue-chip core also makes the stock indexes unstable. As the constituent listed companies fluctuate in their economic performance, the indexes have high turnover rates as they frequently reshuffle the component stocks. The above two factors consequently lead to two special considerations for index investments in China:

❑ **Difficulty in index-based investments**: with limited capital and assets under management, most mutual funds and other institutional investors in China find it difficult to invest in the vast number of stocks required for index replication and more difficult to hold that position over a long period of time. Furthermore, the funds tend to incur substantial tracking costs as the indexes typically experience frequent reshuffling.
❑ **Manipulation concern:** in established markets, the blue-chip core in the indexes makes market manipulation extremely difficult. This is because the largest blue-chip stocks are too big to be manipulated and the fluctuations in the small stocks have little impact on

the overall index movements. But in a market without the blue-chip core, it is relatively easy to manipulate the index by focusing on a few stocks, which challenges the effectiveness of index-based products such as the ETFs. Adding more stocks to the index may alleviate the manipulation issue, but it would adversely impact the index's investability as mentioned above.

Separation of equity ownership

Many widely used indexes such as the familiar S&P 500 index are market-capitalisation weighted. Such an approach, however, faces challenges in China because of the unique share-class structure of the listed companies. As discussed in Chapter 1, the shares of locally listed companies are subclassified into three classes, which are state shares, legal-person shares, and public individual shares. Only the public individual shares – the A shares – are freely float-ing in the open markets. As a result, about two-thirds of the shares of the listed companies are currently not tradable. In other words, the float-to-outstanding shares ratio is approximately 33% on average.

Nontradable shares (China) *versus* restricted stocks (US)
There are so-called "restricted stocks" in the US stock market, which cannot be traded freely. The nontradable share in China, however, is quite a different concept.

The restricted stocks in the US are very different from the nontrad-able shares in China. In the US, most restricted stocks can be traded freely after being held for a sufficiently long holding period, for exam-ple the restricted stocks received from a private security offering. In the case where the restriction cannot be completely removed by a holding period, those restricted shares can still be sold with certain volume and manner limitations, for example the shares held by corporate insiders such as the board of directors.

By contrast, China's nontradable shares are subject to much stronger restrictions. In fact, the nontradable shares could not be traded publicly at all before China in 2005 reinitiated the reform on the separation of equity ownership issue. Even for those companies that participated in the full-flotation pilot programme, their nontradable shares could not be traded until the public shareholder meeting and regulatory bodies approved their shareholding reform plan.

Such an overhang of high government ownership suggests that the free-float market value (related to the actual public trading) is substantially different from the total market capitalisation of the listed companies in China. This raises the complex issue as to which should be used as the appropriate weight for the stock indexes – the free-float, the total capitalisation, or some adjusted amount?

❑ **Free-float capitalisation**: compared with total market capitalisation, the free float of Chinese stocks should reflect their liquidity and investability more accurately, because it represents the shares that are actually available to investors for trading. Using free float directly as a weight has its own issue, however. As China continues its effort to reduce government ownership in listed companies, the free float of the companies is steadily increasing. Simply applying the free float as an index weight would lead to frequent index adjustment, which would increase index maintenance costs as well as index investors' tracking costs.

❑ **Total capitalisation**: this approach makes the index a better benchmark for the general economy. The index weight does not change frequently because the total shares of a listed company typically do not change often. However, the investability of the index is reduced because the total capitalisation includes a substantial proportion of shares that are not tradable on the market. Finally, the index may be manipulated through a leverage manner, ie, the index may be controlled through those stocks whose free float is small (and thus have a volatile trading price) yet whose total market capitalisation is dominating.

❑ **Float-adjusted capitalisation**: this approach combines the two methods above to use an adjusted (based on the float) total market capitalisation as the index weight for the component stocks. This has been adopted by the Shanghai Shenzhen 300 Index and will be discussed in detail below. It is a compromise of the investability and the benchmark character. However, it adds complexity to the index methodology, making it harder for the public to understand. Because the weight needs to be adjusted as the stocks' free float change, this method also requires the authority to keep the index weight adequately disclosed from time to time.

Table 2 Different market capitalisation as index weights

Choice of methodology	Advantages	Disadvantages	Examples
Free-float capitalisation	Suitable for investment	Frequent weight modification when free-float changes Higher tracking costs	S&P/CITIC 300 index, Dow-China Total Market Index
Total capitalisation	Stable weights for component stocks	Less suitable for investment Possible manipulation through leverage effect	Shanghai Composite Index, Shenzhen Composite Index
Float-adjusted capitalisation	Close to float-based method, suitable for investment	More complex methodology	Shanghai Shenzhen 300
	Weight relatively stable if free-float does not change significantly	Harder for investors to understand	Index, SSE 180 Index, SSE 50 Index

THE NEW INDEX – SHANGHAI SHENZHEN 300 INDEX

The Shanghai Shenzhen 300 Index launched in April 2005. Also known as the Unified Index, it is the first stock index to be jointly released by the Shanghai and Shenzhen bourses. It selects 300 yuan-denominated A shares on the Shanghai and Shenzhen Stock Exchanges as constituent stocks. According to statistical data released at the end of March 2005, the Unified Index has a total market capitalisation of approximately 2.18 trillion yuan (US$263 billion), which accounts for about 65% of the total market capitalisation of the two exchanges.

The methodology adopted by the Unified Index provides insight into how the exchanges effectively address the two major challenges discussed earlier in this chapter: the lack of a blue-chip core and the segregation of share ownership.

Constituent stocks selection and replacement

Because of the lack of a blue-chip core, the Unified Index has to use 300 stocks to cover slightly above half of the market capitalisation on the two exchanges. To keep the index components relatively stable for the investors, its constituent stock selection and replacement mechanism is critical.

Table 3 Shanghai Shenzhen 300 Index

Index name	Shanghai Shenzhen 300 Index (SHSE-SZSE300)
Index code	000030 (for Shanghai Exchange) 399300 (for Shenzhen Exchange)
Number of component stocks	300
Weight methodology	Float-adjusted capitalisation
Index base date	30 December, 2004
Base day index	1,000
Index launch date	8 April, 2005

To be eligible for the Shanghai Shenzhen 300 index, a stock must:

❑ be listed on the Shanghai or Shenzhen Exchange for at least one quarter;
❑ not be an ST or *ST stock (no suspended trading);
❑ be of good company performance, with the company having had no material violation of laws or regulations and no material issues with financial reporting;
❑ have a stock price that is not apparently subject to uncommon fluctuations or market manipulations.

The group of eligible stocks is called a "sample space" in statistical terms. The Shanghai Shenzhen 300 index then selects from the sample space 300 large-cap, liquid names as index components. This "scale and liquidity" approach is reflected in a weighted average scoring system that takes into account the following factors in daily average terms:

❑ Total market capitalisation
❑ Market value of floating shares
❑ Number of floating shares
❑ Market value of trading volume
❑ Trading volume

The above factors are 12-month averages, or IPO to date averages for newly listed stocks, and the exchanges assign 20%: 20%: 20%: 10%: 10% weights to the factors. All the stocks in the sample space are then ranked by such weighted-average calculation results, with the highest 300 scores becoming the index component.

The exchanges have taken a few steps to improve the stability of the index composite. The index will be revised biannually, typically each January and July, but no more than 30 stocks (10%) should be changed on each occasion. Additionally, the exchanges adopted a "sampling buffer" mechanism to select new stocks to replace the stocks removed from the index. The buffer gives preference to the top 240 stocks in the new sample space and the top 360 in the old sample space, which aims to reduce the index turnover rate, thus reducing index investors' tracking costs.

Float-adjusted capitalisation weight methodology

As discussed earlier, there are debates on which market capitalisation should be used as the weight for the Shanghai Shenzhen 300 index. On balance, the Shanghai Shenzhen 300 index adopts a float-adjusted capitalisation methodology. Based on a stock's float-to-outstanding-share ratio, the exchanges assign a weight factor. The weight factor is then applied to the stock's total capitalisation to determine the appropriate weight for the stock in the index calculation.

Example 1
Company A's float-to-outstanding-share ratio (ie, float capitalisation to total capitalisation) is 10%. As it is less than 20%, the actual float ratio will apply thus the float capitalisation (10% of the total market capitalisation) is used as the index weight for Company A stock.

Example 2
Company B's float-to-outstanding-share ratio is 35%. As it falls into the (30%, 40%] range, 40% will be used according to the above table.

Table 4 Float-adjusted capitalisation methodology

Float-to-outstanding ratio (%)	≤20	(20, 30]	(30, 40]	(40, 50]	(50, 60]	(60, 70]	(70, 80]	>80
Float-adjusted ratio (%)	Float ratio applies 30		40	50	60	70	80	100

Consequently, 40% of total capitalisation is used as the index weight for Company B stock.

Following this methodology, a stock's weight in the index would not be adjusted should there be a small change in the float, which may be increased by making nontradable shares tradable or be decreased by open-market share buybacks. Take a company with an original 35% float-to-outstanding-share ratio for example. Initially, for index purposes it will use 40% of total market capitalisation as the appropriate weight. If its float moves between 30% and 40%, its index weight will stay at 40% of total market capitalisation. Needless to say, should the company take steps to make large chunks of nontradable shares freely tradable, its weight in the index would be changed substantially.

ETF's NAV Gap: full-float impact on index

Yangtze Power and CITIC Securities are two listed companies involved in Phase II of the full-flotation reform pilot programme, and they are also two constituent stocks of the SSE50 ETF. Their share trading was suspended when they were selected for the pilot programme and was resumed on 15 August, 2005 when the two companies implemented their detailed reform plan.

During the opening minutes on 15 August, 2005, the SSE50 ETF market saw extraordinary value deviation between the ETF trading price and the underlying index value. As a result, many investors busily made arbitrage trades in the morning, only to find at the clearing that the actual ETF share basket value was drastically different from what the investor had in mind when executing the arbitrage trades.

Where does the difference come from? The main reason is that the ETF constituent stocks' weights in the SSE50 Index are changed because of the full-flotation reform. For Yangtze and CITIC, their reform plans involved delivering new shares to the A share investors (1.67 new shares per 10 shareholdings for Yangtze and 3.5 new shares for CITIC).

As a result, the floating share percentage for these two shares changed substantially enough to move their weights to a different level. For Yangtze and CITIC, their weight in the SSE50 ETF moved respectively from 7,000 shares to 9,600 shares and 1,500 shares to 2,200 shares. Those new weights made a significant impact on the ETF's net value calculation on 15 August, 2005 and consequently on the profit and loss for many arbitrage trades on that day.

Source: Guangzhou Daily Newspaper, 18 August, 2005

NEWCOMERS: G SHARE INDEXES

Following the pilot programme in the first half of 2005, more and more listed companies in China started to carry out the share structure reform to make nontradable shares tradable. The concept of the "G share" came to the market because for those companies who had worked out the detailed reform plan, their share listing on the exchange starts with an additional code – G – reflecting the word "*gaige*" or reform in Chinese.

"G share" is not really a new share category added to the existing alphabetical list of Chinese listed companies' ownership structure. G shares are essentially the A shares of the companies that have resumed trading after winning government and shareholder approval for their plans to sell nontradable shares. They have the additional G code to distinguish themselves from other listed companies that have not initiated steps to make all their shares tradable.

As more and more companies are going to or have launched full-flotation reform measures, the number of G shares is on the rise. To monitor the performance of this distinctive market subsection, the market naturally demands stock indexes solely track the G share companies. Meanwhile, a specific G share index is also a benchmark for the shareholding structure reform, as investors will compare the performance of the G share index with that of other companies (the more traditional indexes).

Months after the share reform process started, the two exchanges launched their respective official G share indexes.

Mid & Small-Cap Board Index

On 1 December, 2005, the Shenzhen Stock Exchange launched the first G share index in China, the Mid & Small-Cap Board Index. The index tracks all 50 small and medium-sized enterprises currently listed on the board. The index appreciated by 4.5% in the first three trading days, reflecting market optimism in G share companies.

There are a few important aspects of the Mid & Small-Cap Board Index. Firstly, the Index's base date and launch date have a gap of almost 5 months. The Index's base date was the IPO listing day of the fiftieth component stock, while the index launch date was a few days after all the component stocks completed the full-flotation reform (21 November, 2005). Because the Mid & Small-Cap Board

Table 5 Shenzhen Mid & Small-Cap Board Index

Index name	Mid & Small-Cap Board Index
Index code	399101
Number of component stocks	50
Weight methodology	Up to date free-float capitalisation
Index base date	2 June, 2005
Base day index	1,000
Index launch date	1 December, 2005
Launch day index	1,438.99

Table 6 Developments in the listed Mid & Small-Cap sector

	As of Dec 30, 2005	Increase from Jan 1, 2005	Increase (%)
Number of listed companies	50.00	12.00	31.58
Total capitalisation (100 million yuan)	481.55	68.12	16.48
Floating capitalisation (100 million yuan)	185.29	65.33	54.46
Annual trading volume (100 million yuan)	1,203.92	382.72*	46.61

Source: *Shenzhen Stock Exchange*; *Trading volume in 2004

expanded exponentially in 2005 (see Table 5), that time difference resulted in the index level on the launch date being approximately 43.9% above that of the base date.

Secondly, although all the component stocks in this index are G share companies, the Shenzhen Stock Exchange decided to use the respective up to date free-float capitalisation as the weight for the component stocks. In G share companies, all shares are freely tradable by nature, as they have completed the full-flotation reform. The Exchange however uses free-float capitalisation to exclude shares with other transfer constraints, such as shares held by senior management. By contrast, in the New Shanghai Composite Index to be discussed below, the Shanghai Stock Exchange uses the total capitalisation directly as the weight for its G share index.

Thirdly, compared with the broad stock market, the Mid & Small-Cap Board Index has a relatively high P/E ratio. This certainly reflects the typical "high risk, high reward" profile of fast-growing companies. On the other hand, the average earning per share (EPS) for the Mid & Small Cap Index is far superior to that of

Table 7 P/E and average EPS for Mid & Small-Cap Index and broad market

Mid & Small-Cap Index P/E	20.76
Broad market P/E	16.92
Mid & Small-Cap Index average EPS	0.31
Broad market EPS	0.19

Source: *Shenzhen Commercial Newspaper, 22 November, 2005,* citing unidentified research

Table 8 New Shanghai Composite Index

Index name	New Shanghai Composite Index
Index code	000017
Number of component stocks	All G share companies on Shanghai
Weight methodology	Total capitalisation
Index base date	30 December, 2005
Base day index	1,000
Index launch date	3 January, 2006

the broad market (see box), leading to the argument that the higher P/E ratio may be justifiable.

The New Shanghai Composite Index

The Shanghai Stock Exchange launched its own G share index, the New Shanghai Composite Index on the first trading day of 2006. Similar to the Mid & Small-Cap Index, it closed 1% higher on its first day of operation, a sign of the high expectations among investors for a stock market that is currently undergoing reform.

Compared with the Mid & Small-Cap Board Index, the New Shanghai Composite Index has three distinctive features. Firstly, instead of fixing the number of component stocks, the New Shanghai Composite Index intends to cover all G shares on the exchange. For companies that are currently undergoing the full-flotation reform, they will be included in the index on the second trading day after they complete the share reform. Secondly, this index uses the total capitalisation as the index weight, instead of the up to date free-float capitalisation used in the Mid & Small-Cap Board Index.

Thirdly, large-cap blue-chip stocks dominate the New Shanghai Composite Index, whereas the Mid & Small-Cap Board Index by definition is exclusively comprised of medium and small-sized companies. Bao Steel and China Yangzi Power are the two largest component stocks that carry about 30% of the total weight of the index. Subsequently, the P/E ratio of the New Shanghai Composite Index is at a relatively attractive low level of 12.14x, which is 23.47% lower than that of the broad Shanghai Composite Index (as at 15 December, 2005, Shanghai Stock Exchange data).

G share index characteristics

From the perspective of investment and products innovation, a G share index has a few advantages over traditional indexes.

❑ **Market-based valuation**: traditionally, the A share price includes a "liquidity premium", ie, it is freely tradable whereas the state and legal-person shares are not. Additionally, the A share price reflects the market expectation on future shareholding structure reform, for example, when and how the state regulatory will unload the nontradable shares to the market. As a result, the A share trading price has not been a fully market-based valuation when equity ownership in listed companies is segregated. For a successfully transformed G share company, however, the share price should be mainly driven by the market and more accurately reflect the listed company's intrinsic economic value.

❑ **Stable weight for constituent stocks in index:** as discussed earlier in this chapter, the overhang of nontradable shares makes the weights of constituent stocks in the index unstable. That is, a stock's weight in the index would change every time a large chunk of nontradable shares is sold to the market. This issue does not exist in a G share index, so it could simply use the companies' total capitalisation as the weight for the index, just like the indexes in developed markets such as the S&P 500 index.

❑ **Suitable platform for structured products:** because the nontradable share overhang is removed from a G share index, such an index should be more suitable than a traditional A share index for next-generation index-based structured products. For example, an option on a traditional A share index is likely to have a complex value adjustment mechanism in the event some constituent stocks take on full-flotation reform. This is because a holder of the underlying shares in the index would have received bonus shares as compensation for the full-flotation reform event, and the holder of the index option would probably demand a fair value adjustment upon such event.

In summary, the new G share indexes as well as the Unified Index are cutting-edge innovations to reflect the ongoing reforms in China's stock market. However, it always takes time before even the most active stock market investors adopt a new index. These new indexes' structural virtues, however, should lead to new derivatives products linked to them, for example index futures (to be discussed in more detail below). Investors should become more familiar with these indexes once more products (funds, ETFs, and futures) are developed around them and they should rapidly become benchmarks for the transforming Chinese stock market.

PROSPECT: INDEX FUTURES

The exchanges and securities firms are expected to offer a series of new investment products linked to the Shanghai Shenzhen 300 index in the near future. In addition to regular index mutual funds, the new index may also be applied to innovative fund products such as ETFs and LOFs. Furthermore, investors are eagerly waiting to see whether index futures will be introduced following the new index, providing a new alternative to manage the broad stock market risk.

With China's stock market trading around a multiple-year low, investors are in desperate need of stock market hedging tools. At present, short selling is still banned in China, preventing investors from hedging losses in a sliding market. Thus a futures contract linked to a broad market index could become an important hedging tool for stock investors. The Unified Index could well be a major step towards the introduction of index futures.

Regulators in China, understandably, are taking a very cautious approach on index futures. The stock index futures, if launched, are leveraged investment products, as investment in futures does not require a large amount of initial capital upfront. Because the stock market is characterised by speculation, many investors are likely to view the stock index futures as a new gambling tool, rather than a hedging tool. As the institutional investors' base continues to grow in China, however, this should become less of a concern.

On top of speculation, the regulators probably have strong concerns about potential manipulation in index futures trading, because China's financial industry had some bad experiences with futures trading some years ago. In 1993, China launched the first financial futures government bond (T-Bond) futures market. Unfortunately, trading was forced to a halt in 1995 after rampant manipulation (see Chapter 8), which bankrupted one of China's leading securities companies and almost turned China's financial market into meltdown.

Looking at historical precedents, investors in China should have reason to be optimistic about the prospect for index futures. In the Korean and Taiwanese markets, index futures were introduced after their QFII system substantially increased foreign ownership in the stock market, because the institutional investors needed effective hedging tools to manage systematic risks. As China continues to expand the QFII system and the general institutional investors' base in the A share market, stock index futures are probably at the top of the regulators' agenda.

CONCLUSION

The stock indexes in China reflect the special characteristics of China's stock market. In addition to the typical features of an emerging stock market, China's stock indexes are challenged by the lack of a blue-chip core and the segregated shareholding structure in the listed companies.

Because of the lack of the blue-chip core, a stock index needs a large number of shares to represent the broad stock market. The Shanghai Shenzhen 300 Index, with 300 component shares, is the first stock index jointly issued by the two Exchanges in China, thus providing a truly nationwide benchmark for China's stock market. It adopted a sampling buffer and a float-adjusted capitalisation methodology to facilitate the index maintenance process, which should help index investors reduce tracking costs.

Following the reform of the segregated shareholding structure in the listed companies, G share indexes that exclusively track fully floating companies are on the rise. On the one hand, the Mid & Small-Cap Board Index specifically tracks medium and small capitalised G share companies. On the other hand, the New Shanghai Composite Index covers all G share companies listed in Shanghai, and it will become increasingly representative of the broad market as more companies complete the share reform.

The Shanghai Shenzhen 300 Index and the G share indexes may lead to a new series of index products in China in the near future, including the long-awaited index futures products. Due to the qualities of the Unified Index and the latest addition of G share indexes, coupled with the fact that they are spreading to an increasingly broad audience, these new indexes should rapidly become a benchmark for the market decisions of investors in China.

China's Principal-Protected Investments

Many people are interested in China but worried about the risks involved. Since it peaked in mid 2001, the A share market has lost almost half of its value in the past five years. Capital-protected products appeal to concerned investors as a way to tap into China's growing market with a controlled downside risk.

Capital-protected products made their debut in 2003 and attracted strong retail interest. However, this sector has been growing at a modest pace, as its trading strategies and potential returns are constrained by China's nascent bond and options markets.

In 2005, capital-protected funds delivered higher returns than any other equity-based investment funds in China. They are again attracting investor interest, but it remains a question whether such superior performance can be repeated. The catalyst going forward probably lies in the emerging options market, whose growth could enable financial institutions to offer a variety of capital-protected investments with flexible risk/reward profiles for investors.

PROTECTED FUNDS: RISING IN CHINA'S FUND INDUSTRY

In the US and Europe, the markets for capital-protected products have expanded significantly in recent times in response to turbulent equity market returns. Multinational investment banks, insurance companies, and even the Post Office in some regions, now routinely issue protected products linked to the stock market. The markets see this as a harbinger of product development, exhibiting a wide range of products with dramatically different levels of capital protection, underlying asset class (eg, funds of hedge funds and unit trust funds are a recent addition to the recipe) and potential returns (also known as the "participation rate", reflecting how much investors "participate" in the growth of the underlying asset).

In China, however, capital-protected investments are mostly a new phenomenon. Although the demand for low-risk, stable-return investment vehicles has risen substantially since the market peaked in July 2001, capital-protected products have grown at a slow pace. So far, they are all in the form of capital-protected mutual funds – more specifically, a mere five funds in a fund industry that itself is also in a nascent development stage.

China's fund industry: overview

The first investment fund in China was launched in 1991, even though China's standardised investment-fund industry officially started much later, marked by the *Administration of Securities Investment Funds Tentative Procedures* issued by the State Council in 1997 (codified in 2003 by the legislature in the Securities Investment Funds Law). Despite this late start, China's investment funds have grown rapidly in number and size.

In the coming years the fund industry is expected to expand greatly. First of all, the funds sector mediates between the large amounts of capital available (mainly in the form of retail bank deposits) and the capital needed for China's industrialisation. The high savings rates and the huge capital demand provide powerful catalysts for fund sector growth in China. Additionally, China promotes growth of the fund industry as part of its effort to build up the institutional investors' base in the stock market. The government hopes that investment funds will not only draw people's bank savings into equity investments, but also bring in long-term investment styles to a stock market characterised by short-term churn and speculation.

But the future growth of the fund industry faces its challenges. Despite recent growth in size, China's investment funds have failed to provide the country's investors with a variety of investment styles so far. This is partly due to the limited investment instruments available to the funds, as convertible bonds, options and other innovative financial instruments are very much

Table 1 Major development stages of China's fund industry

Date	Major events
March 1998	First batch of two closed-end funds* listed on the Shenzhen Stock Exchange
	For the following three years, only closed-end funds permitted to trade in China
August 2001	Hua'An Innovation fund launched as the first open-ended fund** in China
May 2003	China Southern Fund Management launched the first capital-protected fund: "Southern Capital Protected Fund"
August 2004	Listed open-ended funds (LOFs)*** started on the Shenzhen Stock Exchanges

*Closed-end funds: funds that exist for a fixed term and that permit no additional investment beyond a predetermined amount.
**Open-ended funds: similar to US mutual funds; new investors may purchase or redeem at any time, with potentially no limit on the maximum capital or time frame of a particular fund.
***Listed open-ended funds (LOFs): open-ended funds that are listed and transacted on a stock exchange. LOF investors can either trade a LOF like a regular stock on the exchange, or redeem it, as in the case of a regular mutual fund. LOFs are discussed in detail in Chapter 5.

newcomers to the A share market. As illustrated in the above table, the innovation process in the fund industry has been fairly slow.

As a result, diversification of risk is difficult to achieve via investments in China's retail funds, which undermines the attractiveness of the funds to investors. Because the funds do not offer access to instruments or, apparently, to better investment strategies, retail investors have an incentive to invest on their own. In addition, this lack of diversification benefits also creates problems for institutional investors such as pension and insurance funds. They mostly rely on retail investment funds for their exposure to the equity market, but currently they are exposed to a single investment style more or less.

In this context, capital-protected funds are coming into their own. The protection on investment capital, needless to say, is attractive as China's stock market struggles with a multi-year bear market. Equally, they are poised to bring diversification benefits to investors, as their performances are not necessarily highly correlated to the equity market.

Protected funds: on the rise

In China, the demand for low-risk, stable-return investment vehicles has been tremendous since the Chinese equities market peaked in July 2001. The A share market has been trading around its multi-year low ever since. Chinese retail investors are thus being more cautious with investing in the equity market. Nevertheless, investors have few alternative investment vehicles available, as illustrated by the trillions of cash (in yuan) that retail households keep in bank savings deposits.

As a result, Chinese retail investors have shown strong interest in principal-protected investment products. These products are expected to generate better returns than those offered by bank savings accounts, and, as importantly, they provide some insurance for investment capital.

Nevertheless, principal-protected funds have developed slowly in China. The main reason probably lies in the conservative approach generally taken by the existing protected funds, due to market trading and liquidity limitations that will be discussed later in this chapter. When their allocation provides less exposure to the markets, it may eliminate or greatly reduce any potential gains the fund can achieve from subsequent gains in the stock market.

However, principal-protected funds posted superior performance in 2005 even though China's stock market was at a multiple-year low. For example, the China Southern Fund distributed 0.63 Yuan per 10 units, making it the largest dividend payout per single term in 2005. Their average return also outperformed funds with other investment styles. As the Chinese stock market still struggles with the multiple-year bear market, the high returns in 2005 should attract investors strongly going forward.

Table 2 Average return of funds (1 January, 2005–15 December, 2005)

Fund types	Average return (%)
Equity funds	−2.07
Money market funds	2.30
Capital-protected funds	4.81
Fixed-income funds	7.51

Source: News Morning Paper (XinWenChenBao), 16 December, 2005

The role of the bond market

In the most developed markets of capital-protected products, one commonly used protection strategy is the Option Based Portfolio Insurance (OBPI) strategy as illustrated below in Figure 1. The OBPI strategy consists of a zero-coupon bond and an equity call option. The zero-coupon bond typically has a present value of about 70–90% of the initial investment, with the precise discount amount dependent on the appropriate interest rate for the currency, the maturity date and the credit rating of the issuer. It will have a redemption value equal to the initial investment at maturity, hence providing the capital protection. The remainder of the initial investment (minus applicable fees) is used to purchase the equity call option on stocks or index, which provides the upside exposure to the equity market for the investor.

The second method is Constant Proportion Portfolio Insurance (CPPI), or its variant Time-Invariant Portfolio Protection (TIPP), as illustrated below in Figure 2. Unlike the OBPI strategy, CPPI or TIPP do not rely on derivatives to produce capital growth. As will be described in detail later in the chapter, they rely entirely on their trading and asset allocation strategies to protect the initial investment amount. In a CPPI/TIPP structure, the exposure to the risky assets is adjusted as the asset price changes. As the price of the underlying asset falls, the manager tends to reduce the exposure in

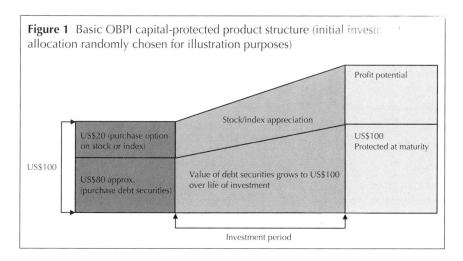

Figure 1 Basic OBPI capital-protected product structure (initial investment allocation randomly chosen for illustration purposes)

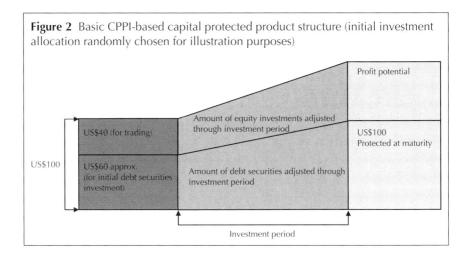

Figure 2 Basic CPPI-based capital protected product structure (initial investment allocation randomly chosen for illustration purposes)

order to reduce the risk in the portfolio, and as the asset price rises the manager tends to add risk in the portfolio.

However, whether the strategy is OBPI or CPPI/TIPP, the underlying methodology is essentially the same for all products. All these strategies involve using fixed-income instruments to generate capital protection. Therefore, the following sections will first review China's current bond market.

BOND MARKET: OVERVIEW

Compared with the A share stock market, China's bond markets are probably even further behind on the development curve. The market started in 1981 when the government resumed issuing government debt, and it has been developing slowly throughout the last 20 years. Like the stock market, the bond market is also state-denominated. The liquidity and range of terms are probably still not sufficient to support sophisticated financial instruments.

Treasury and corporate bond markets

Official T-bond issuance began in the early 1980s. For the most part, only the government via the Ministry of Finance and the two major policy banks have issued bonds. During the past two decades, the Treasury market has expanded gradually in the depth and width of the T-bonds offered, and the percentage of institutional investors is continuously increasing. Still, the maturity term structure needs to

Table 3 Product developments in Treasury bonds market

Time	Major events
Before 1993	Treasury bonds were mainly physical bonds made of printed paper. These disappeared by 1998
1993	Book-entry bonds issued for the first time
1994	Certificate bonds targeted to individual investors introduced
2001	Long-term treasury bonds of 15 and 20 years issued for the first time
2002	Long-term treasury bonds of 30 years issued for the first time

be further developed to promote a workable yield curve and a mature market.

Within the bond markets, the corporate bond market lags far behind the government Treasury bond market. Most companies primarily rely on borrowing from banks instead of corporate bond issuance as the main source of fixed-income financing. The corporate bond issuance system, however, is expected to relax in the near future, particularly in terms of the approval process and coupon rate setting. As discussed in the convertible bond (CB) section in Chapter 3, the bond market should play an important role in Chinese companies' corporate finance decisions once the segregated ownership issue is resolved through the state-share overhaul reform.

Two trading systems
Another important feature of China's bond market is the bifurcated trading system: the exchange bond market and the inter-bank bond market.

Exchange-traded bond market
The Shanghai Stock Exchange and the Shenzhen Stock Exchange list Treasury bonds, corporate bonds and CBs. The exchange market is the marketplace where both institutional and individual investors trade bonds. The secondary market transactions include both spot trading and repurchase ("repo") trading.

Trading in both stock exchanges follows the principle of price and time precedence. The transactions are order-driven and executed at matched price.

Interbank bond market

In 1997, the commercial banks withdrew from the stock exchange and started the interbank bonds market. A majority of book-entry Treasury bonds and all policy financial bonds are issued and traded on this market. It is also the platform where the People's Bank of China (PBOC) – the central bank – performs its open-market operations to achieve monetary policy goals.

The interbank bond market is an OTC one where the institutional investors trade bonds on a wholesale basis. Trading on the interbank bond market is mainly in repos and spot trading. Trading on the interbank market is quote-driven and executed case-by-case at the negotiated price.

In essence, the two markets are separate yet closely related. For example, many innovations were first trialled at the interbank markets before being widely introduced on the exchange market (eg, the buy-out repo discussed in detail in Chapter 8). Many market players suggested unifying the exchange-place bond market and interbank bond market to improve China's bond market liquidity.

Implications for capital-protected products

In summary, the bond market is still at its nascent development stage. As mentioned earlier, the OBPI strategy consists of a zero-coupon bond and an equity call option. Currently, zero-coupon bond supply is scarce in China. Furthermore, the equity derivatives market is a new development; only coming into existence in late 2005 (see earlier chapters for detailed discussion). As such, current market conditions do not sufficiently support the "zero-coupon bond + option" OBPI strategy, even though it is probably the most common type of principal-protected product in developed markets.

Thus in China capital-protected funds have to rely entirely on their trading and asset allocation strategies to protect the initial investment amount. The principal-protected funds launched in China are reported to use two main strategies: CPPI and/or TIPP. The following section will examine these two related yet different strategies.

CPPI AND TIPP TRADING STRATEGIES
CPPI

CPPI is a principal-protection technique that works by dynamically moving capital between a so-called safe asset and a risky asset, depending on the performance of the risky asset. It works by employing a mathematical asset-allocation model designed to prevent a fund price from falling below a set protection level.

Through the investment period, CPPI strategy involves dynamic rebalancing of the allocations between risky (eg, stocks) and less-risky (eg, fixed-income instruments) assets. The risky assets portion gains a desirable exposure to the underlying market, whereas the less risky assets portion provides some insurance for the investment capital. This asset allocation is dynamically adjusted through the investment horizon. For example, if the index rises in value, the portfolio will be rebalanced with an increased weighting in equities *versus* the bonds.

Assuming total capital is invested in two assets only – stocks and bonds – then over time, the desired stock position is created based on the following formula:

$$\text{US\$ invested in risky assets (stock)} = M * (A - F)$$

where

M	= stock investment multiplier
A (assets)	= total assets held in the portfolio
F (floor)	= minimum portfolio value (zero risk level)
A − F	= net amount of cushion or funds that can be put as risk

Using CPPI strategy, the issuer buys more stock as it appreciates and sells when it depreciates. Bonds are purchased as the stock is sold, and vice versa. The investment multiplier is typically established at a value greater than 1. When A − F = 0, the portfolio will stop investing in stocks.

TIPP

TIPP has the same investment amount calculation formula, except that its protection floor level (F) is not fixed at inception. The protection level in TIPP is also adjusted over time, but is only adjusted upwards, never downwards. At any time, the new protection level in TIPP is the larger of (a) the current protection level and (b) the current asset value in the portfolio (or a percentage of asset value, eg, 90% of A, as per investor risk tolerance level).

Thus the protected level at adjustment period T + 1 is

$$Ft + 1 = MAX (A, Ft)$$

where

Ft + 1 = protected level at period T + 1

A　　 = total asset value at the end of period T

Ft　　 = protected level at period t

Similarly, US$ invested in stock for Period T + 1 = M * (A − Ft)

There are two rationales for the adjustable protection level (F) in TIPP: firstly, investor current wealth level should be considered when determining the current protection floor level. When their investments are receiving positive returns, such returns (investment appreciation) should be subject to protection as well. Secondly, investors are risk-averse. When their wealth increases, the protection level should be increased as well; but when total wealth is decreasing, they typically do not want to decrease the protection level. Thus over time, the protection floor level should be adjusted, but only upwards. As such, TIPP is essentially a more conservative investment approach than CPPI.

Bond market constraints

Both the CPPI and TIPP strategies are still subject to the constraints of the bond markets in China. With fairly high volatility in China's stock market, the principal-protected funds need to adjust their equity and debt positions frequently under either the CPPI or TIPP strategies. The limited liquidity of China's bond markets may make it difficult to buy or sell a large volume of bonds quickly. This will be a particularly critical issue when the stock market experiences a significant drop, because funds need to sell stocks and buy bonds in large amounts. Hopefully, the liquidity situation will improve as more debt-markets financial innovations are introduced, such as the new T-bond buy-out repo trading on the Shanghai Stock Exchange (see Chapter 8 for detailed discussion).

Considering the limited liquidity of China's bond markets, many funds have taken a conservative approach by investing a high proportion of capital in bonds for the initial asset mix. For example, the first CPPI fund from China Southern is reported to have 75% of initial assets invested in bonds. Generally speaking, the funds take a conservative approach. The following table shows the ratio for the risk-free assets in those funds.

Table 4 Average return of funds (1 January, 2005–15 December, 2005)

Funds	Minimum risk-free asset (%)
China Southern	75
YingHua Fund	60
TianTong Fund	80
GuoTai JingXiang	70
JiaShi Pu'An	80

Source: Value Magazine, July 2005

This approach puts pressure on potential returns from those funds. As they invest mostly in debt securities, the fund allocation provides less exposure to the markets, which greatly reduces any potential gains the fund can achieve from subsequent gains in the stock market. In addition, there is always a danger of being "cash-locked" in the CPPI/TIPP fund. If the price of the asset falls near to its floor value (ie, when $A = F$ in the formulae discussed in previous subsections), there will be little cash available for purchasing additional risk exposure to the equity market.

OPTION-BASED STRATEGY *VERSUS* CPPI/TIPP
The growth of the bond and options markets in particular could dramatically change the landscape of China's capital-protected products market. There are a few factors that should favour the OBPI strategy over CPPI/TIPP strategies in the near future.

Volatility issue
The CPPI structure tends to produce the best returns for those assets that have the least volatility, but performs less well with assets that have much volatility and move in a trading range. In other words, the asset classes that benefit most from this structure are precisely those for which capital protection is least necessary, since assets with low volatility are unlikely to see significant drops in value.

China's stock market is well known for its high volatility. The ongoing state-share overhaul reform and institution building in the

A share market should eventually bring down the market volatility. In the near term, however, the stock market continues to exhibit high volatility, which will probably stay at least until the nontradable shares are finally floated in the market. This high volatility environment would favour the OBPI strategy for capital protection.

Transparency in structure

At the basic level, OBPI products are extremely simple to understand as they consist of only two elements: high-rating, fixed-income security for capital protection and options on stock (or index) for growth. The option component, of course, could have a degree of complexity. But as the option terms are established prior to the start of the trade, investors have a preview of the precise mix of risk and potential return of such products. Most importantly, once investors understand the option payout formula, they will know the exact performance of the product based on a future level and index, stock price or fund performance (as the case may be).

For example, if the embedded option gives investors 50% participation on any appreciation of the SSE50 Index from a starting point of X, then given the level of the SSE50 Index on the maturity date as Y, investors could easily calculate that they are entitled to payout as:

Payout = 50% * (Y − X), even if they have little knowledge of the behind-the-scene hedging activities of the issuing securities firms

By contrast, CPPI structures are particularly opaque. The potential return from CPPI/TIPP funds is not clear at the outset and the final payout will depend on the trading activities of the securities firms. Trying to understand the investment process of each fund house and the investment style of the particular fund manager is a much more complex task than an option payout formula. Additionally, buying as the price rises and selling as the price falls tends to go against the intuitive investor norm of seeking to buy low and sell high, which makes it further difficult for investors to understand how protected funds work.

Flexible structuring

In the US and Europe, the options markets have developed substantially over the past few decades and are now some of the most liquid financial instruments currently traded. They provide easy access to a universe of stock indexes around the world, and they can be further structured into option combinations flexibly. As such, they are an ideal vehicle through which securities firms can design products to meet a wide variety of investor needs.

The options market in China is young but growing fast. More importantly, the wide array of synthetic exposure that options can provide could be extremely valuable to China's fund investors in terms of diversification benefits. In general, investment funds in China currently lack diversity in investment strategies. When the funds do not offer access to innovative instruments or arguably better investment strategies, retail investors naturally invest on their own. The variety of equity exposure that options-based funds could potentially offer should bring more investor interest to the fund sector.

In summary, CPPI structures are most commonly found where it is difficult to write options on the underlying assets, for example, hedge funds or mutual funds. In China CPPI and TIPP naturally have been used by all existing capital-protected funds so far. But as the options market matures, the OBPI strategy should take off and provide a new catalyst to the principal-protected funds market.

PROSPECT

The capital-protected products proved appealing in 2005, as the stock market continued to struggle. The performance of the principal-protected funds outperformed all other equity investment funds. But it is quite a different picture when viewed from an absolute return perspective. The capital-protected funds have a required three-year investment period and their average return is a modest 4.81% as shown in Table 5 below. By comparison, the yield on a three-year Treasury bond was approximately 2.3% per annum.

Table 5 Average return of funds (1 January, 2005–15 December, 2005)

Fund types	Average return (%)
Equity funds	−2.07
Money market funds	2.30
Capital-protected funds	**4.81**
Bond funds	7.51

Source: News Morning Paper (XinWenChenBao), 16 December, 2005

In addition, the relatively superior performance of the protected funds originated primarily from their exposure to the bond markets. As shown in Table 5, the best performing funds in 2005 were the bond funds and most of the returns of the capital-protected funds were attributable to the exceptional bull market in the bond sector (as well as the bear stock market). Take the best-performing protected fund, the China Southern Fund (with a higher than 8% annual return in 2005), for example. As reported, the Southern Fund correctly predicted the interest-rate movement in the bond market and consequently increased the debt portion in the fund portfolio. The increased exposure to the bond market was a major lift to its performance in 2005.

Therefore, although investors showed strong interest in protected products in 2005, there are substantial hurdles ahead of this burgeoning market. The trade-off between capital protection and potential future growth is the most important one. In a CPPI structure where most of the assets are invested in the bond market, the upside is limited. When the equity market takes off, its limited exposure to equity is unlikely to gain comparable returns.

The emerging options market in China (see Chapter 4) should be a strong catalyst for the protected-products market going forward. With its embedded leverage, options are able to provide high potential returns (with the corresponding risks, of course). The combination of capital protection and a leveraged payout profile could be an attractive approach for investors in the Chinese market.

First of all, capital protection is valuable to investors, in particular for those who are just starting to explore the Chinese market, or simply aiming to gain some global exposure and add some diversification to their investment portfolios. Capital protection is most valuable in a bear market, where the investment capital is protected at a defined level, preventing it from failing sharply. Considering the risks and uncertainties involved in investing in China, this protection should have great appeal to investors.

To illustrate with some sample numbers: if a portfolio drops by 10%, it will need to grow by 11.1% to return to the initial investment level; if it falls by 20%, it will need to appreciate by 25% to recover the loss; and if falls by 50%, it will need a 100% jump. The appreciation level needed for mere breakeven increases at an accelerating pace. By defining a level of protection upfront, the capital-protected products reduce the extent of the fall. Consequently, investors could rely on smaller future growth levels to return to their initial financial situation.

Secondly, capital protection does not necessarily cost investors potential high returns. Once an investor defines a protection level that they are comfortable with, there is great flexibility in structuring the option payout formula, with respect to the rest of the investment capital, to give the investor the desired equity exposure. Instead of investing in the stock market directly, investors could apply the remainder to option structures with a high risk/reward profile for leveraged exposure to the equity market. In other words, investors would still have access to potential high performance levels.

China's options market is poised to become one of the biggest and most active in the world. The gradual opening of the dealers' OTC options market, in particular, should lead to a wide variety of options structures providing a broad spectrum of economic payout. The capital-protected products market, in turn, would be able to offer investors structures with capital protection and customised equity-market exposure. For example, investors could invest in a customised equity-linked note offered by an investment bank instead of a mutual fund with capital protection.

In addition, Chinese CBs, with their bond floor and the embedded option on individual stocks, may also become an interesting asset choice for capital-protected funds to gain equity exposure with a controlled downside risk. The continued innovations in China's options and options-related markets would give the capital-protected markets a strong boost going forward.

CONCLUSION

Capital-protected products offer investors in the Chinese stock market capital appreciation with certain capital protection. Mutual funds with principal protection emerged in the Chinese market and continued to attract interest as the Chinese stock market struggled through a multi-year bear market.

Due to the lack of zero-coupon bond and option derivatives markets, many funds have reportedly adopted CPPI and TIPP strategies for principal protection. TIPP is a more conservative strategy than CPPI, but both require dynamically adjusting asset allocations (stock and bond investments) over time. The bond markets in China are not always liquid, however, thus leading many principal-protected funds to invest a high proportion of capital in bonds at inception.

The growth of China's bond and options markets should provide strong catalysts to the capital-protected products market going forward. With an options-based capital-protection strategy, financial institutions should be able to provide a broad spectrum of capital-protected products (such as equity-linked notes) in addition to protected mutual funds. When an investor' starting point for investing in China is "do not lose my initial investment", then capital-protected products can play a key role in offering the protection level they need and then tailoring the desired exposure to China's stock market.

8

Short, Repo and Futures

The earlier chapters of Part II discussed the new investment vehicles for investors to participate in China's anticipated growth. Chapter 7 looked into principal-protected products as a strategy for participation while controlling the risk to the initial investment capital. Now, what if people take a bearish view on China?

In fact, more and more investors in China are looking into short sales of stocks to take advantage of the volatile stock market. Short sales, by definition, are the opposite of the more typical "long" positions, in which investors purchase shares and hold them for a relatively long investment period, waiting for prices to rise. By contrast, in a typical short sales scenario, an investor borrows shares from financial institutions and sells them, waits for the price to fall, then repurchases them at the lower price to close out the stock borrowing and pocket the trading gain.

To date, unfortunately, a direct stock short selling mechanism is not available in China's domestic share market. Futures and put options on broad market indexes are still nonexistent (although put options on individual stocks have emerged as a result of the state share overhaul reform). Thus for now, foreign investors taking a bearish view on Chinese stocks can only do so with those listed on the New York or Hong Kong stock exchanges.

The positive news is, however, that the emerging ETF and options markets have led to a "synthetic" short sale mechanism under certain circumstances. In addition, the newly introduced buy-out repo in the T-bond market has made short selling officially possible in the fixed-income market. Most notably, the recently amended Securities Law officially removed the legal hurdles for stock lending and short selling. The stock market has good reasons to be optimistic that short sales on stocks or indexes are not far away.

CHINA A SHARES: A ONE-SIDED MARKET

Why short in China? With China's stock market hovering around a multi-year low lately, many believe it is bottoming out and time for bargain hunting. Others, however, argue that China's stock market is still systematically overvalued (thus justifying a trading strategy to short) precisely because there is no official short sale mechanism available on the domestic stock market.

This overvaluation theory goes as follows. When short sales of assets are constrained, the trading market creates a speculative motive for investors, because they know overpriced assets cannot be forced to return to their fair value easily (ie, there is no short selling when the assets are overpriced). As a result, a stock holder expects not only to collect future cashflows from the asset, but also to profit from other investors' overoptimism in the future by selling the share at a price higher than he thinks it is worth.

Therefore, the price of an asset in such a market could be broken down into two components: the fundamental valuation of the asset owner if forced to hold the asset forever and collect all the future cashflows; and a speculative component generated by the asset owner's option to sell the share for a speculative profit. Given the strict short-sales constraints and the lack of trading experience of typical Chinese investors, it follows that the market would be characterised by intensive speculative trading, leading to artificially high stock prices deviating from the fundamental value of the stocks.

The statistical data regarding the frequency of stocks reaching daily up or down limits in recent years (see Table 1 below) provides some empirical evidence to support that hypothesis.

As the data below shows, up limit trading occurred much more frequently than down limit, except for 1997. However, 1997 was an unusual data point, as the stock market suffered sharp declines. The market tumbled twice in the middle of that year, with a 20.41% drop from April to July and 12.08% in September. The collective data from 1997 to 2003 unequivocally proved the point, with the up limits

Table 1 Frequency of stocks reaching up and down limits in 1997–2003

Year	Number of total samples*	Up limit events		Down limit events	
		Number of events	Frequency (%)**	Number of events	Frequency (%)**
1997	150,123	2,300	1.53	3,101	2.06
1998	181,349	1,808	0.99	1,223	0.67
1999	191,432	3,387	1.76	1,294	0.68
2000	212,134	4,345	2.04	908	0.43
2001	230,657	1,861	0.81	635	0.28
2002	241,764	2,422	1.01	989	0.41
2003	254,185	2,364	0.93	1,016	0.40
Sum	1,461,644	18,487	1.26	9,166	0.62

*Number of total samples = sum of the number of the respective effective trading days for all the listed stocks in such year.
**Frequency = number of up (or down) limit events/number of total samples.

Source: Shanghai Stock Exchange.

frequency more than twice that of the down limits. This phenomenon is typically referred to as a "one-sided" market (*dan bian shi*), and arguably the market as a whole has an upside bias.

The trading price of the Chinese stocks, of course, goes into more complex and fundamental issues than the lack of the short mechanism. The segregated ownership structure of the listed companies (ie, the high percentage of state ownership in the form of nontradable shares), for example, has weighed on the A share market for years with extraordinary downward pressure – the opposite to the upward bias caused by the lack of short sales.

In short, it is really debatable (and there is probably no absolutely correct answer at all) whether China's stock market is overvalued or undervalued at this stage. However, even if investors do not necessarily consider the market to be systematically overpriced, they could otherwise develop new trading strategies in China's A share market should a short sale mechanism be readily available.

SHORTING-BASED TRADING STRATEGIES

Short sales allow investors to satisfy several distinct objectives:

❑ betting that the broad market or individual stocks are heading down for macroeconomic or company-specific reasons;

❑ focusing on the absolute "alpha" of relative stocks without much exposure to the broad Chinese economy;

❑ arbitraging on pricing discrepancies between related securities in the market;

❑ hedging the downside risk of shares held long-term in a portfolio.

Downside shorting

Without getting into the fundamental valuation analysis of the individual stocks, some investors may be concerned by the macro factors around China's economic growth and the related sector performance.

For example, an upward revaluation of the Chinese currency against the US dollar may hurt the exports of the manufacturing sectors in the long term. Rising commodities prices are also a big concern. High prices for oil and base metal would increase costs across the economy, reducing companies' earnings. Furthermore, interest rates may increase again as the Chinese government grapples with potential inflation risks, thereby dampening enthusiasm for Chinese stocks.

Shorting allows investors to capitalise on their bearish views on the broad market or individual stocks (which is not possible in a one-sided market). However, naked shorting is a high-risk strategy. Only a relatively small number of funds rely solely on naked shorting as their trading strategy. Shorting strategy usually involves a corresponding long position in a related security to mitigate the risk.

Long-short strategy

Market-neutral strategies are trading strategies that are widely used by hedge funds and proprietary traders. Theoretically, a trader could go long on certain instruments while shorting others so that his portfolio has no net exposure to broad market moves. This strategy aims to profit from relative mispricings between related instruments – going long on those perceived to be underpriced while going short on those perceived to be overpriced – while avoiding systematic risk (the exposure to the broad market).

Such a combination of long-short is also referred to as "pairs trading" or "relative value arbitrage." Typically, a trader seeks to identify two companies with similar characteristics whose equity securities are currently trading at a price relationship that is out of line with their historical trading range. He then buys the apparently undervalued stock while selling the apparently overvalued one short. Relative-value investors typically focus on stocks in the same sector or industry to reduce the risks in this strategy.

Arbitrage trading
Segregated share classes
As discussed in Chapter 1, one unique feature of the Chinese market is that many listed companies have segregated share classes. For example, A and B shares are two classes of common shares with identical voting and dividend rights, listed on the same exchanges (Shanghai or Shenzhen), but traded by different participants because of different currency denominations.

Specifically, Class A shares were restricted to domestic residents, whereas Class B shares were accessible only by foreigners until a rule change in February 2001 allowed domestic residents to purchase B shares using foreign currency. However, the A and B shares still trade very differently, as foreign currency controls continue to limit Chinese residents' access to B shares.

The pricing discrepancy between the different classes of stocks gives rise to potential arbitrage opportunities. The A shares on average enjoyed a substantial premium over B shares, even though they were entitled to the same legal rights and claim to dividends. The 2001 relaxation on domestic investors' purchasing B shares did not eliminate all premiums and it remained at an average level of around 80%, according to the database from Shenzhen GTA Information Technology Inc. As such, arbitrage trading may be implemented with A/B share pairs of the same listed company.

Stock versus derivative trading
Investors may also execute arbitrage trades to take advantage of the interaction of the derivatives market and the stock market. For example, stock short selling may be paired with a CB position to arbitrage. As discussed in Chapter 3, Chinese CBs have a very special value proposition caused by the segregated ownership structure in the listed companies. If short selling is available, investors could potentially hedge out the stock price risk while benefiting from the values of other structural features in the CB.

Arbitraging between mispriced options and related stocks is another example. For example, early in China's equity derivatives history, the market saw situations where options on a stock were traded at a higher price to the underlying stock. That was a blatant violation of any pricing theory for derivatives, but the market had no short selling mechanism to take advantage it. In fact, the most extreme situation involved a warrant (formally "transferable pre-emptive right") trading at a premium to the underlying stock for more than a month with the premium as high as 30% on certain trading days in that period. As the options market in China continues to flourish, arbitrage opportunities may arise between options and stocks or between different options.

Risk management

Finally, the ability to short stocks or indexes is valuable even for the many investors who are positive on the Chinese market. While bullish on the overall market, short selling allows investors to hedge out the risk in areas where the market could be quite volatile. For example, index futures are the most commonly used derivatives instrument to hedge the market risk to which an investment portfolio is exposed.

CURRENT RESTRICTIONS ON STOCK SHORT SELLING

Short selling of stocks is currently unavailable to investors in China's domestic stock markets. Chinese investors' accounts are kept centrally at the stock exchanges and subject to very stringent "short sale" constraints. The exchanges' computer systems always check an investor's position to ensure the physical shares are available before they execute any trade. This trading system makes it very difficult for financial institutions to lend stocks to their clients for short selling purposes.

Historically, short selling briefly appeared in China's capital markets through the early trial of T-bond futures. T-bond futures' trading, unfortunately, was quickly put to a complete halt by China's regulators in 1995 following a price manipulation scandal, discussed below. A decade later, China's capital markets have become sufficiently developed to reintroduce advanced trading tools such as short sales, and the regulatory framework has been gradually relaxed for potential short selling mechanisms in the stock market.

Early trial: T-bond futures trading
"327" T-bond futures event

Launched in the early 1990s, China's Treasury bond (T-bond) futures market did not attract widespread interest until late 1993, when the Shanghai Stock Exchange opened up T-bond futures trading to public investors. The market expanded exponentially in 1994 and early 1995 until the disastrously manipulated trading around the T-bond futures contract No. 327 (which has been widely referred to as the "327 T-bond futures event") led to a complete crackdown on the T-bond futures market.

The No. 327 T-bond futures contract was a three-year contract expiring in June 1995. On 23 February, 1995, the Ministry of Finance announced the new debt offering plan for 1995, which was interpreted by the market as bullish for the Treasury rate market. As a result, the underlying T-bond 327 soared. Facing the risk of catastrophic losses, the major firms holding large short positions sold huge volumes of contracts shortly before close of market, causing the No. 327 contract to tumble 3.8 yuan on that day (contract closing price at 147.50 yuan). At the low closing price, tens of financial institutions holding long positions faced bankruptcy.

The government quickly intervened as the No. 327 contract's disastrous trading threatened the meltdown of Shanghai's financial market. When the dust settled, one of China's leading securities companies went bankrupt, and the futures market was closed soon after in May by the CSRC. As it now stands, futures contracts are available only for commodities trading in China.

Lessons of the 327 event

The weak trading governance, among other factors, was the main cause of the collapse of the Chinese T-bond futures market. The cash collateral for the T-bond futures was set so low that the equilibrium between the T-bond market (spot market) and the T-bond futures market (the derivatives market) was completely destroyed, contributing to excessive volatility and manipulation.

Notably, the T-bond futures market was initially introduced to mainly attract public interest to promote the T-bond spot market, instead of responding to the hedging needs of investors. The contracts were designed as such, and the most illustrative aspect was the cash margin requirement. Considering public investors' limited access to financing, each contract only requires a very low margin (cash collateral) equal to 2.5% of the notional value of the contract, ie, a leverage ratio of an astonishing 40:1.

The futures trading volume grew exponentially as a result. From 1993 to 1994, the daily trading volume of the spot market increased by 665.8%, meanwhile the daily trading volume of the futures market increased by 149 times. Not surprisingly, the scale of the futures market quickly surpassed that of the T-bond market. One direct result was that the T-bonds necessary for futures settlement frequently exceeded the available T-bonds in the spot market, causing manipulation around futures settlement dates.

As an example, the following table compares the T-bond trading value in the spot market and the T-bond face value required for settlement in the futures market, both with respect to the No. 925 T-bond, which had the largest flotation volume in the T-bond spot market.

Using the trading volume as a proxy for the T-bonds available for futures settlement, the table below shows that the T-bonds needed for futures settlement in the most extreme case were more than 18 times that of what was available. This could easily lead to a "short squeeze", where the party holding long spot positions also accumulates a large amount of long futures positions without intention to offset, causing spot prices to rise and leading to higher market volatility.

Therefore, prevention of market manipulation is a major issue for regulators as they contemplate the return of short selling in China's capital markets. This concern has been reflected in many structural features in the recently introduced buy-out repo, which will be

Table 2 Face value of No. 925 T-bond trading volume *versus* required amount for settlement of the corresponding T-bond futures contract

Settlement month	Daily average trading volume	Amount required for futures settlement	Ratio (required *versus* trading volume)
March 1994	1,776	6,802	3.83
June 1994	6,515	23,900	3.67
September 1994	10,462	193,692	18.51
December 1994	9,226	156,218	16.93

Source: Shanghai Stock Exchange Report

discussed in detail below. Meanwhile, China's capital markets have made substantial progress during the past decade and are well poised to manage the complexities involved in short selling of stocks. As such, the regulatory framework took a giant step forward in late 2005 to open the door for potential short selling in China.

Latest regulatory relaxation

Stock short selling had been strictly banned by China's Securities Law until it made sweeping changes in late 2005. The Securities Law was initially formulated in 1998, a time when most parts of southeast and eastern Asia were going through the Asian Financial Crisis. The legislators naturally placed the prevention of financial risks above concerns for the liquidity and efficiency of the market.

In that context, it was probably not surprising that the Criminal Law then held "transactions with shares not physically held" to be a criminal offence. The old Securities Law meanwhile provided stringent measures against stock short selling:

❏ securities transaction must be executed with currently owned shares;
❏ securities firms must not provide clients with capital financing or stock lending services;
❏ securities firms should take transaction orders from clients only when physical shares are actually held in such clients' accounts;
❏ securities clearance institutions must not use clients' shares for pledging or stock lending purposes.

These legal hurdles were removed months ago in the newly amended Securities Law, which now states:

❏ securities transactions can be executed with currently owned shares or in any other forms as provided by the State Council;
❏ securities firms may provide clients with capital financing or stock lending services pursuant to rules provided by the State Council and approvals from the securities regulatory agencies under the State Council.

These Securities Law amendments have removed the obstacles for stock lending and short selling, and they empower the State Council to develop practical rules in the near future. Clearly, as the free market economy in China gains strong momentum, the legislators are turning their focus from administrative control to the development of an investor-oriented stock market.

In essence, the relaxation of stock short selling is also an acknowledgement of the emerging short trading practices in other parts of China's capital markets. In the T-bond market, the Shanghai Stock Exchange launched the buy-out repo in December 2004, a "borrow and short" mechanism in the bond market. In the ETF market, the cash replacement mechanism also makes "synthetically" shorting component stocks possible under certain circumstances. These emerging trading mechanisms – in particular, the buy-out repo – will be discussed in detail below, as they reflect the regulator's current thinking on risk management measures to prevent market manipulation in short selling transactions.

BUY-OUT REPO

The new buy-out repo trading on the Shanghai Stock Exchange is a major financial innovation in China's capital markets. Compared with the existing "closed-end" repo, which is tantamount to a Treasury bond-pledged cash loan, the buy-out repo transfers T-bond ownership between the trading parties. Investors in China thus have a "borrow and short" mechanism available for the first time since T-bond futures were banned years ago.

Background economics of repos

In the US, most market participants lend and borrow securities through repurchase agreements (repos). A participant executing a repo sells securities and simultaneously agrees to repurchase the same securities from the buyer at a negotiated price on a future date. A repo transaction is tantamount to borrowing money against a loan of securities. On the money borrowing side, the proceeds of the sale is the principal amount of the borrowing and the excess of the repurchase price over the sale price is the interest paid on the borrowing. On the securities lending side, the securities receiver acquires the ownership of the securities for the trade term and could use such securities for its own trading purposes.

A new repo trading mechanism on T-bonds was introduced to China's stock markets in late 2004. Its Chinese name literally means "buy-out repo", emphasising the fact that a repo constitutes a temporary transfer of a security by its owner to the repo counterparty.

Before 2004, T-bond repurchase agreements in China ("closed-end repo" in Chinese) were essentially money borrowing with T-bonds pledged as collateral, ie, a device purely for capital financing. Although the money borrower pledged the T-bonds as collateral, the title of the T-bond was not transferred. Thus before the new buy-out repo was available, T-bonds in China effectively became nontradable once they were subject to repurchase agreements.

Trading mechanism in trial period

In April 2004, China's Ministry of Finance, People's Bank, and the CSRC jointly issued the *Notice on Developing Buy-Out Repo Trading on Treasury Bonds*. Consequently, the buy-out repo mechanism was first introduced to China's inter-bank bond market in May (2004), followed by the buy-out repo trading on the Shanghai Stock Exchange for investors.

The trial period on the SSE started in early December 2004, and the exchange chose one specific seven-year Treasury bond issue for repo trading during the trial period. The repo trading trial is on a very limited basis: only 48 institutions are qualified to participate (ie, it is not available to individual investors as yet) and participants must trade through the large order system at the exchange, which has a large minimum size and specific trading hours. Additionally, the current buy-out repo mechanism does not have certain structural features commonly found in more developed markets, such as securities substitution and early termination.

Unlike the margin maintenance requirements in typical repo transactions, China's buy-out repo applies a "performance deposit" mechanism. China's Securities Depository and Clearing Co. Ltd. (SD&C) – the national securities depository and clearing company for securities traded on the Shanghai and Shenzhen Stock Exchanges – is the central intermediary for buy-out repo trading. On the repo trade date, both counterparties have to make deposits to SD&C as collateral for their performance obligation under the repo agreements.

Performance deposit and default reporting system

When entering a buy-out repo, the lender of funds shall make the initial trade price to the lender of T-bond in an amount equal to (a) the clean price of the T-bond at close of trading on T − 1 plus (b) accrued and unpaid interest. The performance deposit for both parties is equal to a percentage of the initial trade price, known as the "performance deposit rate." At the end of the trade (the repurchase date), the lender of funds returns the T-bond and receives a cash repayment equal to the pre-negotiated repurchase price plus accrued interest. That is:

Initial trade price = T-bond closing price on T − 1 + accrued interest
Performance deposit = initial trade price * performance deposit rate
Maturity settlement price = agreed repurchase price + accrued
interest

At trade date:

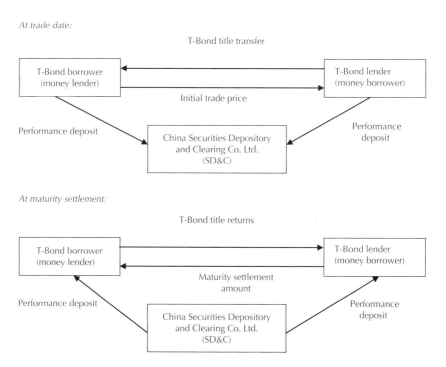

This counterparty-exposure management system differs from typical margin maintenance in two major aspects. Firstly, the performance deposits are not subject to daily mark-to-market based on market price fluctuations during the contract term. Three maturity terms (7 days, 28 days and 91 days) are available for the trial period at the SSE, and the performance deposit rates are 1.5%, 3% and 5%, respectively. According to the public education materials from the SSE, the SSE researchers developed these deposit levels through statistical analysis on certain treasury bonds' price fluctuations within a 12-month span between May 2003 and May 2004. It seems that based on recent historical data, the performance deposits are expected to cover the potential maximum price fluctuations during the trade term.

Default reporting system

Secondly, the SSE's "default reporting" rule limits both counter-parties' contractual liability to the performance deposits. If a repo counterparty is unable or unwilling to perform at the end of the repo trade, the party could simply file a default report with the exchange. Following the default reporting, the non-defaulting party seizes the defaulting party's performance deposit, and the defaulting party is freed from any further performance obligation on the repo contract. If both parties default on the transaction, neither party would receive their deposit back, and the initial per-formance deposits from both parties would be allocated to the Securities Settlement Risk Fund.

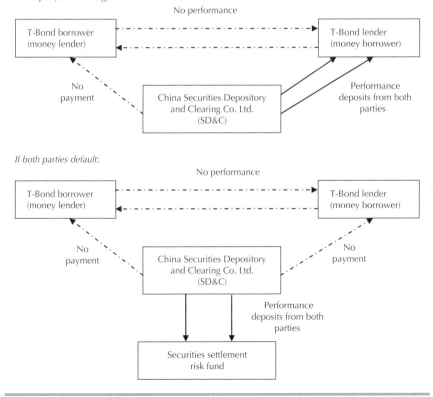

If one party defaults (eg, T-bond borrower defaults):

No performance

T-Bond borrower (money lender)

T-Bond lender (money borrower)

No payment

China Securities Depository and Clearing Co. Ltd. (SD&C)

Performance deposits from both parties

If both parties default:

No performance

T-Bond borrower (money lender)

T-Bond lender (money borrower)

No payment

China Securities Depository and Clearing Co. Ltd. (SD&C)

No payment

Performance deposits from both parties

Securities settlement risk fund

Since the default party is relieved from all obligations under the repo trade after a default report, they are not liable for any amount greater than the original performance deposit amount or for other losses incurred by the non-defaulting party. This differs from the repo mechanism in many developed markets. For example, in the Global Master Repurchase Agreement (2000 version) by The Bond Market Association (TBMA) and the International Securities Market Association (ISMA), the defaulting party is required to pay to the non-defaulting party certain fees, costs and other expenses incurred by the non-defaulting party as a result of the defaulting party's failure.

The rationale for this limited liability setting is apparently to protect trading parties from being "squeezed on the short position." In other words, the T-bond borrower will not be forced to "strictly perform" (in contractual law terms) the repo contract if he sells the T-bond short but cannot recover the security easily prior to the repo settlement.

However, the performance deposits could potentially be considered as a "deposit" (*DinJing*) for contract performance under China's Security Law. According to China's Supreme Court's interpretation of the Security Law in 2000, contracting parties could terminate a contract by giving up the deposit if such a termination mechanism is provided in the contract, and additionally, the parties should follow China's Contract Law for liabilities upon contract termination. How this performance deposit and default reporting mechanism under the SSE rule will be treated within the framework of the Security Law and Contract Law remains to be examined by legal authorities.

Speculation concern on the buy-out repo

The buy-out repo is the first short selling mechanism in China's capital markets since the regulators shut down the T-bond futures market a decade ago. Thus both investors and regulators are keenly interested to see if this fuels a wave of speculative short selling of government bonds. As discussed above, the performance deposit and default reporting are specifically designed to prevent market manipulation and short squeeze in particular. Additionally, the Shanghai Stock Exchange takes extra measures to prevent potential manipulation:

❑ no single institutional investor on the exchange is allowed to have open (unsettled) buy-out positions for more than 20% of the outstanding amount of the underlying T-bond;

❑ investors with 20% more holdings may not participate further in such buy-out repo trading unless they start to reduce their positions;

❑ the Exchange discloses on a daily basis the number of unsettled buy-out repos on each T-bond.

So far, the buy-out repo has not been fully tested. Firstly, investors will take time to become familiar with the new trading method. Secondly, 2005 was a big bull year for the bond market so not many investors were interested in betting on a decline and hence short selling activity was minor. But the interest in short selling could increase in the near future when the bond market reverses its bull-ish trend, and the risk-management concern around buy-out repos would be tested then.

SYNTHETIC SHORT IN ETF MARKET
ETF cash replacement

The ETF redemption and creation system, the arbitrage mechanism that keeps the ETF trading close to the underlying stock basket, effectively involves a short mechanism.

The capital replacement mechanism in the SSE50 ETF creation/ redemption has made it possible for investors to synthetically short the component stocks. As mentioned earlier (see Chapter 5 for detailed discussion on the SSE50 ETF and its trading mecha-nism), for some SSE50 ETF component stocks, investors could use cash (in lieu of the actual physical shares) to subscribe (create) the ETF units.

If investors do use cash to replace a certain component stock, the fund management company that supports the SSE50 ETF will then use the cash to purchase the physical shares. The fund manage-ment and the investors will pay each other any excess cash to make both whole. In other words, if the initial cash payment by investors is less than the share purchase price, the investors will pay the missing amount to the fund company, or if the initial cash payment by investors is more than the share purchase price, the investors will recoup the excess.

When investors take a bearish view on a stock with respect to a forthcoming event, they could effectively short the stock using the following strategies:

1. Subscribe the SSE50 ETF with a basket of the 50 component stocks.
2. Use cash instead of physical shares with respect to the stock in question, if the cash replacement mechanism is available to such stock;
3. Sell the ETF unit on exchange (effectively selling the stock short and receiving the initial stock price as proceeds);
4. The ETF fund company buys the physical share post the event (using the cash initially paid for the ETF subscription) and pays the investors any excess cash (effectively the short position is recovered at the lower stock price post the corporate event);
5. Investors pocket the difference between the initial stock price and the stock price post the corporate event.

Take, for example, the follow-on equity offering by Bao Steel in April 2005. Bao Steel announced its follow-on offering on 19 April and its stock trading halted from April 20 to 26. The closing price on April 19 was 6.02 yuan per share. Purely considering the dilution effect from the follow-on offering, the "ex-event" price of the Bao Steel stock was expected to be around 5.75 yuan per share. So the arbitrage is as follows:

19 April, 2005:	Subscribe the SSE50 ETF, cash replacement for Bao Steel stock. Effectively, shorting Bao Steel stock at 6.02 yuan.
27 April, 2005:	ETF fund company purchases Bao Steel stock as it resumes trading at "ex-event" price. Effectively, buying back Bao Steel stock at the expected price of 5.79 yuan
Profit:	6.02 − 5.79 = 0.23 yuan per share.

As expected, Bao Steel stock tumbled on 27 April and quickly reached the down price limit when it resumed trading. The synthetic short trading proved feasible in connection with the Bao Steel follow-on offering event.

Source: 21st-Century Economic Reports, 18 July, 2005

However, the synthetic short mechanism through ETFs is limited to the component stocks in an outstanding ETF. To date, there is only one ETF – the SSE50 ETF – listed and traded in the public market. In addition, it involves the additional complexity related to the ETF subscription/trading mechanism. Investors would need a system of direct stock or index short selling to implement sophisticated trading strategies on the broad stock market.

PROSPECT

Short sale of stocks is clearly at the top of the Chinese market regulator's agenda, as illustrated by the recent relaxation in the amended Securities Law and the "borrow and short" mechanism being tested in the T-bond buy-out repo market. Additional help also comes from the emerging derivatives market, which has also been officially legitimised by the amended Securities Law. Derivatives securities (eg, index futures, put options) could be flexibly structured to offer a synthetic shorting mechanism on individual stocks and indexes.

But the potential for market manipulation and insider trading as a result of stock short selling will be a major concern to the regulators. In an emerging market with weak corporate governance and risk management, short squeeze and price manipulation may occur and destabilise both the derivatives and spot markets. The unique performance deposits and default reporting system in the buy-out repo market clearly shows that regulators are paying close attention to these issues and have carefully structured the mechanism accordingly.

To that end, stock index futures will most probably be introduced first, as the indexes reflect the broad market and are very hard to manipulate. Then the short sale of individual stocks may occur, probably after the full-flotation reform is complete, as the increased flotation of the individual stocks makes it harder for a few large trading accounts to control and manipulate. In any event, the early failed trials in the 1990s and the recent misdemeanours are still casting a long shadow over the emerging new trading tools – as late as November 2005, a since-detained government trader in London caused the state hundreds of millions of dollars in losses through failed futures bets on copper prices. Thus the index futures

173

and individual stock short selling are unlikely to be rushed to the market by regulators overnight.

CONCLUSION

The introduction of short selling is a natural next step as China continues liberating its capital markets. A short selling mechanism on indexes or individual stocks would reduce speculation trading, improve stock market liquidity and facilitate the development of the derivatives markets. Encouraging developments have gradually emerged: the buy-out repo on T-bonds has created a "borrow and short" mechanism in the fixed income market; the fast-developing ETF and options markets have also led to synthetic shorting opportunities in special situations.

The recent Securities Law amendments have ultimately lifted the ban on stock lending and shorting transactions. With the failed early trial of T-bond futures market still looming over short selling discussions, however, the regulators not surprisingly are taking careful steps as they move forward. The buy-out repo has a unique performance deposit and default reporting system, reflecting the strong focus that the regulators put on the risk-management aspects of short selling to prevent potential market manipulation.

Nevertheless, China's domestic stock market is poised to embrace stock or index short selling in the near future. As China gradually opens its capital markets in line with international standards, short selling mechanisms should become more broadly available for investors. That would bring new trading strategies to the market, and the economic terms and trading behaviour of stocks (eg, interaction of A and B shares) and derivatives products (eg, Chinese CBs) may change dramatically as arbitrage trades emerge.

Part III

Breakthrough in-the-Making

China's stock market was initially launched for financing alternatives to state-owned enterprises (SOEs) and more profoundly, their reform. The reform aims to bring modern corporate governance to Chinese SOEs through the equity capital markets and hence to achieve their improved economic performance.

As China's SOE reform reaches a critical point in the new century, foreign participation in the capital markets is poised to be an increasing necessity. The opening up of its stock market is clearly related to China's WTO commitments, as discussed in Part I. The fundamental reason, however, is that China's stock market needs to incorporate modern corporate governance systems, partly through foreign participation, before they becomes an effective tool for SOE reforms.

China has recently made two substantial moves to increase foreign participation in its stock market. The QFII system, as discussed in detail in Chapter 2, opens up the domestic stock market to foreign institutional investors with respect to tradable shares.

Together with innovative investment products which have recently appeared on China's stock markets, as discussed in Part II, the QFII system provides foreign investors with many more investment opportunities than previously (which were basically limited to cash equity investments in Chinese companies listed on exchanges in Hong Kong or New York).

At the same time, China's multiple regulatory bodies have issued a flurry of important new regulations to bring the framework closer to international norms. These regulatory developments have reopened foreign investor access to the nontradable shares of listed companies (the state-owned shares and legal-person shares). Thus, a large number of state-owned enterprises are being made available for restructuring or partnering with foreign firms, providing foreign investors with greater market entry options.

Therefore, SOE reforms through mergers and acquisitions (M&As) or management buy-outs (MBOs), as will be discussed in detail in Chapters 9 and 10, are expected to offer foreign buy-out and venture-capital firms tremendous opportunities for participation, especially as the regulatory bodies have started the campaign to make the SOE shares fully floatable in the stock market.

For instance, the 2004 China Venture Capital Annual Forum pointed out that central government-controlled SOEs have approximately 10 trillion yuan worth of total assets and 0.5 trillion yuan net earnings. In addition, local government-controlled SOEs should have at least another 3 trillion yuan worth of total assets. Even if only 20% of the total assets are privatised to strategic investors and only a fraction of that is investment-worthy, there are still investment opportunities of the magnitude of tens of billions of US dollars. Foreign investors' abundant capital supply, rich market experience and natural access to the international markets will make them competitive players in this burgeoning privatisation market.

9

M&A and Private Equity Funds

Foreign M&A activities are growing rapidly in China. Following its accession to the WTO, China has opened up many business sectors to foreign ownership, and its recent regulatory enactments have gradually established a viable framework for M&A transactions in China. More and more multinational companies are using the acquisition of Chinese companies as an important strategy to access the Chinese market. The levels of both deal activity and deal size have continued to escalate in recent years.

While M&A appears to be the next wave of foreign investment into China, a strong emerging trend lies in the increasingly active participation by international private equity funds. They compete aggressively with multinational companies in contests for the controlling interests in the Chinese state-owned enterprises (SOEs). For example, in the Carlyle Group's landmark acquisition of Xugong Group Construction Machinery Co. (XCMC), Carlyle reportedly w the deal through an auction process that went through two rounds involving six international bidders. One of the bidders was the US construction manufacturer giant Caterpillar, with whom XCMC already has a joint venture.

Carlyle's successful acquisition of XCMC, as well as other groundbreaking cases to be examined in detail in this chapter, illustrates both the promising and challenging aspects of the booming M&A market in China. On the one hand, foreign investors have managed to acquire controlling ownership in the SOEs as China warms to foreign takeovers. On the other hand, however, many of those acquisitions took years to complete, as the deal processes are complicated by the complex approval system, the dichotomy of tradable and nontradable shares and the high percentage of state ownership in many firms.

OVERVIEW

China's accession to the WTO has opened up many previously closed industry sectors to foreign investment. Many international companies, including highly visible American companies like Amazon.com, Anheuser-Busch, and Yahoo, have started making acquisitions of Chinese companies a key element of their business strategies in China.

Foreign capital acquiring listed companies is particularly on the rise. According to the 2004 Listed Company Annual Statistical Report issued by the Shanghai and Shenzhen Stock Exchanges, by year-end 2004 nearly 100 companies listed on the exchanges had foreign investors among some of their top 10 shareholders.

As shown in the figure below, the number of foreign M&A deals in China and their total deal value have both been moving steadily upward in recent years. (For the purpose of this chapter, foreign M&A in China means "inbound M&A", where the corporate acquirer is a foreign company/investor and the target is a Chinese company.)

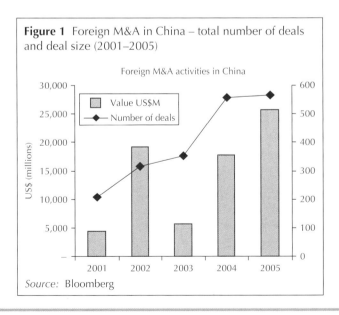

Figure 1 Foreign M&A in China – total number of deals and deal size (2001–2005)

Foreign M&A activities in China

Source: Bloomberg

Driving forces

From a virtually unknown term a decade ago, foreign M&A has become a common feature in China's stock market today. This phenomenal growth of foreign M&A activities has been driven by a number of internal and external factors.

Foreign capital for SOE reform

China has been restructuring its state-owned asset holdings since it started its market economy reform decades ago. In a few industrial sectors, the state is encouraging SOEs to consolidate into large integrated conglomerates, which are intended to be global leaders in their fields, while in other sectors, the state is actively seeking to reduce the level of its equity holding. Overall, the state is aggressively looking for foreign investors (as well as domestic ones) during the SOE reform campaign.

At the same time, as a result of joining the WTO, Chinese companies are increasingly facing more and more foreign competition. They are looking for foreign technology, both manufacturing technology and corporate managerial technology, to increase their competitiveness as the Chinese market opens up in full to foreign companies. M&A with foreign investors thus becomes an attractive (and sometimes necessary) measure for Chinese companies to survive and grow.

To these ends, China's government has issued a series of new regulations to encourage foreign investors to use M&As and capital markets as a new approach to enter and develop business in China. By contrast, for decades China has primarily attracted foreign investment through favourable policies in the foreign direct investments (FDI) sector, such as corporate tax savings for Sino-foreign joint ventures (JVs). Consequently, a large number of SOEs were recently made available for restructuring or partnering with foreign firms through M&A measures.

What is most significant among the recent moves is the capacity for foreigner investors to come in and take controlling stakes in these enterprises. This is a huge shift from the Chinese government's traditional policy towards foreign investment, and it is moving much more into line with the WTO standards. In particular, the permission for controlling interests is a substantial shift from the joint venture mentality which was ever present until a few years ago.

Alternatives to joint ventures

The Chinese market, with its extraordinary size and growth, maintains its strong appeal to international investors. For foreign investors looking for a quantum leap in "China story" exposure, M&A transactions that offer immediate market access are becoming an increasingly attractive alternative to the traditional FDI approach (which is frequently referred to as "greenfield investments").

To be sure, mergers and acquisitions could be complex and potentially risky in China. However, a quick presence in China may be acquired for less than it would take to build the same company from scratch. This is particularly true for sectors that are highly fragmented and already saturated, for instance, a fragmented retail market with many strong regional brands. M&A is fast becoming a third wave of foreign investments in China, following the prevalence of Sino-foreign JVs in the 1980s and early 1990s and the surge of wholly foreign-owned enterprises (WFOEs) over the past 10 years.

Developments in the legal framework

The WTO accession in 2002 has led to significant changes in the Chinese government's attitude towards foreign equity ownership in Chinese companies. The QFII system, as discussed in detail in Chapter 2, opened up the domestic stock market to foreign institutional investors with respect to tradable A shares. Simultaneously, China's multiple regulatory bodies issued a wave of important new regulations to facilitate foreign investors' M&A activities with respect to nontradable shares of the listed companies.

As a result, the new M&A legal framework in China has made considerable advances in the last few years. These recent regulatory developments have expanded the range of target companies and acquisition methods available to foreign investors and the M&A process has become much more transparent and manageable for foreign investors. Although many of the new changes have not been fully tested with transactions, the M&A route by and large offers foreign investors a viable method of entering the Chinese market.

The familiarity factor

Finally, there is the familiarity factor for both Chinese companies and foreign investors. While M&A transactions were virtually unknown a mere 10 years ago, they have quickly become an increasingly common and important theme in China's SOE reform and corporate restructuring.

As China continues its robust economic growth, more and more Chinese companies as well as foreign investors are using M&As as a strategic tool to further their strategies in China. Whether it is domestic Chinese companies making transactions or international companies making transactions into China, the players in the market are becoming increasingly comfortable with the M&A tool. Although M&As still make up only a small portion of total foreign investments in China today, the ratio of foreign M&A activity to total FDI should continue increasing in the future.

Emerging trend

The private equity investors' growing participation is a strong emerging trend in China's M&A markets. They are typically referred to as financial investors, as compared to multinational companies investing in China, who are generally referred to as strategic corporate investors (or sometimes, "traditional investors", because they have been in China much longer than financial investors). The main goal for financial investors is capital appreciation from a quick and profitable turnaround of a Chinese company, whereas a traditional strategic investor's goal is typically to team up with a local partner to make a successful entry into China's local markets.

In general, the exit strategies remain more limited than most foreign financial investors would wish. Overseas listings – mainly the Hong Kong and US markets – have relatively high listing standards in terms of minimum size and reporting requirements for many Chinese companies. China's domestic IPO market has been shut down completely as the existing listed companies have been carrying out the segregated equity ownership reform since early 2005. Most of all, nontradable shares are not freely transferable in the public market, so even a listed company does not necessarily provide a viable "exit" for investors.

The M&A market, however, is seen as a major turning point in the opening up of the Chinese markets for private equity investors in recent years, and investor confidence has changed substantially, becoming more positive. 2004 was a good time for exits by private equity investors through the US public markets. The full-flotation reform, turning nontradable shares into tradable shares, creates an exit opportunity in the public market going forward. Finally, increased M&A activities by the multinational companies also enable private equity investors an exit through the M&A market. Thus in the midst of the explosive growth of foreign M&A activities, more and more private equity investment funds are competing head-to-head with the traditional strategic investors in the battles for controlling interests in Chinese companies.

By November 2005, global buy-out firms led by Carlyle Group and Newbridge Capital had spent more than US$7 billion since 2000 to take equity stakes in Chinese companies, according to data compiled by the Asian Venture Capital Journal. New deal structures have been tried and tested as the investment funds aggressively expand in the Chinese market and foreign investors have started to close a series of landmark transactions:

❑ In December 2004, Newbridge Capital completed the US$149 million purchase of 348.1 million nontradable shares of Shenzhen Development Bank (SDB) Co., whose share ownership is unusually fragmented. Holding 18% of equity ownership, Newbridge is the biggest single shareholder of the bank and SDB became the first Chinese bank controlled by overseas investors.

❑ In October 2005, the Carlyle Group defeated industry giants including Caterpillar to acquire an 85% stake in XCMC, China's largest manufacturer of building machinery, for US$385 million. The deal represents the first time a Western private equity firm has managed to acquire such a high level of control in a leading SOE.

❑ Even in M&A deals by large multinational companies, private investment funds are frequently involved and many have successfully capitalised on this surge of foreign M&A activities in China. Take, for example, the high profile takeover battle between Anheuser-Busch (AB) and SAB Miller for Harbin Brewery in 2004. Global Conduit Holdings (GCH), an investment company registered in the British Virgin Islands, acquired 29.07% of Harbin Brewery's shares early in the process and then it promptly exited with a pleasant premium as AB acquired GCH as part of its campaign to secure a controlling ownership in Harbin Brewery.

These three high-profile cases will be discussed in detail later, as this chapter will focus on financial investors' increasing participation in the fast-growing Chinese M&A market. The increased interest in M&As by the traditional corporate investors, however, is by all means relevant: As more and more multinational companies use acquisitions of Chinese companies as a key strategy to expand in China, private equity investors are finding extra exit opportunities in those M&A activities, as illustrated by GCH's successful exit in the AB and SAB Miller takeover contest for Harbin Brewery.

LEGAL DEVELOPMENTS OPEN DOORS

China's accession to the WTO has led to fundamental changes to its regulatory framework regarding foreign investors' participation in the domestic stock market. Various regulatory bodies have since issued a series of regulations and rules to liberalise takeovers by foreign investors of Chinese companies.

This legal evolution started with the lifting of the ban on foreign investors' acquisition of the state-owned and legal-person shares and further regulatory developments have expanded the range of target companies and acquisition methods available to foreign investors.

Foreign acquisition ban lifted

Foreign acquisition of state-owned equity interests was prohibited for nearly a decade following its brief appearance in the 1990s. This ban was only recently lifted in 2003 so that acquisition of nontradable shares was made available again to foreign investors.

In August 1995, Itochu and Isuzu Motors purchased 4 million legal-person shares of Beijing Light Bus Co., representing 25% of the company's equity. At about the same time, Ford Motor Company purchased 20% of the shares of Jiangling Automobile Company. The two acquisitions stirred up tremendous volatility in China's stock market.

Shortly after the two acquisitions, the State Council moved quickly to issue the *Notice from the State Council on the Suspension of the Transfer of State-owned Shares and Legal Person Shares of Listed Companies to Foreign Investors* in September 1995. The Notice prohibited similar purchases of state-owned or legal-person shares in any listed company until administrative regulations governing such transactions were officially formulated. This moratorium was lifted in late 2002 by the *Circular Regarding the Transfer of State-Owned Shares and Legal-Person Shares of Listed Companies to Foreign Parties* jointly issued by the CSRC, MoF and SDRC.

QFIIs and corporate takeover

Although the qualified foreign institutional investors (QFII) system discussed in Chapter 2 offers QFIIs direct access to China's stock market, it is unlikely that a foreign investor will rely on the QFII system to achieve its acquisition goal.

Firstly, the QFII system is limited to the A share market, ie, the tradable shares of the listed companies, while about two-thirds of the shares of the listed companies are in the form of nontradable state-owned shares. Secondly, a QFII is not permitted to hold more than 10% of the outstanding shares of any particular listed company, and the combined holdings of QFIIs in a company cannot exceed 20% of its listed A shares.

Until recently, foreign takeovers of China's listed companies were not common. Traditionally, foreign investment in listed companies has taken the form of negotiated minority stakes, and has been for the purpose of establishing a strategic relationship or making a financial investment rather than for obtaining corporate control. As the ban on the foreign acquisition of nontradable shares has now been lifted, foreign investors now have the opportunity to acquire sufficient share ownership to gain corporate control.

New M&A legal framework

Over the last few years, China has enacted a preliminary regulatory framework for M&A transactions. The framework, while not complete, provides greater guidance for foreign investors engaging in M&A transactions and standardises practices that have developed over the last few years. The following is a list of the major M&A rules and regulations.

❑ *"Provisional Rules on Mergers and Acquisitions of Domestic Enterprises by Foreign Investors"*, jointly issued by the MoC, SAT, SAIC and SAFE in March 2003, established the first comprehensive regulation aimed at providing consistent standards for all types of M&A activities involving foreign investment.

❑ *"Tentative Provisions on the Use of Foreign Investment to Reorganise State-Owned Enterprises"*, jointly issued by the SDRC, MoF, SAIC and SAFE in January 2003, acknowledged the goal to invigorate SOEs through foreign equity ownership, and the government gave the green light to foreign investors to restructure unlisted SOEs.

❑ *"Issues Relevant to the Transfer of State Shares and Legal Person Shares in Listed Companies to Foreign Investors Circular"*, jointly issued by the CSRC, MoF and SDRC in November 2002, lifted the 1995 moratorium on foreign acquisition of state-owned equity interests from China's listed companies.

❑ Specifically for the financial services sector, *"Administration of Investment and Equity Participation in Chinese-invested Financial Institutions by Offshore Financial Institutions Procedures"*, issued by the China Banking Regulatory Commission (CBRC) in December 2003, established a legal framework and transparency requirements for equity investment by foreign investors.

❑ *"Measures on the Takeovers of Listed Companies"* and *"Measures for the Administration of Disclosure of the Changes in Shareholdings of Listed Companies"*, issued by the CSRC in September 2002, provided fairly detailed guidelines with respect to corporate takeover activities.

Major government agencies in foreign M&A transactions

Ministry of Commerce: the MoC is the principal foreign investment regulator and has general supervisory and approval authority over M&A transactions. Its predecessor was the Ministry of Foreign Trade and Economic Cooperation (MOFTEC).

State Development and Reform Commission: the SDRC is responsible for both approving the foreign investment project application and supervising the restructuring of SOEs. Its predecessor was the SETC (The State Economic and Trade Commission).

State-Owned Assets Supervision and Administration Commission (SASAC): the SASAC has supervisory authority over state-owned assets and it will play a significant role in transactions targeting SOEs. It participates in approving the transaction and may also act as the seller of state assets through one of its designated agencies or companies.

China Securities Regulatory Commission: the CSRC is responsible for monitoring and regulating China's capital markets, and will be involved in M&A transactions related to listed companies.

State Administration of Foreign Exchange (SAFE): the SAFE is involved in M&A transactions that entail foreign-currency related considerations, such as foreign-currency denominated stocks.

State Administration of Industry and Commerce (SAIC): responsible for the registration of enterprises and the regulation of corporate practices such as advertising, trademarks, unfair competition, and consumer protection.

State Administration of Taxations (SAT): the highest tax authority in China.

These recent regulatory changes clearly demonstrate the Chinese government's determination to upgrade the legal infrastructure for foreign investments in China. Its pace in building a M&A legal framework from virtually ground zero has been truly impressive. In a relatively concerted effort, the different governmental agencies have jointly provided a viable framework for foreign M&A activities and have opened up significant new opportunities for the next wave of foreign investment in China.

Meanwhile, existing M&A laws, regulations, and measures, were all enacted piecemeal by different legislative authorities over the past few years. The complex approval system they set out (discussed in detail below as one of the Chinese characteristics of M&As) could be confusing even for experienced Chinese lawyers, and one can certainly be sure that this legal framework will continue to evolve as the existing M&A regulations are tested by forthcoming M&A transactions. 2006 kicked off with the joint release of what some market players understand as the "second QFII rule" (a detailed discussion on this can be found later in this chapter) by five government agencies, and more rules are reportedly in the pipeline to consolidate the existing segregated M&A guidelines. This is probably the beginning of a revamp of the comprehensive M&A framework that may lead to a more consistent and user-friendly M&A playing field for foreign investors in 2006 and beyond.

CHINESE CHARACTERISTICS OF THE M&A MARKET

Part II of this book discussed the Chinese characteristics of many financial products in China's stock market. The unique segregated share-ownership structure of Chinese listed companies has had a substantial impact on the pricing and trading behaviour of those financial products. In the M&A market, the same ownership structure – namely, the high percentage of state ownership and the dichotomy of tradable and nontradable shares – also creates unique features in foreign M&A investments.

Acquisition method: public tender offer or private agreement?

As discussed in Part I of this book, the majority of listed companies in China are SOEs, and they exhibit a unique segregated share-ownership structure and substantial state ownership. Specifically, only about one-third of the shares of the listed companies are freely tradable on the stock exchanges, whereas the remaining two-thirds are in the form of so-called state-owned shares and legal-person shares, which are not listed and are referred to as nontradable shares.

This segregated share-ownership structure leads to the two general approaches to gain corporate control in Chinese companies: one is takeover by public tender offer; the other by private agreement. The tradable shares of listed companies can be accumulated by public tender offer, whereas the nontradable shares (consisting of state shares and legal-person shares) can only be transferred through private negotiation and agreement.

Public takeovers in China: a long way to go
The first batch of hostile takeover cases occurred in China in 1993. Shenzhen Baoan, a company located where the Shenzhen Stock Exchange is based, first attempted to acquire Shanghai Yanzhong Industrial Co., a listed company in Shanghai that had no nontradable shares, through purchasing a large block of Yanzhong stocks on the public market. Soon after, Shenzhen Wanke took a similar measure to try to acquire Shanghai Shenhua Industrial Co., another listed company with no state ownership.

These takeovers all failed to close, as the CSRC quickly intervened and found that the bidders had breached takeover disclosure rules and other relevant securities regulations. But in general, public takeovers of listed companies are rare because in many listed companies the controlling interests are in the form of nontradable shares.

Because the publicly tradable shares typically constitute a mere minority interest in the listed companies, a public tender offer is not a generally feasible method for acquiring corporate control in China. From the first batch of hostile takeover cases in China (see box) to date, successful public takeovers are not only few and far between, but also have only occurred where the target companies had few nontradable shares.

Take, for example, the well-publicised takeover by AB of Harbin Brewery in 2004 (which will be discussed in detail later in a case study). A hostile foreign acquisition via a public tender offer was possible in the case of Harbin Brewery because it had an unusual shareholder base: Harbin Brewery had 40% of its shares listed on the Hong Kong Stock Exchange and more than 50% of its ownership was held by two international investment entities before AB took over corporate control.

Therefore, for a typical listed company with substantial state ownership, an external investor, one way or the other, has to deal with its nontradable shares for a controlling interest in it. For many listed companies, the acquisition of nontradable shares through private negotiation is probably the most direct way of acquiring a controlling or significant interest. Alternatively, foreign investors could also acquire controlling interests in the parent company of the listed company (which holds the nontradable shares) to gain indirect control, which happened in the Carlyle case discussed later in this chapter.

As discussed throughout this book, the Chinese government is currently making efforts to make all shares in listed companies become tradable (the so-called full-flotation reform). As more and more listed companies carry out the reform, the proportion of nontradable shares in listed companies is decreasing. A new rule issued in early 2006, however, essentially keeps those companies reachable by foreign investors via strategic investments (see "Prospect" section later in this chapter). In the near future, therefore, private negotiation should remain the main method of corporate takeover in China whereas public tender offers may gradually gain momentum post the share reform.

Complex approval process

Because of the substantial state ownership in the listed companies, China's government agencies act as both regulator and seller. They play a much broader role in reviewing and approving deal-specific arrangements than the typical role of antitrust or competition regulators in foreign jurisdictions. For instance, the government may have political and social concerns regarding a potential M&A transaction that extend well beyond the deal's direct economic consequences. In some extreme cases, social concerns may even be in direct conflict with the commercial aspects of the transactions.

For example, potential post-M&A employee layoffs may be examined to balance economic interests and social stability. The acquiring foreign company essentially has a social responsibility with respect to the workers in the target company who are likely to become unemployed following the transaction. In fact, the foreign acquiring company in many cases may need to submit a "resettlement plan" for the employees as part of its application package, because potential social unrest is an important concern for China's approving authorities.

Consequently, there is a higher level of government participation in M&A transactions in China than is typical in other jurisdictions. Despite the recent relaxation on foreign investment restrictions, pervasive government approval requirements remain a distinctive feature of M&A transactions in China.

Firstly, while the new regulations have been vastly expanded to permit foreign investors to acquire most types of enterprise in China (including asset or equity acquisitions of foreign invested enterprises (FIEs), domestic enterprises, SOEs and listed companies), distinct regulatory mechanisms are applicable to the acquisition of each type of corporate entity (see a high level categorisation in the table below). Such a corporate form-differentiated legal treatment remains fairly common in China's legal system.

In addition, the state sector provisions also impose stringent requirements with respect to the transfer of state-owned assets. The authorities require state-owned and legal-person shares to be priced through competitive bidding, and the share transfer price should also be based on a compulsory state asset valuation by authorised appraisers. To attract mid and long-term investments instead of short-term speculation, the rules also provide that a 12-month lock-up period applies before foreign investors can transfer their acquired holdings of state and legal-person shares.

Finally, foreign investors need to comply with China's state policies on the direction of foreign investments, which prohibit or limit

Table 1 Various M&A regulatory regimes for different forms of target companies

Form of target company	Applicable rules (non-exhaustive)
Non-foreign invested domestic enterprise	❑ *Provisional Rules on Mergers and Acquisitions of Domestic Enterprises by Foreign Investors*
Foreign invested enterprise (FIE)	❑ The laws and regulations relevant to FIEs ❑ *Several Procedures of Equity Changes of FIEs*
Non-listed state-owned enterprise (SOE)	❑ The laws and regulations relevant to SOE restructurings ❑ *Tentative Provisions on the Use of Foreign Investment to Reorganise State-Owned Enterprises*
Listed company (state-owned, foreign invested or private-owned)	❑ *Measures on the Takeovers of Listed Companies* ❑ *Measures for the Administration of Disclosure of the Changes in Shareholdings of Listed Companies* ❑ *Circular Regarding the Transfer of State-Owned Shares and Legal-Person Shares of Listed Companies to Foreign Parties*

foreign capital in certain sectors. This aspect will be discussed in the next section in detail.

As such, a thorough understanding of the applicable regulatory framework and the regulatory roles is essential for the successful closing of an M&A transaction. The challenge for foreign investors, though, is how to implement the Chinese aspects of the M&A deal on time to meet the global timetable. As M&A market practices become tested, validated and gradually standardised, the approval process should become increasingly efficient to make M&A transactions a truly viable method for accessing the Chinese market.

Industry/sector guidelines

Notwithstanding the opportunities provided by the new legal framework, foreign acquisitions still need to comply with the foreign investment control system in China. The State Council and other regulatory authorities periodically publish and update the Foreign Investment Guidelines and the Catalogue for the Guidance of Foreign Investment. The investment project classification by the Guidelines and Catalogue has an impact on both the approval process and the permissible level of foreign equity holdings.

Table 2 Completed inbound M&A in China with a deal size above US$100 million (2004–2005)

	Target name	Acquirer name	Deal value (US$ million)
1	China Construction Bank-H	Bank Of America Corp.	2,500.0
2	P&G-Hutchinson Ltd	Procter & Gamble Co.	1,800.0
3	Bank Of Communications Co-H	HSBC Holdings plc	1,747.1
4	China Construction Bank-H	Temasek Holdings	1,466.0
5	Ping An Insurance Group Co-H	HSBC Holdings plc	1,039.3
6	Alibaba.Com Corp.	Yahoo! Inc	1,000.0
7	Successful Road Corp.	China Merchants Hldgs Pac Ltd	332.2
8	Huaxia Bank Co Ltd-A	Consortium	326.7
9	Shenzhen Water Group	Veolia Environnement	314.1
10	Hunan Valin Steel Tube & -A	Mittal Steel Co. NV	314.0
11	Hymall Commercial Retail Group	Tesco plc	259.6
12	Meiya Power Co. Ltd	BTU Group	220.0
13	Bank Of Beijing Co. Ltd	ING Groep NV-CVA	215.1
14	Shuangma Investment Group	LaFarge SA	160.0
15	Shenzhen Development Bank-A	Newbridge Capital Ltd	149.3
16	Sewing Machine Business	Kohlberg & Co. Ltd	134.6
17	Plantation Timber Products	Carter Holt Harvey Ltd	134.0
18	Chinese Brewing Unit	Inbev NV	131.5
19	Chinese Brewing Unit	Inbev NV	131.5
20	Huaxia Bank Co Ltd-A	Pangaea Capital Management S	125.0

Source: Bloomberg, as of December 2005

The Guidelines and Catalogue divide foreign investment projects by industry sector into four categories, namely:

❑ Encouraged;
❑ Permitted;
❑ Restricted: no acquisition of a controlling interest is allowed if the target is in a restricted category where the Chinese party must have the controlling interest;
❑ Prohibited: no acquisitions are allowed if the target in a prohibited category.

Thus a preliminary step in any M&A transaction or Chinese investment project is to confirm the status of the industry sector in the foreign investment catalogue.

Reflecting its WTO accession commitments regarding market access, China published a new set of foreign investment guidelines effective from 1 April, 2002, replacing the provisional guidelines promulgated in 1995 and opening up many previously prohibited categories to foreign investors. The guidelines are periodically updated by the governmental authorities.

According to China's WTO accession commitments, the restrictions in respect of most of the industrial or service sectors will be phased out according to different timetables over a period of six years from 11 December, 2001. For example, in 2004 China published regulations that will, for the first time, permit foreign firms to establish trading and distribution companies outside the coastal bonded zones.

The banking and insurance, beverage, retail/consumer goods, and electronic/technology sectors have dominated the recent list of large foreign M&A deals in China. (See table below for transactions with a deal size of more than US$100 million in 2004 and 2005). The case analyses in the following section will examine a few landmark transactions in these active sectors.

CASE 1: BANKING SECTOR – NEWBRIDGE/SDB
Background: China's state bank reform

China has made attracting foreign strategic investors/partners a key component of its banking reform strategy. This policy trend is well supported by the recently issued *Administration of Investment and Equity Participation in Chinese-invested Financial Institutions by Offshore Financial Institutions Procedures* issued by the China Banking Regulatory Commission (CBRC) in December 2003, which significantly improves the transparency of the legal framework for foreign investments in domestic financial institutions.

Equity investments in Chinese banks could be a win-win situation for both foreign investors and China's government. China expects foreign investors to transfer product expertise, risk-management technology and best practices to Chinese banks, and ultimately to enhance Chinese banks' reputations in global and domestic capital markets. Meanwhile, foreign investors could benefit from local partners' established franchise, customer base and distribution network to capture the growth opportunities in China, as the Chinese financial industry is gradually liberalised by relaxed regulation.

After years of hesitancy, American and European financial services companies have been investing aggressively in China's banking sector in recent years. There is a growing sense around the world that now is the time to begin creating a platform to offer financial services products and lay the groundwork for more cross-border deals with Chinese companies in the near future. Many of the largest foreign financial institutions have formed joint ventures or strategic stakes in Chinese banks, brokerage houses and insurance companies, and the list of large foreign investors is growing rapidly and impressively (see table below for a list of major foreign acquisitions in China's banking sector during the past five years).

Of course, China's banking reform is still in the earliest stage and foreign investors will have their own. The Chinese banks' poor asset quality, dysfunctional corporate governance, underdeveloped capacity to manage risk and the complex legal and regulatory

Table 3 Major foreign acquisitions in China's banking sector (2001–2005)

Chinese banks	Investor	Date completed	Deal size (US$ m)	Investment as % of bank (%)
Industrial and Commercial Bank of China (ICBC)	GS, Allianz and American Express	MOU signed in August 2005	Est. US$3.7bn	10.00
Bank of China (BOC)	Royal Bank of Scotland and co-investors	August 2005	3,100	10.00
	Temasek	August 2005	3,100	10.00
China Construction Bank (CCB)	Temasek	July 2005	1,400	5.10
	Bank of America	June 2005	2,500	9.00
Bank of Communications	HSBC	August 2004	1,747	19.90
Shenzhen Development Bank	Newbridge	May 2004	149	17.90
Industrial Bank	Hang Seng Bank	December 2003	208.0	15.98
Shanghai Pudong Development Bank	Citibank	December 2002	72.0	5.00
Bank of Shanghai	HSBC	December 2001	62.6	8.00

Source: public news reports

environment in which they operate all pose thorny issues for foreign investors.

More specifically, foreign investors' management control in the venture is a critical issue. Although China actively attracts foreign ownership to strengthen the competitiveness of its domestic banks, it is still keen to retain control of the banks through Chinese parties. The current regulations have specified 20% as the maximum shareholding a single foreign investor may acquire in a domestic financial institution, and 25% the limit on aggregate ownership by all foreign investors. In the case of Newbridge's acquisition of Shenzhen Development Bank (SDB), the shareholding structure of SDB was unusually fragmented to allow Newbridge to take control of SDB by acquiring close to 20% equity ownership.

Newbridge's acquisition of Shenzhen Development Bank
Initial investment by Newbridge
In December 2004, Newbridge Capital Ltd, a major US-based buyout firm, completed the purchase of 348.1 million nontradable shares of SDB from four government shareholders in 2004 for 1.2 billion yuan (US$149 million). SDB is the smallest of the five Chinese banks traded on the domestic stock exchanges, and the share ownership structure of SDB is unusually fragmented. Holding just 18% of equity, Newbridge has become the largest shareholder of the bank and SDB the first Chinese bank controlled by overseas investors.

Lack of effective control is a major concern for foreign investors in many acquisition deals. Minority ownership significantly limits foreign investors' influence on the management of and operations in Chinese banks, but following its SDB acquisition Newbridge has become the largest shareholder of the bank, which enables Newbridge to bring in good practices and make necessary changes.

As the controlling shareholder of SDB, Newbridge has the right to appoint the chairman and top managers of the bank. In April 2005, SDB received banking regulatory approval to have two foreign professionals head the bank. Frank Newman, chairman of Newbridge, became the first foreigner to lead a commercial bank in China.

Newbridge's turnaround experiences and international contacts are sorely needed at SDB. The bank is working to improve its system ahead of the December 2006 timeline when China will allow foreign banks to operate more freely and conduct local currency business. The restructuring guided by Newbridge intends to change the bank into a more modern financial institution meeting international standards. In general, the private equity business model, with its emphasis on effecting operational change at portfolio company level, fits China's SOE/bank reform blueprint nicely.

How long will it take to turn SDB around? This billion-dollar question intrigues not only the private equity community but also the Chinese government. Once Newbridge has successfully restructured SDB into a modern bank with sound practices, it can certainly expect a stellar return on the way out, as it did earlier in 2005 when it sold its stake in Korea First Bank to Standard Chartered. But there is more to this venture. A successful turnaround of SDB will become an important milestone in China's banking reform campaign and its success could have a ripple effect throughout the Chinese banking system.

Pending stock acquisition by GE

In October 2005, SDB announced that General Electric Co. (GE) agreed to buy a 7% stake in SDB valued at about US$100 million. The two companies have signed the purchase agreement, yet the deal is still pending approval by the Chinese regulatory authorities and SDB's shareholders.

GE's consumer finance unit is expected to acquire its equity ownership in newly issued shares from SDB. If regulators and shareholders approve the deal, GE will become the bank's second-largest shareholder and second foreign investor. Newbridge's holding is expected to drop from 17.9% to approximately 16.58% as a result of the new offering. GE's investment would increase the bank's total foreign ownership to nearly 25%, the maximum permitted foreign ownership in a domestic commercial bank.

GE's investment was priced at a 15 percent discount to the stock's average closing price in the previous 20 trading days. It reflects a purchase price of 5.2466 yuan (US$0.649) per share, which is 47.8% higher than Newbridge's purchase price of 3.55 yuan (US$0.439) per share. GE's price is also more than twice SDB's net asset value (NAV) per share of 2.51 yuan (US$0.310), a price floor that the regulatory authorities set for the transfer of state-owned assets.

The investment by GE Capital could be viewed as another major step by Newbridge to bring international expertise to the struggling SDB. The expertise that GE can bring to the table, particularly in the consumer lending area, should be helpful in moving SDB away from corporate lending toward a retail focus. The new capital from GE will also help SDB's capital adequacy. If GE's investment plan is approved, SDB's core capital adequacy ratio is likely to reach up to 4%, which would qualify SDB to issue subordinated debt to further improve its balance sheet.

Exit through strategic investors?

Meanwhile, the agreement with GE has raised the question in the market as to whether Newbridge is contemplating exiting its investment in SDB through strategic investors such as GE Capital or the like. After all, Newbridge's investment has already shown substantial returns on the book.

Date		Price (in yuan)
October 2004	Purchase price per share	3.55
28 September, 2005*	A share trading price	5.76
	Theoretical return	62%

*SDB trading at the exchange was suspended on 28 September, 2005 for major corporate transactions, ie, the negotiation of the stock acquisition agreement with GE.

At the same time, GE's financing unit, like many other multinational financial institutions, is aggressively seeking partners in China's financial markets. Investment in SDB should pave the way for GE to enter China's evolving consumer finance market, and eventually the commercial lending and banking market. Not surprisingly, many players in the market have the same question in mind: is this the beginning of Newbridge's exit from its SDB investment?

Unfortunately, the market must remain in suspense for a while. The Chinese stock market is currently undergoing share ownership reform to float the nontradable shares, and the CSRC has made it a policy that listed companies must complete the share ownership reform first before they can raise new financing through equity. In SDB's public release in late October 2005, SDB confirmed its agreement with GE but emphasised that the company's first priority is share ownership reform.

Thus in the near term, SDB will most probably first hold a shareholder meeting to approval its share reform plan, to be followed by a separate shareholder meeting to seek approval on the GE investment. Once the next act of the Newbridge/SDB investment unfolds, the M&A market in China will probably see further innovative deal structures in the banking sector.

CASE 2: BREWERY SECTOR: AB/HARBIN BEER
Overview: AB/SAB contest over Harbin Brewery

The brewing industry remains one of the few sectors where China has allowed 100% foreign ownership. However, many large-sized breweries in China are controlled by one large domestic shareholder. It is therefore quite difficult for "external capital" to obtain a controlling interest in those companies.

But the shareholding structure of Harbin Brewery – before being taken over by Anheuser-Busch (AB) – was quite unusual. Harbin Brewery, a company located in a north-eastern province in China, was listed in Hong Kong. The public owns approximately 40% of the equity ownership, and two international investment entities control more than 50% of the shares. Such a shareholding situation provided the right set-up for an acquisition battle.

In 2004, AB and SAB Miller (SAB) launched a bidding war for the controlling interest in Harbin Brewery. AB eventually won the battle by paying a substantial premium over the trading price of Harbin Brewery stocks. This was a major event in China's stock market development, as it is a rare corporate takeover of a listed company via a public tender offer and it marked the first time that a foreign company launched a hostile takeover bid for a mainland company. The following table lists the major events in this saga.

GCH: Little-known winner

The behind-the-scenes player that set the stage for this dramatic takeover contest was Global Conduit Holdings (GCH), a private fund that was little known. From limited public disclosure, GCH is an investment holding company registered in the British Virgin Islands (BVI). It is owned by a group of investors, with no single investor owning more than 20% of GCH interests. The parent company of GCH, Capital Select Enterprise Ltd, fully owns GCH and is

Table 4 Major events in AB/SAB contest for Harbin Brewery

Date	Event
June 2003	SAB, the world's second largest multinational brewery, became the largest shareholder of Harbin Brewery when it purchased a 29.6% stake in the Chinese brewery and signed an "exclusive strategic investor agreement"
March 2004	Forty days before AB's 2 May, 2004 announcement, Global Conduit Holdings Limited (GCH) had purchased a 29.07% stake (in the form of nontradable shares) in Harbin Brewery from the original second largest shareholder for HK$0.947 billion
1 May, 2004	Harbin Brewery unilaterally terminated its strategic cooperation contract with SAB
2 May, 2004	AB, the world's largest brewery and a traditional competitor of SAB, announced that it had purchased GCH, a company registered in the British Virgin Islands, at a price of HK$1.08 billion (US$138 million). GCH was purchasing 29.07% stock in Harbin Brewery from the Harbin municipal government
2 May, 2004	SAB announced a general tender offer in a bid to become the controlling shareholder of Harbin Brewery. SAB offered an attractive price of HK$4.3 (US$0.55) per share, which was 33.3% higher than Harbin Brewery's closing price of HK$3.225 (US$0.41) per share on 30 April
19 May, 2004	AB held a news conference to announce that GCH's acquisition of Harbin shares had been approved by authorities
1 June, 2004	AB made a counter-offer of HK$5.58 per share, approximately 30 percent higher than SAB's tender offer price
3 June, 2004	SAB announced it was terminating its own tender offer and sold its share holdings to its rival and walked away with US$211 million and more than 100% return on its less than one-year investment

also registered in BVI. There was little information available on the ultimate investors in GCH and Capital Select.

Before launching the general tender offer, AB acquired its major shareholding in Harbin Brewery through its purchase of GCH, whose only assets were Harbin Brewery shares that had been acquired from Harbin Brewery. As its name might suggest, GCH functions pretty much as a conduit company in a series of complex transfer transactions.

On 20 March, 2004, the Harbin municipal government sold its Harbin Brewery shares to GCH for HK$947 million (US$121.57 million). The shares that GCH purchased were state-owned shares, representing 29.07% of Harbin Brewery's equity ownership. Because state-owned assets were involved, the purchase was subject to regulatory approval. The approval was granted in May without much complication, as the purchase price far exceeded the book value of the assets (which is a price floor set by the Ministry of Finance for state-owned asset transfers).

The most interesting aspect is that GCH transferred the shares to AB even before its purchase of the Harbin Brewery shares was finally approved and settled. Because GCH had never been the true owner of the Harbin shares at any time, GCH was not obligated to disclose its internal corporate organisation under the corporate acquisition rules in Hong Kong. Post the takeover, GCH and Capital Select are controlled by AB, and the mysterious owners of GCH will probably remain permanently confidential.

But no matter who the ultimate beneficiaries are, the highly structured execution by GCH was truly remarkable. It successfully exited from its shareholding with a substantial premium, leaving the contest to AB and SAB. Without being a true shareholder for a single day, GCH and its investors cashed in more than HK$130 million (US$16.84 million).

CASE 3: MANUFACTURING SECTOR: CARLYLE/XCMC
Foreign acquisition of absolute controlling interest

On 25 October, 2005, global private equity firm The Carlyle Group announced that it had reached a definitive agreement to acquire an 85% stake in XCMC for $375 million. The Carlyle transaction represents the first buy-out of a Chinese state-owned company by a foreign financial investor.

XCMC is the largest construction machinery manufacturer and distributor in China. Its products are widely used in infrastructure construction, coalmines and power plants. In 2004, XCMC had total annual sales of 6.59 billion yuan (US$815 million). The deal represents the first time a leading SOE in China has sold such a high level of control to a foreign private equity firm.

Following the acquisition, Carlyle owned an 85% stake in XCMC, with the state-owned parent company, Xuzhou Construction Machinery Group (XCMG), keeping the remaining 15 percent share. Carlyle's high percentage ownership of XCMC triggered a general offer to the shareholders of a subsidiary of XCMC, which was listed on the Shenzhen Stock Exchange (see box).

General offer obligation in acquisition of listed companies

The PRC Securities Law provides that a mandatory tender offer requirement is applicable to a takeover of more than 30% of the outstanding shares of a listed company. In connection with a takeover, the investor must make a public offer to all existing shareholders unless exempted by the CSRC from such an obligation.

In April 2004, Samsung Corning completed a share acquisition of Seg Samsung Co., which is regarded as the first case of foreign acquisition of an A share listed company. The mandatory tender offer was waived by CSRC in the transaction for case-specific reasons.

The Carlyle transaction will trigger a mandatory general offer to the shareholders of Xuzhou Science & Technology Co. Ltd (XSTC). XSTC is a 43%-owned subsidiary of XCMC and an A share company listed on the Shenzhen Stock Exchange. With 85% ownership of XCMC, Carlyle has acquired more than 30% of the share ownership indirectly, which triggers its obligation to make a public tender offer. This will become the first general tender offer to the shareholders of a Chinese A share listed company executed by a foreign investor.

Additionally, the transaction was the first time that a Chinese SOE had ever been privatised through a controlled auction process pursuant to international standards. XCMC had been in the midst of a restructuring programme aimed at developing an international brand name in a market dominated by multinational giants such as Caterpillar Inc. The company thus was looking into foreign investment to bring in international market exposure, technological innovation and new investment projects.

Amid the two-year-long talks, XCMC reportedly attracted six international bidders including Carlyle and Caterpillar. A professionally run auction process was set up to maximise this SOE's asset value as well as identify the best partners. The company eventually named Carlyle as its preferred bidder, whereas Caterpillar was apparently less attractive because it would have competed directly against XCMC. The deal clearing price from the international auction was two times the XCMC's NAV, which comfortably passed the NAV price floor that regulatory authorities set for transfer of state-owned assets.

Opportunities and challenges in SOE privatisation

China has long sought to revive and privatise thousands of troubled SOEs that are a legacy of its centrally planned economic past. In the midst of China's SOE reform, local governments have sold hundreds of state-owned companies, mainly to private Chinese buyers. This privatisation process has become politically sensitive in recent years and has led to widespread public indignation over the alleged fraudulent transfer of state assets in some transactions (see the detailed discussion in the next chapter on management buy-outs).

As a foreign investor, US-based Carlyle is not expected to raise such controversy in this transaction. The XCMC buy-out is truly a landmark in that for the first time a foreign financial investor was permitted to acquire absolute ownership control over a major SOE. This new development signals that the government recognises that ownership is not always as important as existence. For many loss-making, poorly managed SOEs, China is looking into foreign investors for international capital and technological expertise to make those firms truly competitive in the global market.

On the other hand, the buy-out took more than two years to complete, as Carlyle, the municipal government that owned XCMC and provincial authorities in charge of managing state-owned assets, wrangled over a host of complex deal points, in particular possible staff reductions and cost-cutting at XCMC. Even with the definitive acquisition agreement, the deal still requires final approval from China's central government. The lengthy negotiation and complex approval processes that are ubiquitous in most foreign M&A deals remain a major challenge to international investors.

What next? Carlyle has a multiple-year plan to convert XCMC from a largely domestic operation into a global competitor. According to news reports, the XCMC acquisition agreement has limitations on Carlyle's right to transfer its ownership to industry companies in the same sector. One possible exit for Carlyle could be to transform XCMC and have it listed on overseas exchanges in the future. The private equity funds in Asia are certain to look closely at every aspect of this deal as a case study for tapping the hottest private equity market in the world.

PROSPECT

Going forward, the presence of a rich field of acquisition targets will continue driving foreign M&A growth in China. The restructuring of the SOE sector is a high priority in the next stage of China's economic reform – China currently still has tens of thousands of SOEs that need new capital injection or strategic restructuring. Neither the state banks nor domestic capital markets are sufficiently robust to fund all the capital necessary to restructure the state sector. Foreign M&A activities are set to grow exponentially as China actively attracts international investors to further its SOE restructuring and privatisation campaign.

In the near term, foreign investors still face institutional and political obstacles in the M&A market. Many restrictions stem from the idiosyncratic shareholding structure of Chinese listed companies, which are characterised by a dominant state-owned interest and the co-existence of tradable and nontradable shares. These features have led to difficult issues in deal execution, including regulatory uncertainties, complex due diligence and difficulties in exiting, as well as extensive government intervention and approval requirements.

However, foreign investors have reason to be optimistic. The Chinese government is fully aware of the problems caused by the segregated share-ownership structure, and it has launched the nontradable share reform as its current top priority in reviving the stock market. The ongoing campaign to float the nontradable shares and the recently released foreign A share investment rule should add new catalysts to the foreign M&A market.

Floating nontradable shares

As discussed in more detail in Chapter 1, the Chinese stock market is undergoing a fundamental reform on the "segregated equity ownership" of the listed companies, potentially making all shares of the listed companies tradable in the A share market. The government kicked off the pilot programme in May 2005 with four medium-sized listed companies. By the end of 2005, approximately 300 companies (out of roughly 1,500 listed companies on the domestic stock exchanges) had announced their share reform plans.

Investors have generally reacted positively to the fast expansion of the full-flotation campaign, as they view the bigger than expected size and scope of participating firms as a sign of the government's commitment to, and confidence in, the reform process. If this reform is carried out thoroughly and successfully, the share ownership structure and corporate governance of Chinese listed companies should become more in line with international standards. Combined with the newly issued A share investment rule (detailed in the next sub-section), popular techniques in Western markets such as public tender offers may then become more feasible in China's M&A market.

Furthermore, the full-flotation effort should provide foreign investors with additional exit alternatives. In most of the foreign acquisition deals to date, investors have acquired nontradable shares from government-controlled institutions. By definition, those shares are not freely tradable in the domestic A share market. To repackage the acquired company and list it on the Hong Kong Stock Exchange is a potential option, but listing standards in the H share market may pose a challenge to many Chinese firms with respect to company net asset levels and the size of stock offering. The full-flotation campaign potentially offers a new exit alternative to foreign investors, as they may be able to sell their holdings in the A share market once the share reform is complete.

New rule on foreign A share investment

The reform of "segregated share ownership" also transformed the playing field for acquisition of nontradable shares. As discussed earlier, foreign investors without QFII status used to be able to acquire a stake in listed companies by purchasing nontradable shares through private agreement. With the proportion of nontradable shares in listed companies decreasing through the reform, previously acquirable nontradable shares will suddenly be placed out of the reach of foreign investors not holding QFII status (as those nontradable shares are turning into public A shares).

Apparently intending to ensure that listed companies remain reachable to those investors, five government bureaus issued a joint rule at the beginning of 2006 to allow non-QFII foreign investors to purchase strategic stakes in tradable A shares from companies that have completed the share-reform programme (the G share companies). Under this rule, qualified investors – essentially those with at least US$100 million total capital or US$500 million under management – could purchase stocks from existing shareholders or new shares issued by those companies.

Although the rule imposes a minimum deal size of 10% of the listed company and a three-year holding period, foreign investors that take such strategic stakes would enjoy the liquidity of the public stock market at the end of the investment period. Reflecting market optimism that the new rule may lead a new wave of foreign M&A activity, the stock market responded strongly and positively on the day of the rule release: the New Shanghai Composite Index (a G share index discussed in Chapter 6) rose by 1.24% in magnified trading volume.

CONCLUSION

Following decades of economic reform, the Chinese economy has improved dramatically in its industry structure, legal framework and investment environment. These internal changes in China and the significant interest of foreign investors in accessing the huge Chinese market all led to a new wave of foreign investments in China through M&As (compared to the first wave of JV investments years ago).

The rapid increase in foreign M&A activities is particularly fuelled by the ongoing restructuring and privatisation of the SOEs and a relative newcomer to the stage – leveraged buy-outs by private equity firms. China has embarked on comprehensively upgrading the M&A legal framework to attract foreign investments to its SOE reform, which creates new openings and opportunities for foreign financial investors.

Although investors still face institutional hurdles such as regulatory uncertainties and a complex execution process, China promises to be an exciting M&A market in the coming years. As regulations are relaxed and market access expands, foreign investors will have a greater range of structuring options for pursuing investment opportunities. The ongoing full-flotation programme and the recent rule on strategic A share purchasing post the share reform should create further catalysts for foreign M&A activities. From Newbridge/ SDB and Carlyle/XCMC to many similar landmark transactions, the private equity investors are setting new precedents each and every time: foreign M&A investment in China is entering a brave new world.

10

Management Buy-Outs

The aggregate size of the assets in China's state-owned enterprises (SOEs) is in the order of the magnitude of US$1 trillion. The management executives in the SOEs, however, in contrast to their US counterparts, hold far fewer equity holdings and less personal wealth in their companies. These facts have given investors great hope of opportunities to team up with the Chinese executives in management buy-out (MBO) transactions. However, MBOs in China have sparked unparalleled public debates compared with any other stock market transactions. Since its debut in China seven years ago, MBO development in China has been anything but smooth.

For example, at the beginning of 2003 when MBO growth was at its peak, many stock market participants enthusiastically expected a "year of MBOs", but everything ground to a sudden halt months later following a regulatory moratorium on MBOs. When the prohibition was lifted in 2004, the market saw heated debate on the fairness of such transactions and in some extreme cases, senior management in certain companies arrested for alleged fraud.

In mid 2005, MBOs in China entered into a new era following the first official MBO regulation. The new provisional regulation officially put a brake on MBO transactions with the largest SOEs but simultaneously validated and standardised such transactions with smaller companies. Considering the sheer size of SOEs and the limited financing resources available for company management in Chinese companies, the MBO market in the next few years will undoubtedly become one of the most tantalising challenges and opportunities for foreign investors.

BACKGROUND TO MBOS

In an MBO, the managers and executives of a company purchase the controlling interest in a company from existing shareholders. The management team usually joins hands with financial institutions or investment funds in the acquisition process, because an MBO is a complicated process that requires significant capital as well as transaction expertise.

Thus there are three main parties involved in an MBO: the existing shareholders of the company who hold the controlling interest prior to the MBO, the management team looking to acquire an equity interest and the financial investor seeking a return on the invested capital.

MBOs have assumed an important role in corporate restructurings besides M&As. An MBO often presents a more viable option than a takeover as the depth of knowledge and experience remains within the company. Additionally, MBOs have been widely considered as one path to efficient corporate management because they empower managers to own their own business hence eliminating the "agency" problems in a modern corporation (see box for discussion).

MBOs and the "agency problem"

The "agency problem" in corporate governance theory arises from the separation of ownership (shareholders) and management in modern corporations. The management, in theory, acts as the agent of the shareholder with a fiduciary duty to maximise the shareholders' interests. In reality, however, managers, like other individuals, will act to maximise their own interests when facing an economic choice. In short, management and shareholders generally have different interests.

Modern corporations have tried to deal with this so-called agency problem in several ways. Firstly, performance-based stock option plans or bonuses are introduced to bind the management to serve the shareholders' interests. Secondly, corporations signal to external investors, by linking the managers' incentives to those of the shareholders, the managers' resolve to maximise the value of the firm. Finally, monitoring devices are designed to police management. The total costs of such binding, signalling, and monitoring, as well as the misbehaviour that continues in the face of these steps, are collectively referred to as agency costs.

From a theoretical viewpoint, the MBO deals could potentially minimise agency costs by combining ownership with management. Through an MBO, managers become the sole or dominant owners of

> the company, so the firm's destiny is their own (in other words, the for-
> mer agent is now the owner). Because the management, not dispersed
> shareholders, will enjoy the full benefits of the firm's upside potential
> (as well as the full downside risk), managers have powerful incentives
> to assure the post-MBO company's success.

On the other hand, MBOs present hard questions on management's duty to be loyal to the company shareholders. Debate over
MBOs has centred around two major issues: fairness to shareholders and possible conflicts of interest between the management/
acquirer and shareholders. For one thing, the management has a
superior information advantage about the company over the shareholders. For another, arms-length price negotiations are hard to
imagine when the management is both the buyer and seller in the
MBO transaction.

These two issues have been particularly complex and controversial in China. The agency problem has additional twists in China's
listed companies due to the segregated equity ownership structure,
ie, the majority shareholders of a typical listed company are the state-
owned institutions holding the nontradable shares. The involvement
of state-owned assets further complicates the MBO process (in particular, the pricing of an MBO). MBOs in China thereby exhibit
unique characteristics that set them apart from the MBO practice in
more developed markets and the short seven-year development history has been surrounded by public debate and controversies.

MBOS AND CHINA'S SOE REFORM

MBOs have, in recent years, played an important role in privatising state-owned enterprises in China. In November 2003, the
State-owned Assets Supervision and Administration Commission
(SASAC) released a survey of SOEs in 23 provinces including 16
major cities, which showed that 85 percent of the restructured SOEs
had successfully completed the process of transferring ownership.
According to statistics from the SASAC survey, half of the SOEs
that had completed restructuring had done so through MBOs.

Two factors make MBO an attractive measure for China's recent
SOE reform campaign. Firstly, an MBO theoretically provides an

alternative solution to the agency problem in a company, which is particularly complex in the Chinese context. Secondly, an MBO strengthens the stability of a firm's senior management team, because the current salary system of SOEs arguably cannot provide the necessary incentives for managers and stock-based compensation remains in the experimental stage in China.

Agency problems in SOEs

In China, the agency problem is exacerbated by the segregated equity ownership. The institutional feature that the state holds the controlling but nontradable shares adds a new twists to the principal/agent (shareholder/management) conflict in corporations. Thus, in a listed SOE, there are many conflicts of interest: tradable *versus* nontradable shareholders, government bureaucrats *versus* public investors and state government *versus* corporate managers are among the major ones. All these factors result in a phenomenon typically referred to as the "absence of a true owner".

On the one hand, the majority shareholder of the listed companies in theory is the state. The state as an invisible majority owner, however, cannot directly impose supervision over management. How about the state-owned institutions holding the nontradable shares? SASAC (see box, p. 211), the highest and the most powerful among all, remains in search of its ultimate role: a major shareholder, or a regulatory agency, or both?

On the other hand, investors in the public market are more concerned about short-term trading profits than corporate governance. As discussed earlier in the book, the turnover rate in China's stock market is very high, and the market is characterised by speculative trading instead of long-term investments. Part of the reason is that public market investors, being dispersed minority shareholders, realise they are not really equipped or empowered to act forcefully in enforcing corporate governance.

In short, there is no effective management supervision mechanism in China's listed companies. China has been promoting the institutional investors' base in the stock market of late, but it may take more time before those institutions become a significant force in imposing supervision over management in the listed companies. So, in the near term, MBOs are a direct, though drastic, solution for the agency problem in China's SOEs.

SASAC: regulator or controlling shareholder?

Founded in June 2003, SASAC (http://www.sasac.gov.cn/) is responsible for, among other functions, the appreciation of state-owned assets as well as guiding and supervising SOEs. In China's market economy reform, SASAC – as the supervisory body of state assets – has become one of the most active and important government agencies.

The functions of SASAC, as currently defined, are somewhat mixed. With respect to state assets, it behaves more like a major controlling shareholder. With respect to SOE reform, it acts more like a government regulatory entity.

The goals of SASAC are also manifold. The appreciation of state assets is a commercial objective, whereas promotion of a modern corporate governance system in SOEs is more of a regulatory and social issue. The former is a relatively concrete goal, while the latter is less quantifiable.

According to news reports, the Chinese legislature is currently drafting the State Asset Law, which is expected to further clarify SASAC's functions. Separately, the CSRC is promoting the board of director system in the SOEs to improve supervisory systems. In the future, SASAC will probably focus more on the controlling shareholder's role once the director systems are put in place in the SOEs.

Stability of Chinese companies' management

Compared with the US market where MBOs are mostly an economic activity by corporate managers, the MBOs of China's SOEs have an additional institutional context. That is, the managers of China's SOEs are not truly "hired from the market" as in mature market economies, but are, in effect, government officials appointed by the state.

As such, China's corporate executives have a dual role as managers and government officials. Unfortunately, they do not necessarily enjoy the best of both worlds. In fact, they may, on the one hand, act as managers but be subject to a strict salary system (with no equity-based incentives) for governmental officials. On the other hand, they may act as government officials to follow orders from the above but also be held responsible for the profit or loss of the companies as corporate managers.

Many efforts have been made to solve the conflicts of the managements' two roles. In the 1980s, the emphasis was on granting managers more autonomy in decision-making. However, that approach was soon abandoned because of the massive outflows of state assets to private hands as well as much mismanagement that worsened the financial situations of many SOEs. Then, in the 1990s, the government adopted the new policy of "grab the big, release the small" (*zhuada fangxiao*). The new approach ensures the state continues strict control over the large SOEs while effectively permitting small to medium-size companies to be privatised.

In this context, for the managers of SOEs who have built up their businesses from scratch, an MBO represents the best way to realise their dream of becoming the real bosses of their companies. As equity-based compensation packages such as employee stock options (ESOs) remain few and far between in the SOEs, the MBO has been used on many occasions as an alternative for a management incentive mechanism. Viewed from the other side of the equation, an MBO tends to be less disruptive than other SOE reform measures in maintaining a firm's stable growth, as the management team stays in the SOE's post-MBO restructuring.

MBO MARKET POTENTIAL AND CHALLENGES

Once widely accepted as an effective SOE reform measure, the MBO has grown rapidly in China since it was first imported in 1998. There is still much potential even after years of exponential growth in the MBO market.

For example, in 2003 when the market was full of enthusiasm for a "year of MBOs", a statistical report cited by the official *China Daily* newspaper valued state equity ownership in listed companies at 6 trillion yuan (US$725 billion). Meanwhile, the same report suggested that among all the companies listed on the Shanghai Stock Exchange, only 0.08% of the equities were held by the management of the listed companies. That shows the MBO market in China still has much room and demand for future growth.

However, until very recently there had been a lack of a well-developed legal framework following MBOs take off in China a few years ago. In a sense, it is a classic example of the "crossing a river by feeling the stones underneath" philosophy, a key theme (discussed in Chapter 1) throughout China's financial markets reform over the past two decades. As a result, the Chinese MBO market's brief seven-year history is characterised by many dramatic bumps and sudden turns (see box), which eventually led to the first official MBO regulation in 2005 that set up a new platform for next-generation MBO transactions.

Table 1 MBO development in China: a bumpy road

1998	Stone Group, a hi-tech company originally established as a "collectively owned enterprise" (a corporate form somewhere between a SOE and a private enterprise), became the first Chinese company to use the MBO to restructure its equity ownership structure
2000	GD Midea Holding Co. Ltd, a leading home appliances producer in Guangdong, became the first listed company to implement an MBO, which quickly led to many MBOs in small and medium-sized companies in China
2002	The CSRC and other regulatory agencies issued a series of regulations on corporate takeovers and the related disclosure requirements. The new rules indirectly established a legal framework for MBOs (a form of corporate takeover), leading to a new wave of MBOs that involved listed SOEs
January 2003	The market saw unprecedented enthusiasm in MBOs with SOEs. Many market players expected 2003 to be "a year of MBOs"
March 2003	The Ministry of Finance (MoF) issued its *Proposal on Temporary Suspension on MBO Examination and Approval."* This new policy effectively put all MBO applications (whether for listed or unlisted companies) in sudden suspension, pending on the future issuance of more detailed regulations
Late 2003	SASAC was established and in December 2003 the General Office of the State Council issued *"Opinions On Standardization of State Owned Enterprise Restructuring"*, which was interpreted to provide a conditional permit for MBO. A dozen leading listed companies launched MBOs soon after
Early 2004	The MBOs in listed companies reached a record high, including many well-known companies, such as home appliances giant Haier, drawing wide public attention to those transactions
Late 2004	Economist Larry Lang Hsien-ping, a professor at the Chinese University of Hong Kong, strongly questioned the fairness of the MBO transactions with large SOEs. His views sparked a nationwide debate among regulators, market participants and academics on whether MBOs are suitable for China's SOE reform
December 2004	The State Council expressly stated its view that MBOs of large SOEs should be forbidden whereas small and medium-sized companies could only execute MBOs with further regulations and guidance issued by SASAC
April 2005	SASAC issued the first official regulation on MBOs in China, which, interestingly, avoided the popular term MBO and used "transfer of state ownership to management" instead. The new rule officially puts a ban on MBOs of large SOEs, while acknowledging and permitting MBOs for small and medium-sized SOEs

UNIQUE CHARACTERISTICS OF CHINESE MBOS

A few major Chinese characteristics differentiate MBOs in China from their counterparts in more developed markets. Those include the pricing gap between nontradable shares and the publicly tradable A shares, the legal restrictions around the acquiring party in MBOs, the limited funding alternatives and the controversies around post-MBO cash-dividend policy.

MBO price – dichotomy of tradable and nontradable shares

Because of the segregated share ownership structure, the controlling ownership of China's listed companies is typically in the form of nontradable shares. Thus in most MBO transactions of listed SOEs in China, the shares are not acquired through the public A share market but rather the negotiated transfer of nontradable shares.

The prices of the nontradable shares and the corresponding A shares are drastically different. In the A share market, the demand for share investments far exceeds the supply so the A shares tend to trade at high P/E ratios and for many years were believed to be heavily overvalued. By contrast, there is no liquid market for the nontradable shares and the only possible reference for valuation is the shares' NAV.

As would be expected, in most completed MBOs so far, the acquisition price for the non-tradable shares was highly correlated to the NAV of the shares but had little correlation to the corresponding stock trading price in the A share market. Because of the large gap between the prices of the two markets (furthermore, many MBOs were priced at huge discounts even to the NAV), existing MBO practice has raised much public concern on the fairness of pricing.

The regulation in point is a rule by the MoF, which enforces a minimum price floor for state asset transfers at their NAV. However, the NAV floor neither guarantees that the state assets will be protected nor that state income from sales of state assets will be maximised.

For one thing, many state firms worth a lot more than their NAVs were sold off at less than their real market value, since a sale at just above NAV could legitimately take place (thus fulfilling the minimum requirements of the central government). For another, in cases where legal-person shares (a subsection of the nontradable shares) rather than state shares are involved, the NAV floor has not been universally applied, because some market participants argued that the NAV rule does not apply if no state asset is involved.

As the following table of selected cases shows, the MBO purchase price for nontradable shares was generally at a discount or on a par with the NAV per share. In cases where legal-person shares were transferred (technically no state-owned shares were involved), the MBO purchase prices were mostly at a significant discount to their respective NAV per share. These include GD Midea Holding Co., Shenzhen Fangda and Foshan Plastic Group Co. in the following table. On the other hand, in MBOs of state-owned shares, the NAV per share has been used as the MBO purchase price (ie, little or zero discount). These include DongTing Aquatic Products Co. and Shengli Investment Co. in the table below.

Additionally, compared with the public trading price for comparable A shares, the MBO price listed above only represents a small fraction of the A share trading price, as shown in the table below.

The NAV-based valuation approach, which has been prevalent in China's MBO market, raises a few issues. Above all, many in China believe that with the NAV method, state-owned assets are deeply undervalued when transferred through MBOs because the corresponding A shares are trading at a huge premium in the open market. Furthermore, the NAV method focuses more on the assets'

Table 2 Comparison of share purchase price and NAV in selected MBO transactions (yuan)

Listed companies with completed MBO		MBO purchase price per share	NAV per share	MBO price discount to NAV (%)
GD Midea Holding Co.	1st round	2.95	3.81	22.5
	2nd round	3.00	4.07	26.3
Shenzhen Fangda A	1st round	3.28	3.45	4.93
	2nd round	3.08		10.73
Foshan Plastic Group Co.		2.95	3.19	7.52
DongTing Aquatic Products		5.75	5.84	1.5
Shengli Investment		2.27	2.27	0

Data source: Securities Times (ZhenQuan Shi Bao), 11 December, 2002 and calculations by author

Table 3 MBO price as a percentage of corresponding A share price in selected MBO cases (yuan)

Listed companies with completed MBO	EPS at MBO	MBO purchase price/EPS	A share trading price	A share P/E	MBO price as % of A share price (%)
GD Midea Holding Co.	0.63	4.8	13.16	20.9	22.4
Shenzhen Fangda A	0.23	15.4	5.64	24.5	62.9
Foshan Plastic Group Co.	0.27	11.0	8.91	33.0	33.0
DongTing Aquatic Products	0.26	22.1	17.75	68.3	32.4
Shengli Investment	0.14	16.2	6.93	49.0	32.7

Data source: Securities Times (ZhenQuan Shi Bao), 11 December, 2002 and calculations by author

original or replacement cost, but pays little consideration to post-MBO cashflow analyses. From a valuation perspective, future cash-flow generation is obviously much more important than the NAV on the accounts.

Legal form of the purchasing party

MBO literally means management buy-out, so one would assume it is obvious that the party who acquires the shares of the target company in a MBO (the "purchasing party") is the management team. Under the current legal framework in China, however, who and in which legal form the purchasing party should be is not a rhetorical question.

For a start, there are legal hurdles for the management as natural persons to be the acquiring party in a MBO. In the "*Tentative Measures on Stock Offering and Trading Regulations*" issued by the CSRC in 2002, it provides in Section 46 that no individual person shall be permitted to hold more than 0.5% of the publicly issued common stocks for any individual listed company. As such, natural persons are not likely to be the purchasing entity in an MBO transaction to seek the controlling interest in a listed company.

In many completed MBOs so far, a shell company has been typi-cally used as the purchasing entity in those transactions. In this form, the management as the controlling shareholders of the shell company ultimately controls the target company being acquired. But even a shell company has legal issues for the following reasons.

Firstly, China's Company Law limits the number of shareholders in a shell company. A shell company is typically set up as a limited company and, under China's Company Law, a limited company cannot have more than 50 shareholders. The MBOs in China, however, frequently involve more than 50 individual persons, because in addition to senior management, broad mid-level management and sometimes the general employees may also participate in an MBO.

Secondly, there are also limits on external investment by the shell company. According to China's Company Law, a company's investment in other companies may not exceed 50% of such a company's NAV, except for the investment companies or controlling companies organised according to the State Council rules. Clearly, if a shell company is established for the sole purpose of buying out another company, the 50% investment limit is a potential issue. Relating to this issue, the shell company also needs to deal with issues such as "main business operation" and "ongoing operation" for corporate registration purposes.

For the reasons above, many completed MBOs used a form of trust as the purchasing entity in those transactions. Pursuant to relevant laws, a trust has high flexibility in the maximum trust arrangements it may have – therefore it does not run into issues such as the limitation on the number of shareholders in a limited company. Furthermore, the management of assets in trust is not subject to company law regulations so the limitation on external investment is not applicable. Finally, a trust has the additional benefit of keeping the ultimate benefactors – the company management – undisclosed when it executes the MBO transaction.

However, the new 2005 MBO Regulation (discussed in detail later in this chapter) has prohibited company managements from using trusts to execute an MBO. As the MBO market moves into a new phase, how to structure the purchasing entity will become a crucial issue, and new solutions will probably come from both market innovations and regulatory developments.

Limited funding alternatives

The MBO market in China is also characterised by the lack of funding alternatives. In developed markets, various financing sources provide executives with greater options to finance their MBOs. More specifically, bank loans and high-yield corporate debts are the most common financing vehicles in foreign MBOs, but they are not really practical in China.

On the bank loan side, China's Company Law expressly stipulates that directors and managers of companies cannot use company assets as a pledge for the loans by company shareholders or other individuals. Therefore, it is not possible to use the target company's assets as collateral for management to take out individual loans.

Furthermore, in the *"General Rules for Lending"* issued by the People's Bank of China, the rule prohibits borrowers from using bank loans for stock-related investments or speculation in securities or futures. It further sets strict limitations on inter-company loans. In other words, even if a MBO is executed through a shell company, it will still face many legal hurdles to apply for bank loans or to seek inter-company loans for MBO financing.

On the corporate debt side, debt offerings currently require an application and approval process. Generally speaking, these are not permitted for MBO purposes. As with individual loans, it is also questionable whether corporate assets could be used to secure corporate debt for MBO purposes. Furthermore, there are also limitations on the premium of corporate bond yields over equivalent bank deposit rates. Corporate debt, therefore, is unlikely to be a key financing tool for MBOs in China.

Thus, unsurprisingly, for many listed companies that have completed MBOs, their disclosure related to their financing source has been literally nothing or mostly vague – for example, a casual reference to "financing through financial institutions." However, the new MBO regulation in 2005 firmly requires that MBO transactions occurring since the introduction of this new rule must expressly disclose their source of funding, which will make funding an extremely critical issue for future MBO deals.

Post-MBO conflict between tradable and nontradable shareholders

No matter what the financing tool is, the management no doubt will take on some level of debt one way or another, because the corporate managers in China's SOEs generally do not have sufficient (or sometimes any) funds for their MBO share purchases. The debt repayment pressure typically leads to a high cash dividend payout after the MBO.

In China's stock market, however, the stockholders on the public market do not typically welcome a cash dividend payout (see box).

The main issue is the dichotomy of tradable and nontradable shares. The holders of nontradable shares prefer high cash dividends, because they are not able to cash in stock dividends on the public trading market. On the other hand, the holders of tradable shares prefer stock dividends, because cash dividends imply a much lower dividend return to them than that for the nontradable shareholders. This conflict of interests has long existed in China's stock market.

Cash dividend puzzle in China's stock market

In mature markets, a cash dividend increase is typically a bullish sign for a stock. But in China, high cash dividends are greeted with mixed responses by different shareholders. Generally, the stock market in China shows a zero or negative reaction to cash dividend increases, but a positive reaction to a cash dividend decline, especially for firms with a high percentage of nontradable share holdings.

To explain this unusual phenomenon, the common western corporate finance theories (such as the clientele theory, signalling theory and agency theory) are mostly irrelevant. Because of the segregated share ownership and the price gap between the tradable and nontradable shares, cash dividends have been widely viewed as a way used by nontradable shareholders to earn a return on their illiquid holdings.

YongYou Software Co.'s dividend event in 2002 (also known as the "YongYou phenomenon" in China's stock market) was an illustrative example. YongYou announced superior performance of 0.70 yuan earnings per share for fiscal year 2001 and declared a cash dividend of 0.60 yuan per share. The market reacted quickly with a sharp drop in the stock price in public trading.

The strong disappointment of the A share market in the YongYou case is quite obvious: the initial cost for the nontradable shares was approximately 1.1 yuan per share only, whereas the IPO price for the corresponding A share was 36.68 yuan per share. In other words, the return on the nontradable shares was a stunning 54% whereas the return on A shares was merely 1.6%.

Data source: Shanghai Securities Newspaper (3 April, 2002)

The tension on cash dividends will become most obvious for a post-MBO company in China. When a MBO is highly leveraged, ie, a large portion of the MBO purchase price is borrowed from financial institutions, a high cash dividend payout is probably essential for the management to support the post-MBO loan repayments.

However, if MBO purchases are priced at or near the NAV per share, ie, significantly below the A share trading price, A share holders will very probably oppose post-MBO high cash dividend payouts because their per share dividend rate will be substantially lower than that of the management.

In summary, the above Chinese characteristics make MBOs an extremely controversial topic in China. The public questioned the fairness of MBO prices as well as the transfer process in general. Many alleged malpractices and fraudulent transactions have triggered a nationwide debate on whether MBOs are suitable for China to begin with. In the midst of the raging debate, SASAC in early 2005 issued the first specific MBO regulation in an effort to standardise MBO practice in China.

NEW ERA: 2005'S NEW REGULATION

Since their 1998 debut in China, MBOs have experienced fast growth under a regulatory framework providing few legal guidelines or principles. The public has constantly called for more transparency and fairness during the seven-year history of MBOs in China, which has been accompanied by many issues such as self-dealing, dubious financing resources, loss of state-owned assets and erosion of the interests of ordinary employees due to, allegedly, legal loopholes in the MBO market.

On 14 April, 2005, SASAC and the MoF jointly issued the first official regulation on MBOs of SOEs. In this *Provisional Regulation on Transfer of Enterprises' State Ownership to Management* (the MBO Regulation), the Chinese authorities for the first time expressly clarified the criteria for the transfer of SOEs' state shares to their management. The MBO Regulation, however, curiously chose to use the term "transferring state ownership to management", instead of the popular term MBO that has been ubiquitously used in market practice, media reports and academic research.

Under the new MBO regulation, MBOs of large SOEs, including their wholly owned or controlling subsidiaries, are prohibited. Instead, MBOs can only be carried out by small and medium-sized SOEs under the strict supervision of local state-assets management agencies and according to a clearly defined set of standards. While putting a brake on the MBOs involving largest SOEs, the MBO Regulation also formally recognises the MBO practice, thus putting an end to the prolonged debate on MBO feasibility for SOEs. In short, MBOs in China have entered a new era.

Ban on MBOs of large SOEs

According to the MBO Regulation, management may not acquire state-owned property either in large state-owned or state-controlled enterprises or in major subsidiaries that are wholly owned or controlled by such enterprises and engage in the primary business of such enterprises. As in similar regulations, the interim MBO regulation prohibits MBOs in large SOEs in the light of their dominating importance in the nation's economy.

When releasing the MBO Regulation, SASAC mentioned three reasons for the ban on MBOs in large SOEs. Firstly, market conditions are not sufficiently mature (eg, pricing mechanism for state-owned assets, poor corporate governance system, etc) for MBOs in large SOEs. Secondly, the combination of ownership and management in an MBO is inconsistent with the state's efforts to establish modern corporate systems in large SOEs. Thirdly, because of the large asset size, management typically cannot secure adequate capital for MBO transactions with large SOEs, which potentially leads to illegitimate financing and undervaluation of state-owned assets.

Because large SOEs are prohibited from MBO transactions, the categorisation methodology of the SOEs becomes a critical issue. The MBO Regulation adopts the methodology in two existing rules related to SOE reform (see box), while leaving the door open for future new standards on this issue.

What is a large SOE?

The MBO Regulation refers to the method of classifying SOEs defined in two earlier regulations issued by the National Bureau of Statistics of China while keeping the door open.

One of the regulations is the *"Provisional Regulation on Standards of Small and Medium-Sized Enterprises"* (issued jointly by the State Economic & Trade Commission, the State Development Planning Commission, and the MoF in February 2003). The other is the *"Provisional Regulation on Division of Large, Small and Medium-Sized Enterprises for Statistical Purposes."*

> Pursuant to existing regulations, "small and medium-sized companies" refer to companies:
>
> ❏ that employ less than 2,000 employees;
> ❏ whose sales revenue is less than 300 million yuan (approximately US$36.2 million), or;
> ❏ those whose total capital is less than 400 million yuan (US$48.3 million).
>
> Companies above those standards are deemed to be large SOEs.

Strict standards for MBOs on small and medium-sized SOEs

The MBO Regulations permit MBO transactions with medium or small SOEs pursuant to strict standards, and require local state-asset management agencies to strictly supervise such MBOs. The detailed standards include auditing requirements, procedures and venues for dealings, permitted financing channels, and information disclosure obligations.

Auditing requirements

In connection with a sale of state-owned assets, the institution holding the state-owned assets is required to follow the relevant state regulations to appoint advisory firms to audit the target companies. Furthermore, if the management participates in the sale (an MBO), then the management's economic performance should also be audited.

According to the MBO Regulation, management teams found liable for their company's declining performance during the auditing process cannot take part in the transfer of state-owned assets. Should the management be found to have intentionally removed or concealed assets or arranged related transactions to depress the target company's net assets, they would also not be allowed to purchase the state-share ownership.

No management participation in sale decision

The MBO Regulations attempt to prevent management teams from serving as both the seller and the buyer in a MBO. To avoid potential self-dealing, the MBO regulation prohibits the management of the smaller SOEs from participating in the design of state-assets transfer plan, relevant audits, asset evaluations and pricing matters.

Consequently, the institutions holding the state-owned assets will determine the procedures of asset transfer and related important actions, such as a general check-up of assets, financial statement auditing, assets evaluation, the minimum transfer price and the appointment of intermediaries (eg, auditing firms, valuation advisors, etc). As a result, the management must compete with other potential buyers through an open bidding system.

Broader definition of corporate management

The State Council, in a 2003 rule on SOE reform, defined "corporate management" to include the chairman and vice-chairman of the board of directors, directors, general managers, vice-general managers and chief accounting officers. The MBO Regulation broadens the concept of management to include all those holding managerial positions in companies conducting MBOs as well as in entities that directly or indirectly hold state-owned assets in those companies.

Thus for the MBO Regulation, the concept of management includes not only those stipulated in the 2003 regulation, but also positions such as party secretary of the company, chairman of the workers' union, chief legal officer, and others who participate in the company's decision-making. The broadened definition further covers management in both the MBO target company and the institutions holding controlling interests in such a target company.

"YaoJiang Union" – is that "management"?

Yaojiang Group Co. in ZheJiang Province completed its MBO in 2004. The market called this transaction the "Yaojiang model." One important feature of this MBO was its structured purchasing entity.

The purchasing entity in the Yangjiang MBO was a group – the so-called "Yaojiang Union." This Yaojiang Union consists of 39 natural persons and 2 legal persons (ie, institutions). The group overall is controlled by the target company's CEO.

Because the legal form of this Yaojiang Union had never been tested, it was unclear whether it would be subject to the broadened concept of management. Structural innovations like the Yangjiang model are certain to be seen more frequently in the new MBO era.

Bidding system

It is widely believed that MBOs need to increase competition and transparency to better protect state-owned assets. The MBO Regulation thus provides that the management must compete with other potential buyers through an open bidding system for state equity ownership. As such, MBO trades must be conducted through ownership exchange agencies and all transfer information must be made public.

The regulators obviously expect that through a fair and transparent public bidding system, all potential buyers will be fully informed about the underlying assets of the target company and consequently, competitive bidding should result in the best price for state assets. In practice, however, third-party bidders often do not have sufficient time or full access to the MBO company's core information before participating in the bidding and the public financial reporting by the company is typically far from helpful for a purchase decision. In other words, the management unavoidably has a superior information advantage.

Disclosure and transparency of funding sources

The MBO Regulation particularly tightens up the regulation around MBO funding sources. In China's SOE market, managers

---

Information in MBO bidding

The leveraged buyout of RJR Nabisco is still the largest buy-out transaction in history. The deal illustrates the importance of information flow in efficient bidding.

RJR's shares had been selling at about US$55 before the transaction. A group led by the CEO offered a price of US$75 per share in a highly leveraged MBO. Following six weeks of intense negotiation, the corporation was sold to another investor group at a price of US$109 per share, more than 45% higher than the MBO price.

The major factor attributable to the high bid price was probably the information disclosure initiated by the board of directors. The board actively promoted the bidding process through a special committee. In particular, the special committee instructed the management team to provide confidential business information to serious competing bidders. Without such information, outside bidders would have been at a substantial disadvantage, compared with the management team, in making their investment decision.

---

typically do not have sufficient (or in many cases, any) funds for their purchases (see box). In some earlier MBO cases, managers were able to acquire a company without putting in any of their own money, relying on undisclosed sources of funding or bank loans obtained by using the company assets as collateral.

A few steps have been taken in MBO Regulation to improve disclosure and transparency in this matter. Firstly, corporate management must present evidence for the funding source in an MBO transaction. Without adequate evidence of the funding sources, the management will be forbidden from purchasing the state-share ownership. Secondly, the management may not borrow from state-owned or state-controlled enterprises (including the target enterprise) or use these enterprise's assets as collateral for commercial loans to finance the MBO.

Finally, the Regulation expressly prohibits the management from purchasing the state ownership in an indirect manner such as through a trust or agent arrangement. This echoes the requirement for management to disclose the funding source, because through a third party such as a trust, the management could execute an MBO transaction anonymously. According to SASAC, a third-party arrangement conceals not only the identity of the true buyer, but also other important information such as its credit credibility and the reason for the buy-out, which could hamper SASAC's supervision of the underlying assets.

Show me the money

At a press briefing on the provisional MBO Regulation, a senior official from SASAC used numerical examples to illustrate the funding issue around MBOs.

According to statistics, he said, only a few managers in large SOEs can earn an annual salary of 1 million yuan (approximately US$121,000) or more. Using 1 million yuan as an example, that equals 10 million yuan (US$1.2 million) for 10 years' work. Yet transfer of properties of a large SOE involves at least 100 million yuan (US$12 million), which makes it hard, if not impossible, for managers to use their own funds (without embezzlement or taking bribes) to complete a MBO.

Because there are not enough financing tools available for MBOs, the SASAC official concluded his example by saying that the salary

> history in SOEs was also a reason "why we do not think market condi-
> tions are mature for [an MBO of] SOEs." On the other hand, it would
> be easier for small and medium-sized enterprises to pursue MBOs
> because the funding requirements there are much less.

In summary, these provisions intend to set up a competitive bidding system to find the best price for state-owned assets transfers. At the same time, it adds in some checks and balances to prevent the management from manipulating the company's financial situation during the MBO process. Above all, the most significant changes are the requirement to disclose funding sources and the prohibition on using third-party arrangements such as trust structures. In the new MBO era, MBO investment funds will become one of the few legitimate funding resources (if not the only one) available in the MBO market.

PROSPECT

SASAC's recent move regarding the MBO Regulation creates a milestone in China's growing MBO market. Although MBOs of large SOEs are prohibited, this provisional rule officially recognises MBO practice and permits MBOs of small and medium-sized SOEs. MBOs are here to stay and there is still potential for their further growth.

A number of factors may lead to future growth of the MBO market. Firstly, the MBO Regulation provides clearer guidance on transactions with small and medium-sized SOEs. The added clarity should help MBO transactions pass the finishing line in the midst of public controversies. Secondly, many local governments remain interested in privatising SOEs. In connection with the SOE reform, the central government has suggested revitalising small and medium-sized SOEs by various methods, including reorganisation, mergers, shareholding cooperatives and sales. But in practice, many local governments have chosen to sell SOEs.

Thirdly, there is a cultural evolution around private ownership. Private business owners are a very recent phenomenon given China's decades-long planned economy. Private enterprises were forbidden in the past and the private sector was a non-factor in China's economy until two decades of market economy reform. It takes time for the public to understand and accept MBOs, even when those transactions are properly structured and fairly priced.

Finally, the MBO Regulation offers a clearer legal framework for foreign investor strategic participation in MBOs in China. There is nothing in the Regulation that prohibits the management from borrowing from abroad for the buy-out. In fact, considering the limited funding alternatives and the legal hurdles around many of them, foreign investment capital funds could become one of the few legitimate funding sources available in the MBO market.

All in all, the MBO market should remain an interesting investment field in the years to come. Meanwhile, MBOs may be further driven by the growth in the M&A market discussed in the previous chapter. Chinese companies, whether listed or private, generally lack transparent financial reporting or corporate governance. In some cases, teaming up with management for an MBO may be an appropriate alternative to a pure takeover.

Will the large SOEs become available for MBOs again in the near future? There is no easy answer to this billion dollar question. However, it is quite an interesting coincidence that in April 2005 when SASAC issued the MBO Regulation, the CSRC at about the same time unveiled the full-flotation plan to make state-owned shares become tradable in the A share market. This really shows that SOE reform will continue to chug along and the only question is whether state-owned shares should be brought to the open market or monetised through private transactions.

CONCLUSION

The huge size of the state-owned assets in SOEs and the limited shareholding by their managements suggest substantial potential in MBOs. However, the segregated equity ownership structure in the listed companies exacerbated two major issues surrounding MBO transactions: fairness to shareholders and possible conflicts of interest between management/acquirers and shareholders.

As such, MBOs in China exhibit many unique characteristics that make them substantially different from those in more developed markets. Those characteristics include the pricing gap between nontradable shares and the public tradable A shares, the legal restrictions around the acquiring party in MBOs, the limited funding alternatives, and the controversies around post-MBO cash dividend policies.

Following its 1998 debut in China, the MBO market saw tremendous growth with few legal guidelines. However, the Chinese characteristics of the MBO market also triggered a nationwide debate on whether MBOs are suitable for China to begin with. In an effort to standardise MBO practice in China, SASAC in early 2005 issued the first official regulations for MBOs.

Under the new MBO Regulation, MBOs of large SOEs are prohibited. Nevertheless, this provisional rule officially recognises MBO practice and permits MBOs of small and medium-sized SOEs and a number of factors may lead to future growth of the MBO market. The MBO standards intend to set up a competitive bidding system to find the best price for state-owned asset transfers and they also add in some checks and balances to prevent the management from manipulating the company's financial situation during the MBO process.

Above all, the most significant changes are the requirement to disclose funding sources and the prohibition on using third-party arrangements such as trust structures. Considering the limited funding alternatives and the legal hurdles around many of them, foreign investment capital funds could become one of the few legitimate funding sources available in the MBO market. In the post-MBO Regulation era, the MBO market will surely become one of the most interesting and challenging investment areas for foreign investors.

Bibliography

Angel, J., 2005, "Shorting Mechanism in International Markets and Possible Models in China Market", Volume 1, Shanghai Exchange Research 2005 Reports.

China CSRC Fund Regulatory Department and Tsinghua University Joint Research Team, 2004, "Research on QFII Market Impact and Regulatory System", Volume 1, Shanghai Exchange Research 2004 Reports.

Gao, S., 2002, "China Stock Market in a Global Perspective", Research Report of Dow Jones Indexes, September.

Girardin, E. and Z. Liu, 2003, "The Chinese Stock Market: A Casino with 'Buffer Zones'?", *Journal of Chinese Economic and Business Studies*, Vol. 1, No. 1, pp. 57–70.

Graham J. and C. Harvey, 2002, "How Do CFOs Make Capital Budgeting and Capital Structure Decisions?", *Journal of Applied Corporate Finance*, Vol. 15, No. 1, Spring.

Haitong Securities Company Inc., 2005, "The 'Tunnel Effect and Excessive Financing under the Segregated Equity Ownership", 2005 Shenzhen Stock Exchange Member Reports.

Hong Kong University School of Economics Research Team, 2002, "The Capital Structure of China's Listed Companies", Volume 2, Shanghai Exchange Research 2002 Reports.

HuaTang Law Firm, 2003, "Certain Legal Issues relating to Ownership Transfer and Reorganization in Listed Companies," Volume 4, Shanghai Exchange Research 2003 Reports.

Joint Research Team – China Europe International Business School (CEIBS) and the Chinese University of Hong Kong Department of Finance, 2004, "Internal and External Investors: Choices among Bank Loan, Corporate Debt and Convertible Corporate Debt", Volume 1, Shanghai Exchange Research 2004 Reports.

Kalok Chan, Albert J. Menkveld, and Zhishu Yang, 2002, "Evidence on the Foreign Share Discount Puzzle in China: Liquidity or Information Asymmetry?", NCER working paper No. 200218.

Kutan, A., Z. Wang, and J. Yang, 2003, "Information Flows Within and Across Sectors in China's Emerging Stock Markets", EMG working paper series WP-EMG-03-2003, Cass Business School, June.

Liu, D., 2005, "Feasibility Research on T+0 Trading in China", Volume 1, Shanghai Exchange Research 2005 Reports.

Lu, W., 2003, "Foreign M&As in China and the Driving Forces", Volume 1, Shanghai Exchange Research 2003 Reports.

Lu, W., 2005, "To Launch Warrants in the Shanghai Stock Exchange", Volume 1, Shanghai Exchange Research 2005 Reports.

Ma, W., 2000, "The Misappropriation Theory under the Chinese Securities Law – A Comparative Study with its U.S. Counterpart", *Richmond Journal of Law and Business*, 1 Rich. J. Global L. & Bus. 33 (2000), URL: http://blj.ucdavis.edu/article/546/.

Ma, W., 2004, "Convertible Bonds: A New Approach to China's Stock Markets", *U.C. Davis Business and Law Journal*, 5 U.C. Davis Bus. L.J. 4 (2004), URL: http://blj.ucdavis.edu/article/546/, December.

Ma, W., 2004, "China's Convertible Bonds", *Derivatives Week,* September.

Ma, W., 2005, "China's Warrants and Options", *Derivatives Week,* November.

Ma, W., 2005, "China's Stock Index and Index Futures", *Derivatives Week,* July.

Ma, W., 2005, "China's Innovative Fund Products: ETFs and LOFs", *Derivatives Week,* April.

Ma, W., 2005, "China's Principal Protected Investments", *Derivatives Week*, March.

Press conference and Q&A session by the Index Working Group of the Shanghai and Shenzhen Stock Exchanges regarding Shanghai Shenzhen 300 Index, *See* http://www.sse.com.cn/sseportal/ps/zhs/sczn/zstx_home.shtml (05 April 2005).

Shanghai JiaoTong University and GuaDa Securities Co. Joint Research Team, 2002, "Research on Abnormal Volatilities in Shanghai Stock Market", Volume 3, Shanghai Exchange Research 2002 Reports.

Shanghai Stock Exchange Research Center, 2003, "ETF Design: Global Experiences and Theories", Volume 2, Shanghai Exchange Research 2003 Reports.

Shenyin & Wanguo Securities Co. Inc. and the Statistics Department of Eastern China Normal University, 2003, "Research on the Chinese characteristics' impact on Index Computation," Volume 3, Shanghai Exchange Research 2003 Reports.

Situ, D. and H. Fu, 2004, "Research on Equity-Based Incentives for Senior Management in Listed Companies", Volume 2, Shanghai Exchange Research 2004 Reports.

The Hong Kong Polytechnic University Research Team, 2004, "Behavioral Analysis on Chinese Retail and Institutional Investors", Volume 1, Shanghai Exchange Research 2004 Reports.

Tsinghua University School of Management Research Team, 2003, "International Comparative Studies on Management Buy-Outs (MBO)", Volume 2, Shanghai Exchange Research 2003 Reports.

Wang. J., 2004, "Dancing with Wolves: Regulation and Deregulation of Foreign Investment in China's Stock Market", *Asian-Pacific law & Policy Journal*, June.

Yu, Y., 2005, "Research on Index Options in China Markets", Shenzhen Stock Exchange Report No. 0108, March.

Index

Securities instrument 7
Securities Investment Licences 51,
    56–7
Segregated equity ownership
    structure 3, 23–8
Separation of equity ownership 7
Shanghai Composite Index 111
Shanghai Shenzhen Stock
    Exchange 44
Shanghai Stock Composite Index
    113
Shanghai Stock Exchange (SSE)
    86, 97, 107, 111, 118, 124, 147,
    212
    180 Index 117
    Dividend Index 117
Shares
    legal-person 8, 22
    public individual 9
    state-owned 8, 22
Shenzhen Development Bank
    (SDB) 182, 194
Shenzhen Mid & Small Cap Board
    Index 117
Shenzhen Stock Exchange 44, 86,
    97, 117–18, 134–5, 147
Short
    China A shares 158–9
    current restrictions on stock
        short selling 162–6
    shorting-based trading
        strategies 159–62
    synthetic short in ETF market
        171–3
Standing Committee of the
    National People's Congress
    84
State Administration of Foreign
    Exchange (SAFE) 40
State-owned Assets Supervision
    and Administration
    Commission (SASAC)
    209
State-owned enterprises (SOEs) 7,
    33, 175, 177, 207
State-owned shares 187
State-share overhaul reform 23
Strike price 79

Subscription Rights Certificate
    (SRC) 79

T
T-bond borrower 170
The Bond Market Association
    (TBMA) 170
The Great Leap Forward 31
Time value 79
Total capitalisation 129
Transferable pre-emptive right
    (TPR) 80, 162
Treasury bonds 147
Trial and error approach 6

U
US generally accepted accounting
    principles (GAAP) 34

V
Vega hedging 102
Volatility 79

W
Warrants and options
    background on option trading
        77–9
    Bao Steel 87–92
    dealer options market 99–103
    options/warrants in China
        79–82
    prospect 103–5
    return of warrants 83–7
    Shenzhen Stock Exchange
        options 97–9
    Wuhan Steel 92–6

X
Xugong Group Construction
    Machinery Co. (XCMC) 177,
    200

Y
Yahoo 178
Yield to maturity 62

Z
Zero-coupon bond 155